OUR COMMON LAND

sixth edition

the law and history of common land and village greens

Paul Clayden MA

Open Spaces Society
25A Bell Street, Henley-on-Thames, Oxon RG9 2BA

Tel: 01491 573535 Email: hq@oss.org.uk Website: www.oss.org.uk

Registered Charity 214753

Published in January 2007 by the Open Spaces Society, 25A Bell Street, Henley-on-Thames, Oxon RG9 2BA, registered charity no 214753.

International Standard Book Number (ISBN) 978-0-946574-21-6

Typeset and printed by Higgs Group, Caxton House, Station Road Corner, Henley-on-Thames, Oxon RG9 1AD, telephone (01491) 419400

About the author

Paul Clayden, a solicitor, was the society's secretary from 1976 to 1984. He subsequently worked for the National Association of Local Councils and was its director from 1995 to 1998. He is now a freelance legal consultant and author.

PREFACE TO THE SIXTH EDITION

In 1971 the society published *A Guide to the Law of Commons* by the late Ian Campbell LLB, the then secretary of the society. The third edition (1980) was co-authored by Paul Clayden, Ian Campbell's successor as the society's secretary, and renamed *The Law of Commons and Village Greens*. The fourth edition, entitled *Our Common Land*, appeared in 1985 and was re-printed with a supplement in 1992. The fifth edition thoroughly revised and updated the fourth edition to include, in particular, the important legal changes made by the Countryside and Rights of Way Act 2000 and the appearance of the government's Common Land Policy Statement 2002. This, the sixth, edition explains the changes made by the Commons Act 2006—the first piece of major commons legislation since 1965—and the effect of recent decisions by the House of Lords on the nature and status of village greens. Most of the 2006 act did not come into force on the day the act received the Royal Assent (on 19 July 2006), but will be brought into force in stages as the regulations which are necessary to implement the act are made. In the interests of clarity and simplicity, the text generally states the law as if the 2006 act was in force and omits earlier legislation repealed or superseded by the act. However, the provisions of s194 of the Law of Property (works on common land) and s147 of the Inclosure Act 1845 (exchange-land procedure) are included because they will continue to be operated until the relevant parts of the 2006 act come into force.

One of the immediate results of the passing of the 2006 act has been the establishment of an association of commons registration officers called the Commons and Greens Registration and Management Association of England and Wales. Their job will become more complex as the various parts of the 2006 act are brought into force and the establishment of the association (with some vital core-funding from Defra) is to be welcomed. The association can be contacted at Endeavour House, 8 Russell Road, Ipswich IP1 2BX (website: www.cgrma.org.uk).

The Government of Wales Act 1998 set up the National Assembly for Wales. In 1999 most of the powers formerly exercised by the Secretary of State for Wales were transferred to the assembly, including those powers relating to commons and greens. Although the basic law of commons and greens is the same in both England and Wales, differences of detail between the two countries have emerged, and will continue to emerge, both in subordinate legislation and in governmental advice or guidance.

In England, the powers formerly exercised by the Secretary of State for the Environment and the Secretary of State for the Environment,

Transport and the Regions are now exercisable by the Secretary of State for Environment, Food and Rural Affairs.

The following abbreviations are used throughout the book:

the 1965 act	the Commons Registration Act 1965
the 1925 act	the Law of Property Act 1925
the 1981 act	the Acquisition of Land Act 1981
the 2000 act	the Countryside and Rights of Way Act 2000
the 2006 act	the Commons Act 2006
the CLF	the Common Land Forum
the CLPS	the Common Land Policy Statement 2002 published by Defra in July 2002
appropriate national authority	the secretary of state in England and the National Assembly for Wales in Wales
Defra	the Department for Environment, Food and Rural Affairs
local council	parish, town or community council
principal authority	county, district or unitary council in England; county or county borough council in Wales
s	section (of an act of parliament)
secretary of state	the Secretary of State for Environment, Food and Rural Affairs (in England) or the National Assembly for Wales (in Wales)
SI	statutory instrument
the society	the Open Spaces Society
subs	subsection (of an act of parliament)

The abbreviations used in the citation of cases are listed in Halsbury's *Laws of England* (fourth edition 2001 reissue), volume 54.

Copies of commons commissioners' decisions can be obtained from Defra, Zone 1/05, Temple Quay House, 2 The Square, Temple Quay, Bristol BS1 6EB.

Every effort has been made to ensure that the extracts from the acts and statutory instruments are reproduced precisely and accurately, but readers are advised to make their own checks before placing legal reliance on them.

The first chapter of the book covering the distribution of commons was contributed to the previous editions by Len Clark. It has needed very little revision to bring it fully up to date. I am very grateful to Len for the work he put in then, and it is a tribute to his knowledge of commons that so few alterations have been necessary.

Paul Clayden
Henley-on-Thames
November 2006

CONTENTS

Table of statutes and statutory instruments V
Table of cases V
Table of commons commissioners' decisions VII

I An introduction to common land
Distribution of commons 4

II Commons registration
1. Rights of common 10
2. Waste land of a manor not subject to rights of common .. 13
3. The initial registration process 13
4. Registration authorities 15
5. The registers 15
6. Registration of ownership of common land 16
7. Creation of new rights of common 18
8. Commons where no person is registered as owner 19
9. Alteration of common rights 21
10. Exemptions from registration 26
11. Amendment of the registers 28
12. Conclusiveness of the registers 30
13. Correction of the registers 32
14. Information about the registers 33
15. Official copies of the registers 33
16. Rectification of mistakes 33

III Common land—the rights of the parties
1. The owner's rights 41
2. The rights of the commoners 45
3. Driveways across commons 48
4. The rights of the public: summary 51

IV Management and control of common land
1. Metropolitan commons 53
2. Commons Act 1876 55
3. Commons Act 1899 55
4. Section 193 of the Law of Property Act 1925 57
5. Commons subject to special acts 60
6. National Trust commons 60
7. Commons subject to an access agreement under the National Parks and Access to the Countryside Act 1949 .. 62
8. Commons purchased by a local authority 62
9. Countryside Act 1968 63
10. Commons Act 2006—commons councils 64
11. Manorial courts 65
12. Commons Act 1908 65

13. Crown commons 66
14. Caravans 66
15. Removal of trespassers....................67
16. Unauthorised agricultural activities 67

V Countryside and Rights of Way Act 2000—access provisions

1. Access land 69
2. Registered common land 69
3. Excepted land....................69
4. Section 15 land....................70
5. Maps of access land 70
6. The right of access 70
7. Dedication of land as access land 71
8. Management of registered common land 72

VI Statutory protection of common land

1. Section 194 of the Law of Property Act 1925 73
2. Section 19 of the Acquisition of Land Act 1981 82
3. Sections 38-44 of the Commons Act 2006 88
4. Exchange-land procedures 92

VII Town and village greens

1. Registration of greens during the initial registration period 94
2. The ownership of greens 99
3. The management of greens 99
4. Rights of common over greens....................100
5. Greens and highways 100
6. Damage to and encroachment on a green 101
7. Car parking 102
8. Appropriation and exchange of greens for other purposes. 103
9. Driveways across greens 104
10. Non-registration of greens 106
11. Greens wrongly registered as common land....................107
12. Buildings registered as town or village green 107
13. Removal of other land from the registers of town or village greens 108
14. New greens....................108

VIII The future of common land and village greens....................112

Appendix 1 - Common Land Forum: summary of unimplemented recommendations 113

Appendix 2 - Common Land Policy Statement 2002: summary of unimplemented proposals 114

Extracts from statutes and statutory instruments (listed below) 117

Bibliography 205

Index 207

TABLE OF STATUTES AND STATUTORY INSTRUMENTS

Prescription Act 1832 ss 1, 4 117
Inclosure Act 1845 ss 11, 147, 167 118
Inclosure Act 1857 s 12 119
Metropolitan Commons Act 1866 ss 3, 4 and 5 120
Commons Act 1876 ss 7, 10(4), 19, 29, 37 120
Commons Act 1899 ss 1, 2, 3, 5, 6, 7, 9, 10, 11, 12, 14, 15, 18..........122
Open Spaces Act 1906 ss 9, 10, 14, 15, 16, 20 124
National Trust Act 1907 ss 4(1), 29 126
Commons Act 1908 126
Law of Property Act 1925 ss 193, 194..........128
Caravan Sites and Control of Development Act 1960 s 23 130
Compulsory Purchase Act 1965 sch 4, para 1(1), (2)..........131
Ministry of Housing and Local Government Provisional Order Confirmation (Greater London Parks and Open Spaces) Act 1967 sch, articles 7 (part), 8-12 and 17 132
Countryside Act 1968 s 9, sch 2..........138
National Trust Act 1971 s 23 141
Local Government Act 1972 ss 122 (part), 123, 126 (part), 127, 189(3), 270(1) (part) 142
Acquisition of Land Act 1981 s 19 144
Dyfed Act 1987 s 42 146
Road Traffic Act 1988 s 34 147
Town and Country Planning Act 1990 ss 229, 336(1) (part)..........148
Countryside and Rights of Way Act 2000 ss 1, 2, 15, 16, and sch 1..148
Commons Act 2006 (except sch 6) 153
The Commons (Severance of Rights) (England) Order 2006 202
The Commons Act 2006 (Commencement No 1, Transitional Provisions and Savings) (England) Order 2006..........203

TABLE OF CASES

(numbers refer to paragraphs in the text)

Abercromby v Town Commissioners of Fermoy [1900] 1 IR 302 ..7.12
Abbot v Weekly [1665] Levinz 176 ....7.09
AG v Antrobus [1905] 2 Ch 188 ....3.46
AG v Hanmer [1858] 2 LJ Ch 837 ....2.14, 2.120
AG v Reynolds [1911] 2 KB 888..........2.10

AG v Southampton Corporation [1969] 68 LGR 288 ....6.10, 6.12
Anon, Year Book 15 Hy 7 [1499-1500] 3.17
Arlett v Ellis [1827] 7 B & C 346 ....3.8, 3.18
Bakewell Management Ltd v Brandwood & others [2004] UKHL 14 ....3.37-45, 7.48-53
Bettison v Langton [2001] 1 All ER (D) 223 ....2.66
re Box Hill Common [1979] 2 WLR 177 ....2.122
Central Electricity Generating Board v Clywd County Council [1976] 1 All ER 251 ....2.82, 4.27, 7.3
Chesterfield v Harris [1908] 2 Ch 397 ....2.11
re Chewton Common [1977] 1 WLR 1242 ....2.122
Chilton v London Corporation [1878] 7 Ch D 562 ....2.8
Corpus Christi College v Gloucestershire County Council [1982] 3 WLR 849 ....2.95-96
Cresstock Investments Ltd v Commons Commissioner [1992] 1 WLR 1088 ....2.115
Davies v Davies [1974] 3 WLR 607 ....3.35
De la Warr v Miles [1881] 17 Ch D 535 ....2.9
Earl of Coventry v Willes [1863] 9 LT 384 ....7.16
Eaton v Kurton [1966] Cheltenham County Court, 14 October 1966, (reported in the Society's Journal, Spring 1967, page 175) 6.11
Edwards v Jenkins [1896] 1 Ch 308 ....7.17
re Ellenborough Park [1956] 1 Ch 131 ....3.46
Fitch v Fitch [1797] 2 Esp 543 ....7.31
Fitch v Rawling [1795] 2 Hy Bl 393 ....7.10
G & K Ladenbau Ltd v Crawley and de Reya [1978] 1 WLR 266 ..2.35
Gateward's case [1607] 6 Co Rep 59b 2.13, 3.30
Goodman v Mayor and Corporation of Saltash [1882] 7 App Cas 633 ....3.33
Hall v Byron [1877] 4 Ch D 667 ....3.4
Hall v Nottingham [1875] 1 Ex Div 1 ....7.10
Hammerton v Honey [1876] 24 WR 603 ....7.17
Hampshire County Council v Milburn and others [1991] AC 325 ..2.122
Hanning v Top Deck Travel Group Ltd [1993] 68 P & CR 14..3.37-39, 7.50
Harris v Chesterfield [1911] AC 623 ....2.11
Heath v Deane [1905] 2 Ch 86 ....2.12
Hereford and Worcester County Council v Pick [1995] 71 P & CR 23 ....3.41
re land at Freshfields [1993] 66 P & CR 9 ....2.116
Massey and Drew v Boulden [2002] EWCA civ 1634 ....3.38-39, 7.50
Mercer v Denne [1905] 2 Ch 538 ....7.21
Musgrave v Inclosure Commissioners [1874] LR 9 QB 162 ....3.7

National Trust for Places of Historic Interest or Natural Beauty v Ashbrook and others [1997] *The Times*, 3 July 1997 ....3.18, 4.38
Neaverson v Peterborough Rural District Council [1902] 1 Ch 55 ....3.41
Newman v Bennett [1908] 3 All ER 229 ....2.7
New Windsor Corporation v Mellor [1975] 3 All ER 44 ....7.17, 7.20, 7.23
Oxfordshire County Council v Oxford City Council & another [2006] UKHL 25 ....7.3, 7.34, 7.50
Portland v Hill [1866] LR 2 Eq 765 ....2.12
R v Dyer [1952] 36 Cr App Rep 3.19
R (on the application of Alfred McAlpine Homes Ltd) v Staffordshire County Council [2002] EWCA 76 (Admin) 7.67, 7.71
R v City of Sunderland [2001] ex parte Beresford [2003] UKHL 60 ..7.68
R v Norfolk County Council ex parte Parry [1996] 74 P & CR 12 ....2.96
R v Oxfordshire County Council and another ex parte Sunningwell Parish Council [1999] 3 All ER 385 ....7.19, 7.69, 7.70
R v Secretary of State for the Environment ex parte Billson [1998] 2 All ER 587 ....4.22, 4.26
R (Ashbrook) v Secretary of State for Environment, Food and Rural Affairs [2004] EWHC (Admin) 2387 ....6.19
R v Teignbridge District Council ex parte Street [1989] *The Times*, 9 July 2.51
Robertson v Hartopp [1889] 43 Ch D 484..................................3.26-28
Robinson v Adair [1995] *The Times*, 2 March......................................3.37
re the Rye, High Wycombe, Bucks [1977] 3 All ER 521.....................7.6
Samford and Havel's case [1612] Godb 184 ....3.6
Sheringham v Holsey [1904] 91 LT 225 ....3.41
re Turnworth Down, Dorset [1977] 33 P & CR 192 ....2.48, 2.82
Tyson v Smith [1838] 9 A &E 406...7.21
re 1-4 White Row Cottages, Bewerley [1991] 3 WLR 229.............2.114
White v Taylor [1968] 2 WLR 1402 ....3.21
Willingale v Maitland [1866] LR Eq 103 ....3.31

TABLE OF COMMONS COMMISSIONERS' DECISIONS

Bridge Green Hargrave, Suffolk (35/D/1) 31 May 1972 ....7.13
Bryniau, Dyserth, Clwyd (52/D/5) 9 Mar 1976 ....4.30
Carn Brea, Redruth, Cornwall (206/D/720) 7 Apr 1981 ....4.29
Cheesewring Common, Henwood Common and Longstone Downs, St Clear, Cornwall (D206/D/4-13) 5 Jun 1975 ....2.7
Forest of Dartmoor, Devon (209/D/287, 288) 30 Jun 1983 ....2.7
Gunwalloe Church Cove Beach, Gunwalloe, Cornwall (no 2) (206/D/479) 26 Jan 1978 ....2.13

Hudnalls, St Briavels, Gloucestershire (no 1) (213/D/1)
16 May 1977 .... 3.32,3.34
Knowstone Inner Moor, Knowstone Outer Moor etc, Devon
(209/D/217224) 5 Oct 1981 .... 3.6
Maenporth Beach, Falmouth, Cornwall (206/D/864-867) 29 Oct 1980.. 2.13
Medstead Village Green, Medstead, Hampshire (214/D/113) 14
Sep 1979.......... 7.32
Northam Burrows, Northam, Devon (no1) (209/D/91) 21 Nov 1977 ..3.33
Pasture End, Murton, Cumbria (262/D/277-9) 8 Jan 1981 ....2.2, 3.7
Snettisham Beach Shingle Fields, Snettisham, Norfolk (225/D/7)
11 Jan & 5 Mar 1982 .... 3.34

CHAPTER I

An Introduction to Common Land

1.1 The one and a half million acres (600,000 hectares or 2,300 square miles) of common land in England and Wales are the most underrated and misunderstood, though not unappreciated, part of the countryside. This may be in part a matter of semantics. Ask ten people in the street who owns common land, and nine will probably reply 'the Queen', 'no one' or 'everyone'. And for the great majority of commons they would be wrong. All common land has an owner; the ambiguous term 'common' refers to the rights held in common by certain people to use the product of the soil of the common, by grazing, cutting turf and so on. Yet commons may be said to belong to the people, for although the commoners have an economic interest in the land no doubt they have always used commons, like village greens, for their festivals and holiday activities, a use which has gradually extended to the wider public and is today of considerable importance.

1.2 Pursue your inquiries with the ten people in the street and ask whether they have a right in law to walk on commons. Again virtual unanimity can be expected in the affirmative. Until very recently, this was not true; only about a fifth of our common land was legally open to the public. However, now that part I of the 2000 act is fully in force, the public has a qualified statutory right of access on foot to all registered common land (see chapter V). Even more misconceptions will emerge if you press your inquiries into the law of commons, for it is very complex. Indeed many well-intentioned folk, including a number of our legislators, have set off with hopes of rationalising the law only to discover that, as on many of our commons, they are soon entangled in the legal thickets and retreat hastily. The main aim of this book is to provide at least some waymarking through those thickets.

1.3 Commons are a remnant of the manorial system which from mediaeval times had been the basis of the country's economy. The manor was the basic unit and was supposed to be self-sufficient. Crops were grown on the better soil and the poor land was the 'waste' used for grazing and gathering fuel. The lord of the manor owned the whole of the land but others had rights recognised by the courts. In turn this meant that the lord of the manor could not enclose land without the consent of the commoners or parliamentary authority, hence the unfenced open spaces which we still recognise as the hallmark of a common. The obligation to provide land for commoners' rights derived from the Statute of Merton of 1235 and was reflected in the variety of courts leet which determined the dates for grazing and rotation of crops. One writer described the common as the lowest rung of the social ladder leading to the occupation of the land.

1.4 The importance of commons was not entirely agricultural or domestic. This is illustrated by an act of 1593 which sought to prevent the enclosure of commons, waste grounds and great fields within three miles of the gates of the City of London, to the 'hindrance of training or mustring of souldiers, or of walking for recreation, comfort and health of her Maiestie's people, or the laudable exercise of shooting'. Like many other attempts, the act failed to prevent the spread of London. By the eighteenth century, even in rural areas, commons were associated with horse racing (eg Epsom Downs and Newmarket Heath) and cricket (eg Broadhalfpenny Down, Hampshire). The surveyor of highways for each parish and the turnpike trusts were also authorised to take material from commons and wastes for the maintenance of their highways.

1.5 Inevitably there were clashes of interest, and attempts at enclosure were frequent. But the system persisted largely unchanged until the agrarian revolution in the latter part of the eighteenth century. By then the prospects of more profitable agricultural methods had become too attractive to ignore. Pressure came from the Board of Agriculture and its advising economists who were concerned with more efficient food production for the growing urban and industrial population, especially during the Napoleonic wars. Inclosure acts for individual commons were quickly in vogue, usually promoted by the owners. Although the full parliamentary procedure was involved, including the hearing of counter petitions, the system was loaded heavily against the humble commoner. In true English fashion however the enclosure movement produced a number of articulate and vigorous middle-class champions of the rural poor.

1.6 At first an inclosure act might become law without ordinary people knowing anything about it, and it was only at the end of the eighteenth century that it became obligatory to post notices of an intended bill to enclose on the church door. This provoked public interest notably at Otmoor in Oxfordshire. The promoters of the enclosure had an eye to agribusiness though they professed higher aims, including an uplift to the morals of the poor with this touch of piety: 'God did not create the earth to lie waste for feeding a few geese, but to be cultivated by man, by the sweat of his brow'. The commoners were unimpressed and Otmoor saw several riots. Today the common has disappeared.

1.7 There had been more than 4,000 individual inclosure acts before a general act was passed in 1845, providing that the lord and former commoners would each receive a freehold parcel of land in compensation for the loss of rights. A final residue was to be left for communal use, including land for a poorhouse or field for fuel, a gravel pit for road making and an area for the 'exercise and recreation of the inhabitants'. However, in the 20 years which followed, over 61,000 acres were enclosed and only 4,000 allotted for recreation or the benefit of the poor.

1.8 But social and economic changes were to cool the ardour for increased enclosure during the Victorian era. The attraction of turning over commons to arable was lessened by the development of corn growing in America's mid west which led to cheap imports. As technological advances moved to the industrial scene the towns grew rapidly and there was a demand for open spaces to which people could go for leisure. It was at this point that the Commons Preservation Society entered the scene, attracting the interest of many progressive public figures such as John Stuart Mill, George John Shaw-Lefevre (later created Lord Eversley), Thomas Huxley and Sir Charles Dilke. The society campaigned to rescue commons from enclosure and speculators, especially in the south-east. The sagas of Berkhamsted, Banstead and Wimbledon were some of those enacted in the courts and in direct action on the ground. A more positive approach to the retention of commons was seen in the Metropolitan Commons Act of 1866 and the Commons Act of 1876, both of which provided important frameworks for managing commons.

1.9 In the twentieth century there was a surge in public interest in preserving commons, with the emergence of the National Trust as a major landowner (it owns more than 200 commons including some of the most important open space areas in the country). The national park authorities and local authorities own and manage many of the most scenic commons.

1.10 In the early 1920s there was a major reform of the law of property. This abolished the historic manorial system of copyhold land which had been governed by manorial courts In future, land was only to be owned freehold or leasehold. The society foresaw the danger this might cause to the future of commons, which also had been protected by the manorial courts, and parliament was persuaded to pass sections 193 and 194 of the Law of Property Act 1925. Section 193 is still in force

(4.20-30 and page 128). Section 194 will be repealed and replaced by ss 38-44 of the 2006 act.

1.11 In 1958 a Royal Commission published its erudite and widely praised report on the state of common land and its recommendations for sustaining what it called 'this last reserve of uncommitted land in England and Wales'. It proposed a register of all common land, a general public right of access to commons, and effective schemes for management. The first was achieved with the passing of the 1965 act (although was shown to have been defective in a number of respects); the second was achieved when part I of the 2000 act came fully in force in May 2005 in Wales and in October 2005 in England; the third has been achieved in part 2 of the 2006 act. Some of the proposals in Defra's Common Land Policy Statement 2002 (see appendix 2) and some of the Common Land Forum's recommendations in its 1986 report remain unimplemented (see appendix 1).

1.12 The commission recognised, and it has been even more widely appreciated in the 58 years since, the diverse attractions of common land. In addition to the agricultural and recreational interests, commons are precious for their landscape, history, archaeology, flora and wildlife. Many are sites of special scientific interest (SSSIs) and they comprise vital parts of our national parks and areas of outstanding natural beauty. The small commons and village greens, even wayside verges, are no less important to local communities. The diversity and richness of our commons are briefly indicated in the following notes on their distribution throughout the country.

Distribution of commons

1.13 There is common land in every county of England and Wales (none in Scotland or Northern Ireland) though its incidence is sometimes surprising. Thus a quarter of the former county of Brecknock is registered common as are vast areas of the Lakeland fells in Cumbria. Conversely the High Peak moorlands, so beloved of walkers, are not common land, and there are few commons in the East Midlands, because the enclosure movement was early and thorough in those parts.

1.14 Commons come in all shapes and sizes but there is a broad distinction between the great upland commons of the Pennines and Wales and the smaller commons of lowland Britain. The former are mainly used as pasture. Physical access to common land *de facto* is rarely a problem for the simple reason that its denial, by many miles of fencing, would present a much greater one. There are nevertheless on occasion acute landscape and access problems caused by fencing, some of it unlawful.

1.15 On the lowland commons, rights (where they exist) may or may not be exercised, but the recreational interest is now usually a primary and often a dominant one because of the proximity to the towns. It is here that divergence of interest between types of visitor use and between visitors and commoners is likely to emerge, although this can often be mitigated by some degree of management.

London and the south–east

1.16 ***Greater London*** contains the well-known Wimbledon and Putney Commons, Clapham Common, Blackheath, Hampstead Heath and Wormwood Scrubs among its commons The total estimated area is some 2,800 acres, a remarkable total for such a densely built-up environment. All the commons in London are used for recreational purposes usually governed by special acts or statutory schemes; rights of common have been extinguished on nearly all.

1.17 ***Kent*** is better known for its village greens but it has some varied commons. In the north are the marshlands of Studland and Cliffe and on the western border the high wooded commons of the Weald. Tunbridge Wells is rightly proud of its commons which are the dominating feature of the town, and administered by conservators under their own Tunbridge Wells Improvement Act 1890. Even its public lavatories have a touch of imperial glory. Stelling Minnis near Canterbury has an attractive common which has been especially popular at various times with the army, farmers, gypsies, horse riders and commuter residents.

1.18 In ***East Sussex*** the major common is the 6,000-acre Ashdown Forest with its own act (1974) and elected board of conservators. It is also an SSSI which survives the millions of visitors it attracts each year. Elsewhere in the county are important open spaces at Bexhill Down and Marstakes, as well as several commons used as golf courses.

1.19 ***Surrey*** has a greater proportion of common land in public or quasi-public ownership than any other county, for the tradition of public enjoyment is strong and of long standing. It is here that the roots of the National Trust open space acquisitions are deepest, and the favourable impact on residential property value is marked. Commoners' rights are relatively rare. Historically the Surrey commons were a special interest of the pioneers of the Commons Preservation Society; indeed, the society bought three of the commons and gave them to the National Trust. Lawsuits to safeguard Banstead Common from enclosure by speculative developers lasted for 13 years and vie with the victories at Berkhamsted Common (Herts) and Epping Forest (Essex). Many of the commons, such as Thursley and Hindhead, are of outstanding importance for nature conservation.

1.20 These sandy heathlands of Surrey do not respect county boundaries and continue into the adjacent areas of ***West Sussex*** and ***Hampshire***. Ludshott and Bramshott belong to Hampshire, and Blackdown and Woolbeding are two of the largest commons of ***West Sussex***. Elsewhere in that county there is a scatter of small commons, several of them nature reserves, with an occasional larger one, as at Henfield.

1.21 ***Hampshire***, by contrast, is a county rich in commons of many types, but the largest heathland area, the New Forest (now a national park), was exempted from registration under the Commons Registration Act. It has special status as an Ancient Royal Forest, and is administered by Verderers and the Forestry Commission. Around the Forest 'Perambulation' are important commons at Cadnam, Half Moon, Plaitford and Hightown. There are SSSIs at Gilbert White's Selborne Common and Bransbury, one of a group of riverside marshes in the valley of the Test. At Stockbridge, where the National Trust owns both the marsh and downland commons, the annual court leet continues. The jury is sworn in annually with due ceremony and the aid of silver regalia, and determines the dates of grazing and arrangements for litter clearance and takes other decisions in the interest of the community.

Wessex and the south–west

1.22 The heathlands of east ***Dorset*** are a natural extension of the New Forest and Hampshire basin. Scrub heathland is widespread here. The west of the county has a complex geology and commons are few and scattered. Sadly a large number of commons in Dorset have been lost during the registration process.

1.23 ***Devon*** is a county rich in commons both numerically and by type. The Dartmoor National Park comprises a large group of commons, many owned by the Duchy of Cornwall: they are important for grazing and to walkers and holiday-makers. They are now managed under the Dartmoor Commons Act 1985, the first modern legislation for that purpose. Some of the commoners have special rights 'in venville' over the Forest of Dartmoor and surrounding Commons of Devon. In the north of the county are the West Exmoor commons and less well known, but very attractive, are those of the culm measures towards the Cornish border. Torrington has its own conservators for a fine, hilltop town common. Hatherleigh Moor is documented in Domesday Book and is said to have been given by John of Gaunt to the local people for pasture. The story is apocryphal but at all events the common is now stinted (see 2.2) and firmly managed agriculturally by a local association known as the Potboilers. By contrast the Torridge estuary has attractive grazing marshes at Northam Burrows where the commoners are known as Potwallopers. Finally, East Devon has a number of large recreational commons, notably those managed by the Clinton Devon estate with deeds of access for the public granted by the owner.

1.24 In ***Cornwall*** the analogue of Dartmoor is Bodmin Moor, whose commons include Brown Willy, with its own association of commoners. Elsewhere Cornish commons are mostly small but often of interest. Forrabury, near Boscastle and owned by the National Trust, is said to be a unique survival of the Celtic tenure of land in 'stitchmeal', that is tenanted separately in strips from March to November and grazed in common during the winter months.

1.25 ***Somerset*** commons are in three areas—Exmoor, the Quantocks and the Mendips. Withypool on Exmoor extends to almost 2,000 acres and has stinted pasturage. The Quantock commons illustrate the problems of multiple interest and it is not easy to maintain the right balance. The Mendips include Burrington and Blackdown, with conservators. In ***Gloucestershire*** there is a notable sense of remoteness on the Chipping Sodbury commons north of Bristol. Many popular commons straddle the Cotswold scarp from Minchinhampton (bought by the society and given to the National Trust) near Stroud, to Cleeve Hill high above Cheltenham.

East Anglia and the northern Home Counties

1.26 ***Norfolk*** commons include the popular areas of saltings on the north coast, stretching from Hunstanton to Cromer. Here the local interests include wildfowling and the taking of samphire. Ornithologists and sailors are drawn to these commons as well as the graziers. In ***Suffolk*** too there is a wide range of common land, perhaps the most important being the Sandlings, north of Woodbridge. A great deal of voluntary conservation work is being done in this area. Some heathland, such as Dunwich, is not common.

1.27 ***Essex*** and the northern Home Counties also have a wide scatter of attractive commons, with recreational interest highest near to the towns.

The Welsh Marches

1.28 East of Offa's Dyke it is possible to find as representative a selection of common land as anywhere. The Long Mynd—9,000 acres belonging to the National Trust—and the Clee Hills are large upland grazing areas where the mobile population of the West Midlands cheerfully spills out in great numbers at weekends, and sporting activities like hang-gliding are popular. Similarly the Clent Hills and Hartlebury Common above Stourport are both country parks, the latter also part SSSI.

1.29 ***Herefordshire*** and ***Worcestershire*** offer many magnificent lofty outlooks from commons at Hergest Ridge, Bromyard Downs and Bringsty. These are all in their differing ways honey-pots. More elusive but no less appealing in a tightly drawn landscape are some of the wayside verges of the Welsh Marches, the remnants of old common field, and the flood-plain commons of the Severn at Tewkesbury, Kempsey and Powick. As to the Malvern Hills, the Royal Commission called them 'the long narrow ridge rising majestically from the plain and presenting a skyline unique in Britain'. Its conservators also take care of certain lowland commons nearby.

Wales

1.30 In ***Wales***, where the uplands are sheep country, common land is closely identified with the agricultural interest. Much of this area, though not all, is registered common land. The registers reveal a very large number of commoners, with claims to pasture which, in some cases, could not possibly sustain the number of sheep for which rights are claimed. Registration units are sometimes very large, sometimes very small, and those for the Black Mountain of Carmarthenshire have a sequence reminiscent of the opus numbers of Beethoven's string quartets. Some of the uplands are the haunts of the red kite and the connoisseur walker; others, like the Brecon Beacons and Sugar Loaf, are honey-pots.

1.31 Welsh commons are frequently part of large ownerships, such as the Crown Estate Commissioners and the gathering grounds of Dwr Cymru (Welsh Water). In the 1930s, at the suggestion of the society, the former made a deed granting public access to their 75,000 acres of Welsh commons.

1.32 More recently the national park authority has acquired large areas of common land in the Brecon Beacons and the National Trust has bought the 16,000 acres of the Abergwesyn Commons, the quintessence of mid-Wales wilderness. Many small commons were formerly owned by the Church in Wales, but on disestablishment these passed to the University of Wales which in turn has transferred many to the National Trust, including 50 small areas east of St David's. The lowland commons of Lleyn and Gower are much used by both commoners and visitors, and the urban fringe of the South Wales valleys has some important 'lungs' such as Mynydd Maen near Cwmbran. Much of the Snowdonia National Park is common, although the Snowdon massif itself is not.

The north

1.33 The Pennine commons share some of the features of the Welsh uplands in that they are important for the commoners. Some are very large such as those at Allendale, Hexhamshire and Stanhope. The Lakeland fells are substantially common land with a tradition of hefted sheep, that is sheep which belong to a particular area and which are often the landlord's flock, let with the farm. Public access is, of course, widespread in Lakeland and is accepted on all sides. The North Yorkshire moors are widely stinted and many have their own courts leet. In West Yorkshire, the recreational and water-gathering ground interests loom large and it is surprising that about a third of the metropolitan district of Bradford is common land, including the famous Ilkley Moor. Commons in the north with special historical roots include the Town Moor at Newcastle where the Freemen have in the past often crossed swords with the town over the people's rights, and at Beverley where the commons that surround the town are also often on the local political stage.

1.34 Enough has been said about the diversity and appeal of common land. The recital too easily tends to a catalogue, whereas the reality is the ever-new personal discovery. Each year millions of people go out to enjoy their commons without even thinking about them. They experience the uplift of spirit that motivates the desire to conserve Britain's landscape and wildlife, our most precious endowment.

CHAPTER II

Commons Registration

1. Rights of common

2.1 A right of common has never been comprehensively defined in a statute, but a good definition is quoted in Halsbury's *Laws of England* (4th edition, 1991 reissue) vol 6, p 197: 'a right, which one or more persons may have, to take or use some portion of that which another man's soil naturally produces'. S55(2) of the 2006 act extends this to include cattlegates or beastgates (by whatever name known) and rights of sole or several vesture, herbage or pasture.

2.2 Cattlegates and beastgates are generally exercisable over what is known as gated or stinted pasture, an essential characteristic being that their exercise is limited, usually to a certain period of the year. Rights of sole or several vesture are rather different from other rights of common in that the person enjoying them is entitled to take the product in question to the exclusion of the owner of the soil. With most commons, however, the owner of the soil, in addition to enjoying the mineral and shooting rights, is entitled to what is left of the product after commoners' rights are exercised. For example, if a common will support, say, 1,000 sheep and there are seven commoners with the right to turn out 100 sheep each, the owner of the soil could turn out 300. But the owner of the common is not himself a commoner, for a right of common, as already stated, is a right over 'another man's soil' and the rights of the owner in the common spring directly from his ownership and are not 'common' rights. However, he may have quasi-rights of common which can be recorded in the commons registers: see *In the matter of Pasture End, Murton, Cumbria,* a decision by Mr Commissioner Baden Fuller, discussed below, 3.7.

2.3 There are six generally recognised rights of common: pasture, pannage, estovers, turbary, piscary and common in the soil. Far and away the most important remaining today is the right of pasture, but all the others are still found and many claims have been registered.

2.4 **Common of pasture**: the right to turn stock on to the common to graze. This may be a right appendant, a right appurtenant or a right in gross. An appendant right is in origin a manorial privilege attached to a grant of arable land. The right must have existed before the limit of legal memory (3 September 1189). Appendant rights are rare. An appurtenant right is a right of one person to turn out cattle (and sometimes other animals) on the land of another. Most rights attached to land are in origin appurtenant rights. Both appendant and appurtenant rights must attach to a farm or other land held by the commoner; the more rarely held right of common in gross can be held by a person without land. There are today very few practical differences between rights appendant and rights appurtenant, but the former are usually limited to the right to graze beasts of the plough, such as horses or oxen, or those which manure the ground, such as cattle or sheep. This right is somewhat less easily lost by abandonment. Rights appurtenant may be for goats, geese or any livestock which the custom of the area allows and which can be proved by prescription.

2.5 By s15 of the 1965 act (repealed by s53 of the 2006 act) a right of common of pasture had to be for a definite number of animals—the pre-1965 rights to graze animals *sans nombre*, ie without limits, can no longer exist.

2.6 In many parts of the country, especially in upland areas such as the Lake District, Pennines or in Wales, rights of common of pasture are extremely important and the existence or not of a right may make all the difference to the viability of a hill farm.

2.7 It sometimes happens that, where two commons adjoin each other without being physically separated, animals stray from one common to the other. This is a recognised legal right, known as a right of common by reason of vicinage. However, it is not a separate right, but arises only from the right to graze the 'home' common, and it can be terminated by the owner of the adjoining common erecting a suitable barrier. For these reasons Mr Commissioner Settle decided, in *In the Matter of Cheesewring Common, Henwood Common and Longstone Downs, St Cleer, Cornwall,* that the right to stray was not a right of common capable of registration under the 1965 act. In *Newman* v *Bennett* [1980] the High Court held that the right was a right of common and that N, whose cattle strayed from the 'home' common into the New Forest, was rightly convicted of a breach of the New Forest by-laws relating to the marking of animals belonging to those with rights of common in the Forest. It should be noted that, by virtue of s5(2) of the 2006 act, the New Forest is exempt from registration, so that this case cannot be taken to overrule Mr Commissioner Settle's decision, a view shared by Mr Commissioner Baden Fuller in *In the Matter of the Forest of Dartmoor*.

2.8 **Pannage**: the right of pannage was succinctly described by Jessel MR in *Chilton* v *London Corporation* [1878] as 'a right granted to an owner of pigs to go into the wood of the grantor and to allow the pigs to eat the acorns or beech mast which fall to the ground'. The commoner has no right to pick the acorns or even shake the trees for his pigs—the right is limited to what actually falls to the ground (Jessel MR in the same case at page 565). Quite a number of rights of pannage have been registered over the Wealden commons of southern England.

2.9 **Estovers**: the right to take underwood and small branches, either for fuel or for repairing fences or buildings, or bracken and similar growths for litter for the benefit of the commoner's animals. The nature of estovers was discussed by the Court of Appeal in *De la Warr* v *Miles* [1881] where a right of the defendant to cut furze and small branches from trees on the extensive Ashdown Forest was successfully upheld.

2.10 **Turbary**: the right to dig turf or peat for use as fuel in the commoner's house. The various cases on turbary were reviewed in the leading case of *AG* v *Reynolds* [1911] which made it clear that turbary can only exist for the benefit of a house, but that if an old house enjoying the right is pulled down, the right can continue for the benefit of a new house which replaces it.

2.11 **Piscary**: the right to fish in another person's lakes, ponds or streams. The fish must be taken in reasonable quantities for consumption in the commoner's own household. The authorities on piscary were noted in *Chesterfield* v *Harris* [1908], upheld on appeal to the House of Lords as *Harris* v *Chesterfield* [1911]. Piscary cannot exist in the sea or in tidal rivers since there is a public right of fishing there.

2.12 **Common in the soil**: the right to take sand, gravel, stone or minerals for use on the commoner's holding. Thus in *Heath* v *Deane* [1905] the right to take stone from a quarry on the common was successfully upheld. The right can include the right to take coal, which has been upheld in *Portland* v *Hill* [1866]. Such a right is rare. The digging of coal now requires a licence under the Coal Industry Act 1994.

2.13 A local variant of the right of common in the soil is the right for all persons resident in Devon and Cornwall to take sea-sand from the foreshore 'for bettering of their land, and for the increase of corn and tillage'. The right was granted in the thirteenth century and confirmed by the Sea-sand (Devon and Cornwall) Act 1609. It is not clear, however, whether the right is a right of common capable of registration under the 1965 act (or the 2006 act). The chief commons commissioner declined to express a view in his decision, *In the Matter of Gunwalloe Church Cove Beach, Gunwalloe, Cornwall (no 2)*, because he had not seen the original grant. Mr Commissioner Baden Fuller held in his decision, *In the Matter of Maenporth Beach, Falmouth, Cornwall*, that the right was not a right of common because it was enjoyed by a fluctuating body of people (*Gateward's case* [1607] discussed below, 3.30).

2. Waste land of a manor not subject to rights of common

2.14 S22(1)(b) of the 1965 act (repealed by s53 of the 2006 act) included 'waste land of a manor not subject to rights of common' in the definition of common land subject to registration under the act. This phrase was not defined in the act, so that, in dealing with disputed or conflicting registrations, the commons commissioners and the courts had to rely on judicial definitions. The classic definition was given by Watson B in *AG* v *Hanmer* [1858]:

> The true meaning of 'wastes' or 'waste lands' or 'waste grounds of the manor' is the open, uncultivated and unoccupied lands parcel of the manor, or open lands parcel of the manor other than the demesne lands of the manor.

2.15 This was interpreted by the commissioners and the courts to mean that land qualified for registration as waste land of a manor provided that it was:

(a) waste land, as opposed to enclosed, occupied or cultivated land, and
(b) physically within a manor, and
(c) in the ownership of the lord of the manor.

2.16 This interpretation of the phrase (which has been overturned (2.122)) is no longer of practical importance so far as the registration of new land as common land under the 2006 act is concerned. Any land which might have been waste land of a manor and which was not registered under the 1965 act lost its status as a result of non-registration. It is no longer possible for land to become waste land of a manor. The manor as a legal entity ceased to have any significance when the tenure of land by copyhold was abolished by the Law of Property Act 1922.

2.17 However, the concept of waste land of a manor, and its interpretation, still has relevance in the context of rectification and amendment of the register in accordance with sch2 to the 2006 act, discussed at 2.120-125 below.

3. The initial registration process

2.18 The 1965 act provided for the registration of common land, common rights and town and village greens. Applications for registration could be made between 2 January 1967 and 2 January 1970. Registration authorities could make registrations without application up to 31 July 1970. All registrations were initially provisional, thus allowing for objections to be made. The periods for objection ran from 1 October 1968 to 30 September 1970 for provisional registrations made before 1 July 1968 (first period registrations) and from 1 May 1970 to 31 May 1972 for provisional registrations made after 30 June 1968 (second period registrations). First period registrations to which no objections were made became final and conclusive on 1 October 1970 and second period registrations to which no objections were made became final and conclusive on 1 August 1972.

2.19 Where objections were made and not withdrawn (before 18 December 1971 for first period registrations and before 31 July 1973 for second period objections), the resulting disputes were referred to a commons commissioner. He conducted a hearing into the dispute and gave a written decision. (The office of commissioner was abolished on the repeal of the 1965 act by s53 of the 2006 act; copies of the commissioners' decisions can be obtained from Defra: for address, see preface.) It was possible to appeal against a commissioner's decision to the High Court, but only on a point of law.

2.20 The commons commissioners were also responsible for adjudicating on disputes relating to the ownership of commons (2.36) and those arising from the Common Land (Rectification of Registers) Act 1989 (2.111-116).

2.21 Where a registration became final, s10 of the 1965 act provided that the registration of the land as common land or as a town or village green, or the registration of any rights over such land, was conclusive evidence of the matters registered.

2.22 The final registration of ownership of a common or green was not subject to s10, but the longer such a registration remains unchallenged the more difficult it will become for the correctness of the registration to be proved wrong.

2.23 S21(2) of the 1965 act provided that s10 was not to apply in deciding whether or not land forms part of a highway.

2.24 S10 of the 1965 act has been replaced in effect by s18 of the 2006 act (2.97-103).

2.25 Although the initial period of registration is long since over, it is possible to apply to rectify the register in accordance with sch2 to the 2006 act to correct mistakes made under the 1965 act (2.129-131), to register manorial waste that was wrongly not registered under that act (2.120-125) and to register new common land and new common rights (2.45-49).

4. Registration authorities

2.26 The original registration authorities were the Greater London Council, county councils and county borough councils. As a result of several changes to the structure of local government in both England and Wales, the current registration authorities are: in England, London borough councils, county councils and district councils in areas without a county council; in Wales, county and county borough councils.

2.27 The responsibilities of the registration authorities are to compile, maintain, and (where authorised) amend the registers.

2.28 In 1993 East Sussex County Council's common land registers were burnt. The council obtained a private act (the Commons Registration (East Sussex) Act 1994) which required the council to reconstruct the registers. The new registers have been prepared and were validated on 18 June 2004.

5. The registers

2.29 The form and content of the registers whether of common land or of town or village greens are prescribed by regulations made under s3 of the 2006 act. The registers are required by s20 of the 2006 act to be open to inspection by the public, subject to the conditions set out in regulations (which have not yet been made).

2.30 Copies or extracts from the registers may be taken and registration authorities charge a fee for any copies of documents which they provide.

2.31 Each registration comprises a separate register unit, with its own number. For each unit, the register consists of three parts—

(a) The land section: this describes the land by reference to the register map, which is part of the register.
(b) The rights section: this sets out the nature and extent of the rights of common registered over the land.
(c) The ownership register: this gives details of the registered owner(s) of the land (if any, see part 6 below for 'ownerless' commons), so long as the title to the land is not registered under

the Land Registration Act 2002. If the title is registered, or becomes so after registration in the register of common land, the entries in the ownership section are deleted. However, that does not mean that the public cannot find out about ownership: an official copy of the register and plan relating to a title can be applied for on form 109 sent to the appropriate District Land Registry serving the area in which the land is situated, with the necessary fee. The form should be accompanied by a plan showing the boundaries of the land concerned. It is also possible to search the Land Registry's index map to see whether or not land has a registered title. The relevant forms can be downloaded from the Land Registry's website (www.landreg.gov.uk), which also gives details of the fees payable.

2.32 S21 of the 2006 act provides that an official copy of any part of the register is admissible as evidence in court to the same extent as the original and enables regulations to be made to prescribe the form etc of official copies.

2.33 S24 of the 2006 act sets out in detail the matters which may be prescribed by regulations with reference to applications to amend the registers to reflect changes made in accordance with part 1 of the act.

2.34 S25 of the 2006 act enables regulations to be made for the registers to be kept in electronic form.

2.35 In *G & K Ladenbau Ltd* v *Crawley and de Reya* [1978] it was held that a solicitor who negligently failed to search the registers of common land was liable in damages to a client who suffered loss as a result.

6. Registration of ownership of common land

Under the Commons Registration Act 1965

2.36 The 1965 act provided for the registration of claims to the ownership of commons (and greens) which had already been registered in the initial registration period, except where the title had been registered at HM Land Registry under the Land Registration Acts. However, para 8 of sch3 to the 2006 act provides for regulations to be made to require the removal of ownership details from the register where the Chief Land Registrar notifies the registration authority that the title to the land in question has been registered under the Land Registration Act 2002. Regulations will prescribe the way in which this is indicated in the register and what the registration authority must do with documents relating to ownership entries. This latter point is presumably intended to enact the CLPS proposal that all registered information should be retained at the county-based level.

2.37 The procedure in relation to applications for registration of ownership was the same as for registering common land or rights of common (2.18-22). Where a registration was objected to, or where there were conflicting claims, the resulting dispute was referred to a commons commissioner.

2.38 Where a registration of land as common land became final, but no one was registered as owner, the registration authority was required to refer the question of ownership to a commissioner (1965 act s8). If the commissioner was satisfied that a person or body was the owner, he directed registration of that person in the ownership register. If the commissioner was unable to discover an owner, the land became subject to s9 of the 1965 act (now s45 of the 2006 act: see 2.51).

2.39 Failure to register ownership during the initial registration period did not prejudice a person's title. This was in marked contrast to the position of a commoner, whose rights were extinguished by operation of statute (s1(2)(b) of the 1965 act) if an application to register was not made before 3 January 1970. The reason for this different treatment of owners and commoners was not made clear in the act, but appears to be connected with the fact that under the general law an owner of land cannot lose his title unless he has failed to assert his ownership for at least 12 years (Limitation Act 1980 s15). Those who drafted the 1965 act presumably felt that as the registration period was only three years, loss of title through failure to register would have amounted to a drastic shortening of the limitation period.

2.40 A final registration of ownership was not made conclusive by s10 of the 1965 act, but the longer such a registration is unchallenged the more difficult it would become to assert and prove that the registration was wrong. A challenge would have to be made by way of appeal to the High Court under s19(7) of the 2006 act (2.107).

2.41 Where common land (or a village green) was transferred (whether by sale or gift) after ownership has been finally registered, the title had to be registered at HM Land Registry and the 1965 act registration of ownership deleted (1965 act s12).

2.42 The Land Registration Act 2002 (in force from 13 October 2003) consolidated the existing Land Registration Acts and made a number of changes to the law. The 2002 act gave greater encouragement to register with HM Land Registry the ownership of land which still remains unregistered there, but s33(d) excluded from registration there any notice of an interest which is capable of being registered under the Commons Registration Act 1965. Presumably, this was meant only to exclude rights of common but it seems to have been overlooked that the ownership of a right of common might also be recorded there if not already in the Land Registry.

Under the Commons Act 2006

2.43 Where common land (or a town or village green) is transferred (whether by sale or gift) after ownership has been finally registered, the title must be registered at HM Land Registry (s4 of the Land Registration Act 2002) and the registration of ownership under the 1965 act or the 2006 act deleted (para 8 of sch3 to the 2006 act). However, that does not mean that the public cannot find out about ownership (2.31).

2.44 The CLF recommended that unclaimed common land should be vested in the appropriate local authority. The CLPS made similar proposals about the vesting of unclaimed common land. The 2006 act does not enact these recommendations.

7. Creation of new rights of common

2.45 Common rights can be created by the following methods:

(a) express grant, but only if the right is attached to land and is not over a registered town or village green (2006 act, s6(2)(a));
(b) pursuant to any enactment other than the 2006 act (2006 act, s6(2)(b)).

It is no longer possible to create a new right of common by prescription or long usage. That right was abolished by s6(1) of the 2006 act.

(a) Express grant

2.46 An express grant must comply with any requirements as to form and content prescribed by regulations (2006 act, s6(4)) and does not take effect in law until registered. If the land over which the right is granted is not registered as common land, that land must be registered as well (2006 act, s6(5)).

2.47 The registration authority must refuse an application to register a right to graze an animal if the authority thinks that the land is unable to sustain the exercise of the right or, where the land is already registered as common land, to sustain the exercise of any other rights of common exercisable over the land. The purpose of this provision is to enable the authority to control overgrazing. In order to be in a position to determine whether or not the exercise of the right is sustainable, the registration authority will be able to take appropriate expert advice; s24 of the 2006 act enables regulations to be made covering, among other things, the persons who must be consulted or whose advice must be sought in relation to an application.

(b) Act of parliament

2.48 Any rights of common created by or under an act of parliament before 31 July 1970 should have been registered under the 1965 act in the initial registration period. Failure to register then resulted in extinguishment of the rights (*re Turnworth Down, Dorset* [1977]).

2.49 The Greenham and Crookham Commons Act 2002 resurrected rights of common lost when the commons were taken by the Ministry of Defence for an airfield and which itself has now been given up and cleared. The act allows new rights to be granted to any owner of a residence within a defined area. These rights will be recorded in a register to be kept in accordance with this act, not the 2006 act.

8. Commons where no person is registered as owner

2.50 Where a commons commissioner was unable to discover the owner of a registered common there was no procedure (as there was in the case of village greens, see 7.25) for vesting the common in a local authority or other person.

2.51 If nothing further had been done, such commons would have been at considerable risk of encroachment from nearby properties, for no man's land is in danger of being 'every man's land'. Therefore s45 of the 2006 act (which came into force on 1 October 2006 in England only by virtue of the Commons Act 2006 (Commencement No 1, Transitional Provisions and Savings) (England) Order 2006 (SI 2504), and replaces s9 of the 1965 act in virtually identical terms) provides that any local authority (county, county borough, district and local council) in whose area such an 'ownerless' common is situated may take such steps against unlawful interference as an owner in possession of the land could take. This means that the authority can take criminal proceedings, eg under the Criminal Damage Act 1971, and also civil action to prevent trespass (in *R* v *Teignbridge District Council ex parte Street* [1989] the council successfully relied on s9 of the 1965 act in taking possession proceedings against trespassers), but it is doubtful if the authority could sue for damages since the section gives it no legal interest in the soil.

2.52 The section does not empower an authority to spend money on clearance or improvement (eg removal of litter or planting trees), but such expenditure could be covered by other statutory powers: for principal authorities, ss2 and 3 of the Local Government Act 2000 (power to promote the well-being of area) and for local councils s137 of the Local Government Act 1972 (power to spend up £5.30 per elector (in England) and £5 per elector (in Wales) per year for the benefit of the area; these amounts are regularly revised upwards). Furthermore, a principal authority may be under a duty to keep the land free of litter under s89 of the Environmental Protection Act 1990. Such an authority also has power under s89 of the National Parks and Access to the Countryside Act 1949 to plant trees for preserving or enhancing natural beauty and to treat derelict, neglected or unsightly land, but the society will wish to be consulted on any proposals affecting common land.

2.53 In practice, s9 of the 1965 act has not been very effective because it confers no duty on an authority to take protective action, nor does it specify which level of authority is empowered to act. In consequence, authorities can readily avoid responsibility. There is no reason to believe that s45 of the 2006 act will be any more effective than its predecessor.

2.54 The section is without prejudice to other powers the authority may have to protect common land, eg part 3 of the 2006 act (discussed at 6.63-76).

2.55 'Ownerless' commons are in a legal limbo because no provision for vesting them in a local authority or some other body has been made by parliament. The opportunity offered by the 2006 act to do this was not taken up. The CLF (appendix 1) recommended that they should be vested in the local council or, if there was none, in the district council (which would now include the county or county borough council in Wales).

2.56 The CLPS proposed that: (1) unclaimed common land should be vested in a suitable body which is able to deliver effective management, and (2) claimants who prove they had title to common land which was vested in a local authority should be able to reclaim their land on production of suitable evidence and within the limitation period (currently 12 years under the Limitation Act 1980).

2.57 It may be possible for a local authority to acquire ownership of an 'ownerless' common by adverse possession. This could happen if the authority took complete control of the land and acted as if it were the true owner. In such circumstances, it might be possible to apply to HM Land Registry for registration of a possessory title which, if not challenged, could in due course be converted into an absolute title. However, any authority (or other person) contemplating such action should take legal advice. The topic is outside the scope of this book.

9. Alteration of common rights

Variation

2.58 The owner of common land or a green may agree to vary rights of common registered over the common or green. Such a variation only takes effect if it complies with the requirements as to form and contents prescribed by regulations and does not take effect in law until the variation is registered (s7(4)).

2.59 S7(1) of the 2006 act enables an application to be made to amend the register to record a variation of common rights in the following circumstances:

(a) where a right of common becomes exercisable over new land instead of all or part of the land over which it is exercisable;
(b) where a right of common becomes exercisable over new land in addition to the land over which it is already exercisable;
(c) where there is an alteration of what can be done by virtue of the right.

S7(2) provides that a variation under (a) or (b) cannot be made whereby the new right is exercisable over a town or village green and s7(3) prohibits the variation of a right over a green so as to extend what can be done in exercise of the right.

2.60 S7(5) empowers the registration authority to refuse to register a variation if the authority thinks that the land would be unable to sustain the exercise of the varied right and the exercise of any other registered rights over the land. Thus, for example, a variation to enable 300 cattle to graze instead of 100 sheep would almost certainly be rejected by the authority because of the likelihood of overgrazing.

2.61 A variation of rights does not include a reduction in the area of land over which the rights are exercisable other than in accordance with s7(1)(a) (2.59). A reduction in that area may be achieved by means of a surrender under s12 (2.80).

Apportionment

2.62 Apportionment occurs (if at all) where land to which rights of common are attached is divided into two or more separate ownerships. S8 of the 2006 act enables regulations to be made whereby the register can be amended only when:

(a) a disposition relating to an apportioned right must itself be registered under the 2006 act (2.64); or
(b) the register must be amended under s11 of the 2006 act (2.77).

This somewhat opaque wording is intended to ensure that, generally speaking, apportionment of common rights are not to be registered. Rights of common will be shown as attached to the land with which they were enjoyed at the time when an entry relating to those rights was last made in the register. Subsequent changes to that land will not be recorded (but see s9(5) with regard to *pro rata* apportionment; see 2.69).

2.63 The following is an example of how the regulations are intended to operate. A common is subject to rights to graze 100 sheep, the rights being divided equally between farms A and B (ie 50 sheep per farm). The owner of farm A dies and the farm is divided equally between the owner's two children. Two new units—A1 and A2—are created and part 1 of the act ensures that each unit enjoys the right to graze 25 sheep. Farm B is developed for housing in 50 separate plots, each with one house built on it. Each of those plots has the right to graze one sheep. The register will show a common subject to two separate rights to graze sheep attached to the two original farms A and B. Following the subdivision described above, the owners of the new properties formerly comprised in farms A and B will be able to trace their entitlement to exercise their rights of common by reference to those farms. For example, the owner of a house built on farm B will be able to show that he occupies $1/50^{th}$ part of the area of the original farm, and (applying the rules of *pro rata* apportionment) thus has $1/50^{th}$ of the rights shown in the register as attached to farm B. The owner will be able to show that he is entitled to exercise the rights by virtue of the attachment of the rights to his house (the attachment will be shown in the commons register), and by his ownership of the house (which may be registered in the register of title to land kept by the Land Registry).

2.64 However, regulations may provide that the register is to be amended where an apportionment results from the variation (2.58-61 above), severance (2.66-75) or surrender (2.80-82 below) of rights in accordance with part 1 of the 2006 act.

2.65 S8(3) provides that, where the commons register has not been amended to reflect an apportionment of rights, the rights which arise as a result of that apportionment are treated as if they were separately registered. This is designed to ensure that each of the rights arising as a result of the apportionment is treated for the purposes of part 1 of the act as if it were registered, so that, for example, application may be made under s13 (2.80-81 below) to surrender and extinguish the right even though the right is not itself reflected in an individual entry in the register at the time of the application.

Severance

2.66 If a commoner disposes of the land to which his rights of common are attached the normal rule is that the rights pass with the land. By s62 of the 1925 act a conveyance of land is deemed to include *inter alia* all rights appertaining or reputed to appertain thereto, unless the conveyance expresses a contrary intention. Where the conveyance expressly reserves the rights of common, the traditional view was that they were extinguished unless they could be measured exactly, in which case they became rights in gross. Prior to the passing of the 1965 act, the measurement of grazing rights depended largely upon the rules of levancy and couchancy (ie the capacity of the commoner's land to sustain the grazing animals of the commoner), but s15 of the act provided for such rights to be quantified numerically. In the leading case on this point—*Bettison* v *Langton* [2001]—the House of Lords held that a right to pasture a fixed number of animals was severable from the land to which the right was originally attached. On severance, the right became a right in gross (ie not attached to any land).

2.67 S9(2) of the 2006 act prohibits the severance of rights of common from the land to which they attached except where authorised under schedule 1 to the act (2.71) or under any other act. (S8 of the Dartmoor Commons Act 1985 enacted such a prohibition in relation to rights of common exercisable over registered common land on Dartmoor and s33 of the Greenham and Crookham Commons Act 2002 prohibited the severance of common rights from the land to which they were attached, but allowed them to be transferred to the freehold of another residence in the area entitled to be granted such rights. These have been repealed by the Commons Act 2006.)

2.68 S9(3) of the 2006 act renders void any instrument, or part of an instrument, which seeks to sever common rights from the land to which they are attached. S9(4) provides that where land to which common rights are attached is disposed of, any purported reservation of those rights to person disposing of the land is void. In other words, the purported severance of the rights by the disposer of the land retaining them is of no effect.

2.69 S9(5) provides that common rights must be apportioned *pro rata*. Thus, for example, where a farm is sold as two lots, the rights attached to the farm must be apportioned to each of the lots according to area. If the farm has rights to graze 50 sheep, and is sold as two lots of equal area, a right to graze 25 sheep is attached to each lot.

2.70 S9 of the 2006 act is deemed to have come into force on 28 June 2005 (the day after the introduction of the Commons Bill into Parliament) and thus has retrospective effect. The reason for this was to prevent severance of rights between that date and the date on which the bill received the royal assent.

2.71 Paras 1 and 3 of sch1 to the 2006 act make provision for the authorisation of permanent severance of common rights in the following circumstances:

(a) where the right is transferred on its own to:
   (i) a commons council (chapter IV, part 10 below);
   (ii) Natural England (where the land or part of it is in England);
   (iii) the Countryside Council for Wales (where the land or part of it is in Wales).

   The procedure for transfer is laid down in detail in para 1 of the schedule.

(b) where the appropriate national authority (defined in the preface) makes an order authorising permanent severance. Again, the procedure for severance is set out in detail in para 3 of the schedule.

2.72 Para 2 of sch1 to the 2006 act authorises the temporary severance of rights of common from the land to which they are attached by means of a lease or licence. Authorisation is given either by an order made by the appropriate national authority (defined in the preface) or in accordance with rules made by a commons council (chapter IV, part 10 below). The Commons (Severance of Rights) (England) Order 2006 (SI 2145) came into force on 9 September 2006 but has effect as from 28 June 2005. The order does not apply in Wales. The order allows temporary severance of common-grazing rights in the following circumstances:

(a) by leasing or licensing the right of common on its own, provided that the period of the lease or licence does not exceed two years; or

(b) by leasing or licensing the land, or part of the land, to which the right of common is attached, without the right of common.

Where a right of common is temporarily severed from any land pursuant to (b), any disposal of the retained right of common on or after the grant of the lease or licence of the land and before its termination is of no effect unless

(a) the disposal is made to the grantee of the lease or licence of the land; and
(b) the disposal is made for a period expiring not more than two years from the expiry of the lease or licence of the land.

2.73 Sch1 came into force on the day on which the act received the royal assent (19 July 2006).

2.74 S54 of the 2006 act is also deemed to have come into force on 28 June 2005. It makes transitional provision for the lawful severance of rights of common made between that date and the date on which s1 of the 2006 act comes into force to be registered in accordance with the 1965 act.

2.75 The provisions relating to severance in the 2006 act have relevance mainly to rights to graze or turn out animals. As indicated above (2.66), grazing rights must be quantified, but there is no such requirement in relation to other rights of common. Under the common law, where a right cannot be exactly measured, its severance from the land will result in extinguishment. However, since severance can now only take place under statutory authority, it is submitted that the common law has been overruled and severance will no longer result in extinguishment.

Attachment

2.76 At common law, a right of common held in gross cannot be attached to land. S10 of the 2006 act enables the owner of such a right and the person entitled to occupy the land (if different) to apply to register the right as attached to land.

Re-allocation of attached rights

2.77 S11 of the 2006 act enables the owner of land to which common rights are attached to apply to amend the register so that the rights do not attach to a specified part of the land (called 'the relevant part') in any of the following circumstances:

(a) the relevant part is not used for agricultural purposes;
(b) planning permission has been granted for a non-agricultural use;
(c) a compulsory purchase order has been made, the land is not

vested in the acquiring authority and the land is to be use for non-agricultural purposes.

The purpose of this provision is to enable rights of common to be detached from part of a register unit which is going out of agricultural use on a permanent basis, thus freeing the land from those rights.

2.78 Regulations may prescribe what is and what is not use for agricultural purposes and whether or not the consent of any other person is required before an application to amend the register is granted.

Transfer of rights in gross

2.79 S12 of the 2006 act provides that a transfer of registered rights held in gross (ie not attached to land) does not take effect unless its form and content comply with requirements prescribed by regulations. S12 also provides that the transfer does not operate in law until the transferee is registered as the new owner of the rights.

Surrender and extinguishment of common rights

2.80 S13(3) of the 2006 act abolishes all the common law methods of surrendering and extinguishing rights of common. Instead, s13(1) provides that a surrender of common rights does not take effect unless its form and content comply with requirements prescribed by regulations. The subsection also provides that the surrender does not operate in law until the right is removed from the register.

2.81 S13(2) provides that a surrender does not include a disposition of a right of common made under s7(1)(a) (2.59).

2.82 S1(2)(b) of the 1965 act provided that, after the initial registration period, 'no rights of common shall be exercisable over any ... land unless they are registered under this act or under the Land Registration Acts 1925 and 1936'. It was decided in *Central Electricity Generating Board* v *Clwyd County Council* [1976] that the effect of s1(2)(b) was to extinguish unregistered rights of common. The subsection applied to all rights of common which were capable of being registered before the end of the initial registration period, including rights created by an inclosure award (*re Turnworth Down, Dorset* [1977]).

10. Exemptions from registration

2.83 S11 of the 1965 act exempted from registration the New Forest, Epping Forest, the Forest of Dean (an exemption continued by s5(2) and (3) of the 2006 act) and land included in an exemption order made by the minister. An order could only be made for land (a) which was regulated under the Commons Act 1876, the Commons Act 1899, the Metropolitan Commons Acts 1866 to 1898 or under a local act; (b) over which rights of common had not been exercised for at least 30 years, and (c) of which the owner was known.

2.84 Exemption orders were made for the following commons: The Links Common (Whitley Bay, North Tyneside, formerly Northumberland); the Stray (Harrogate, North Yorkshire); Cippenham Village Green Common (Slough, formerly Berkshire); West End Road Recreation Ground (Southampton); Whitley Common, Hearsall Common, Keresley Common, Stoke Commons, Sowe Common, Radford Common, Gosford Green, Stivichall Common, Top Green, Greyfriars Green (all in Coventry); Victoria Gardens (Portland, Dorset); Otterbourne Hill Common (Hampshire); Cassiobury Common (Watford, Herts); Shenfield Common (Brentwood, Essex); Ley Hill Common, Coleshill Common, Austenwood Common, Gold Hill Common, Hyde Heath (all in the vicinity of Amersham, Bucks); Thorpe Green (Egham, Surrey); Downside Common, Old Common, Little Heath Common, Upper and Lower Tilt Commons, Brooks Hill Common, Leigh Hill Common, Oxshott Heath (all in Esher, Surrey); West Wickham Common, Spring Park (London Borough of Bromley); Kenley Common, Coulsdon Common, Farthing Down Common, Riddlesdown Common (all in the London Borough of Croydon); Mitcham Common (London Borough of Merton); Micklegate Stray (York).

2.85 It should not be assumed that this list of commons covers all the commons which might have been exempted. Some local authority owners or managers (such as the former Greater London Council) did not seek exemption orders although a number of their open spaces would have been eligible. These were registered, sometimes including extensions which had been enclosed land for centuries and were not eligible for registration in any event. Nevertheless, there were no objections and so the registrations became final. Occasionally, the opposite happened. Applications for exemption were not made in respect of a few commons or parts of them that might have been eligible, but neither were they registered. Some recreational allotments were also not registered as town or village greens. It might be possible to use the rectification provisions in sch2 to the 2006 act (2.104-108) to correct any errors made during the initial period of registration. While the point has not been tested in the courts, it is submitted that the original acts and statutory schemes remain fully in force, unless specifically repealed, rescinded or amended, to the extent that they gave rights to the public, despite non-registration under the 1965 act. Under sch2 to the 2006 Act it is possible to register common land exempted from registration (2.118).

11. Amendment of the registers

Statutory dispositions of common land

2.86 S14 of the 2006 act provides for regulations to be made to enable the registers to be amended where a 'relevant instrument' is made in relation to common land or to any rights of common. Regulations may also provide for the registration of land given in exchange. A relevant instrument is:

(a) an order, deed or other instrument made under the Acquisition of Land Act 1981 (ie compulsory acquisition);
(b) a conveyance made for the purposes of s13 of the New Parishes Measure 1943 (no 1) (power of the Church Commissioners to acquire land for churches etc)
(c) any other instrument made under any enactment (eg a power under a private act to acquire land).

2.87 Regulations may also require an application to be made to amend the register when a relevant instrument has been made and to provide that the instrument does not operate in law until the requirements laid down in the regulations are complied with.

Deregistration and exchange of common land under statutory powers

A Applications

2.88 S16 of the 2006 act enables the owner of registered common land to apply to the appropriate national authority for the land (called in the act 'the release land') to be removed from the register. If the area is more than 200 square metres the application must include provision for exchange land (called in the act 'replacement land'). If the area is 200 square metres or less, the application may include a provision for replacement land. The replacement land must not already be registered common land or a town or village green and the owner of the replacement land must join in the application if he is not also the owner of the release land.

2.89 The appropriate national authority must have regard to the following matters when determining the application:

(a) the interests of persons having rights in or over, or occupying, the release land, especially those of commoners;
(b) the interests of the neighbourhood;
(c) the public interest;
(d) any other matter considered to be relevant.

2.90 Where the release land does not exceed 200 square metres and the application does not include the provision of replacement land, the authority must have particular regard to (a) to (c) above when determining the application.

2.91 Where the release land or the replacement land is subject to a legal charge or is let for a term of more than seven years, an application under s16 can only be made with the consent to the chargee or the leaseholder. A legal charge is defined in s15(9) as:

(a) a registered charge within the meaning of the Land Registration Act 2002 (in the case of land with registered title);
(b) a charge registered under the Land Charges Act 1972; or
(c) a legal mortgage within the meaning of the Law of Property Act 1925 which is not registered under the Land Charges Act 1972.

B Orders

2.92 S17 of the 2006 act provides that where the appropriate national authority grants an application under s16 (2.88-91) it must make an order requiring the registration authority to remove the release land (defined at 2.88) from the register and to register any replacement land (defined at 2.88). Where rights of common existed over the release land the order must require the registration of those rights over the replacement land. Any rights registered over the release land are extinguished on the date on which the register is amended in pursuance of an order (called the 'relevant date').

2.93 Where release land is subject to any provision in a specified statute (called the 'relevant provision'—see 2.94), that provision ceases to apply to the land on the relevant date and any replacement land is made subject to that provision on the same date, unless the order makes alternative provision. Thus, for example, if the release land is subject to s193 of the 1925 act (page 128) the replacement land becomes subject to s193 on the relevant date.

2.94 The relevant provisions are—

(a) S193 of the 1925 act (chapter IV, part 4);
(b) A scheme under the Metropolitan Commons Act 1866 (chapter

IV, part 1);

(c) A provisional order confirmation act made under the Commons Act 1876 (chapter IV, part 2);

(d) A scheme under the Commons Act 1899 (chapter IV part 3);

(e) Section 1 of the Commons Act 1908 (chapter IV, part 12).

12. Conclusiveness of the registers

Commons Registration Act 1965

2.95 S10 of the 1965 act provided that the final registration of land as common land or as a town or village green, and the registration of rights of common thereover, was conclusive evidence of the matters registered. The significance of this provision was highlighted in *Corpus Christi College* v *Gloucestershire County Council* [1982] in relation to an application to remove finally registered common land from the register on the ground that it had ceased to be common land. The Court of Appeal held that land could only cease to be common where a relevant event occurred after the registration had become final, for example where the ownership and possession of the common and of the rights of common registered over it came into the same hands. The facts were that rights of common were provisionally registered over Temple Ham Meadow, Little Rissington, Gloucestershire by the parish council and, in accordance with s4(2)(b) of the 1965 act, the land was also provisionally registered. The college objected to the rights registration but not to the land registration. Following a hearing in 1976 a commons commissioner refused to confirm the rights registration, but the land registration had become final on 1 October 1970. The college applied to the county council under s13(a) of the 1965 act on the ground that the land had ceased to be common land, at the latest, on 15 May 1976 when the rights registration became void. The application was refused and the college sought a declaration from the county court that the land had ceased to be common land. The judge held that the registration was conclusive by virtue of s10 and refused to make the declaration sought. The Court of Appeal upheld the decision of the county court judge on the basis that, since the date of registration, the land had not 'ceased' to be common land. The land registration was made solely in consequence of the rights registration and there was no evidence that the land was manorial waste; it could not therefore be shown that the land was manorial waste before registration and, without such evidence, it could not be said that the land 'ceased' to be common land after registration. In the words of Kerr LJ, 'the appellants' application to amend the register in effect involves them in seeking to show that the land had never been common land (because it had never been waste land of a manor), but this is clearly precluded by s10'.

2.96 The Corpus Christi case was followed in a village green case in *R* v *Norfolk County Council ex parte Parry* [1996], where the facts were as follows. A piece of land which formed part of a recreation ground had been closed off for many years and used for agriculture. Norfolk County Council registered the whole of the recreation ground as a village green. The registration became final in 1972. In 1974 P began to build a bungalow on the land. In 1994 he applied to remove the land from the register. The application was refused on the ground that the registration was conclusive and the register could only be amended if the land ceased to be a green after the date of final registration. P appealed to the High Court by way of judicial review. The court upheld the council's interpretation of the law and followed the *Corpus Christi* case (2.95 above). P's real complaint was that the land should not have been registered in the first place, but an application made under s13 could not attack a registration made immune from challenge under s10.

Commons Act 2006

2.97 S18 does not in terms apply to land registered as common land or as a town or village green over which no rights of common are registered. In such a case, s10 of the 1965 act applies to land finally registered under that act (2.95-96 above) (ie before the 2006 act came into force). In practice, all currently registered commons and greens over which there are no rights fall into this category.

2.98 It is not possible under the 2006 act to register land as common land where there are no rights of common, except in accordance with sch2 (rectification of mistakes) (2.117).

2.99 The registration of new village greens is dealt with in chapter VII below.

2.100 S18 applies in terms to common land or a town or village green over which rights of common are registered. Subs 2 deems the land to be subject to the registered rights and subs 3 deems any rights registered with the land to have become attached thereto upon registration of that land. Subs 3 needs to be read in the light of s9 (2.67-2.75) which effectively prohibits severance of rights from land save in limited circumstances.

2.101 S18(4) provides that, in the case of a right of common in gross (not attached to land), the person registered as owner of the right, if not otherwise the owner, is deemed to become the owner on registration.

2.102 S18(5) is intended to preserve the position under the 1965 act whereby customary and similar restraints on the exercise of rights of common (eg those imposed lawfully by manorial and customary courts) continue to apply although not recorded on the register. For further details about manorial courts, see chapter IV below.

2.103 S18(6) applies the provisions of the section to registrations both before and after the coming into force of the 2006 act.

13. Correction of the registers

2.104 S19 of the 2006 act enables a registration authority to amend the registers for the purposes of:

(a) correcting a mistake by the authority in a register entry;
(b) correcting any other mistake, so long as the extent of the register unit or the quantification of a right of common are not altered;
(c) removing a duplicate entry from the register (eg where both the landlord and the tenant have registered rights of common attached to a farm);
(d) updating names and addresses in the register.

A mistake may be an omission or an unclear or ambiguous description. The authority may correct a mistake on its own initiative or on the application of any other person.

2.105 A mistake may not be corrected if the authority considers that it would be unfair to do so where someone had reasonably relied on the incorrect entry, or for any other reason. This could happen where the authority mistakenly excluded land from a register unit and the purchaser of that land relied on the incorrect entry when making his purchase.

2.106 Regulations may be made to establish the criteria to be applied in determining an application or a proposal under the section.

2.107 Subs 7 empowers the High Court to order an amendment of the register if satisfied that:

(a) any entry in the register or any information in an entry was the result of fraud; and
(b) it would be just to amend the register.

This provision is in effect identical to s13 of the 1965 act.

2.108 In addition, the High Court has a general supervisory role over registration authorities and may judicially review their activities.

14. Information about the registers

2.109 S20 of the 2006 act provides that members of the public may inspect and take copies of the documents relating to registration (not only the registers themselves, but also any document referred to in a register and documents relating to applications to amend the register). Regulations may provide for exceptions to the right and for the impositions of conditions, including the charging of fees.

15. Official copies of the registers

2.110 S21 of the 2006 act provides for official copies of the registers and related documents to be admissible in evidence to the same extent as the original. Regulations may prescribe the procedure for issuing official copies, their form, applications for them and the conditions for their issue (including payment of a fee).

16. Rectification of mistakes

The Common Land (Rectification of Registers) Act 1989

2.111 The Common Land (Rectification of Registers) Act 1989 allowed the common land and village green registers to be amended in limited circumstances. This was repealed, in England only, by s53 of the 2006 act on 1 October 2006 by the bringing into force of the entry in part I of sch6 relating to the 1989 act under the Commons Act 2006 (Commencement No 1, Transitional Provisions and Savings) (England) Order 2006 (SI 2504).

2.112 The act enabled anyone to object to the inclusion, in the registers of common land and village green, of any land on which there had been a dwelling house, or which had been ancillary to a dwelling house, continuously since August 1945. Land ancillary to a dwelling house is defined as 'a garden, private garage or outbuildings used and enjoyed with that dwelling house', and the term 'dwelling house' includes a building consisting of two or more separate dwellings.

2.113 Any objection to registration had to be made within three years of the passing of the act (ie before 21 July 1992, the act having been passed on 21 July 1989) in accordance with the procedure in the Common Land (Rectification of Registers) Regulations 1990 (SI 311).

2.114 The meaning of 'dwelling house' was considered by the High Court in *re 1–4 White Row Cottages, Bewerley* [1991]. The commons commissioner rejected an application to deregister land at White Row

Cottages, Bewerley, in North Yorkshire. The commissioner considered that as the cottages had been 'condemned' and unoccupied for 20 years and were now derelict, they had not been dwelling houses at all times since 1945. On appeal, the court said otherwise. Although dilapidated and unoccupied they were still dwelling houses. Thus the row of cottages and their tiny front-gardens, which had been registered as village green along with surrounding land, came off the register.

2.115 The meaning of 'garden' was considered by the High Court in *Cresstock Investments Ltd* v *Commons Commissioner* [1992]. An area of land comprising unfenced woods and shrubs adjacent to a dwelling house was registered as common land. The applicant claimed that the area was part of the garden of the dwelling house and had been enjoyed with the dwelling house since 1933. The commons commissioner rejected the application on the basis that continuous enjoyment since 1945 had not been proved since the land was not fenced in. On appeal, the court held that the commissioner had construed 'garden' too narrowly and there was no evidence to show that the land had not been enjoyed with the dwelling house even though unfenced. The appeal was therefore allowed and the land removed from the register.

2.116 By contrast, in *re land at Freshfields* [1993], the High Court held that land consisting of fields of pasture which had been used for grazing cattle and growing hay could not be described as a 'garden' within the meaning of the act and an application to remove the field from the register was rejected.

Commons Act 2006

2.117 Sch2 to the 2006 act provides for the rectification of mistakes made during the initial period for applying to register land as common land or as a town or village green under the 1965 act (2 January 1967 to 2 January 1970). The provision does not extend to registrations made by a registration authority without application between 3 January and 31 July 1970.

A Non-registration of common land

2.118 Para 2 of sch2 to the 2006 act enables an application to be made to the registration authority, or for a proposal to be made by the authority without application (in both cases within the time limit laid down by regulations), to register land as common land in these circumstances:

(a) the land was not at any time finally registered as common land or as a town or village green;

(b) the land is–
  (i) regulated under a provisional order confirmation act made under the Commons Act 1876 (chapter IV, part 2);
  (ii) subject to a scheme under the Metropolitan Commons Act 1866 or the Commons Act 1899 (chapter IV, parts 1 and 3);
  (iii) regulated as common land under a local or personal act; or
  (iv) otherwise recognised or designated as common land by or under an enactment;

(c) the land is land to which part 1 of the 2006 act applies (ie all land in England and Wales except the New Forest, Epping Forest and the Forest of Dean);

(d) the land satisfies any conditions specified in regulations.

Under these provisions, it will be possible to seek registration of the commons exempted from registration under the 1965 act (2.83-85).

B Non-registration of town or village green

2.119 Para 3 of sch2 to the 2006 act enables an application to be made to the registration authority, or for a proposal to be made by the authority without application (in both cases within the time limit laid down by regulations), to register land as a town or village green. This topic is covered in chapter VII.

C Waste land of a manor not registered as common land

2.120 S22(1)(b) of the 1965 act (repealed by s53 of the 2006 act) included 'waste land of a manor not subject to rights of common' in the definition of common land subject to registration under the act. This phrase was not defined in the act, so that, in dealing with disputed or conflicting registrations, the commons commissioners and the courts had to rely on judicial definitions. The classic definition was given by Watson B in *AG* v *Hanmer* [1858]:

> The true meaning of 'wastes' or 'waste lands' or 'waste grounds of the manor' is the open, uncultivated and unoccupied lands parcel of the manor, or open lands parcel of the manor other than the demesne lands of the manor.

2.121 This was interpreted by the commissioners and the courts to mean that land qualified for registration as waste land of a manor provided that it was:

(a) waste land, as opposed to enclosed, occupied or cultivated land, and

(b) physically within a manor, and
(c) in the ownership of the lord of the manor.

2.122 This interpretation of the phrase was overturned by the House of Lords in *Hampshire County Council* v *Milburn and others* [1991], long after the end of the initial registration period. The essential facts of the case were that Hazeley Heath and Mattingley Green, near Hartley Wintney in Hampshire, were registered as common land as manorial waste, no rights of common having been registered over them. In 1981 the owner sold the titles of the manors in which the land lay but retained the land itself. He then applied to Hampshire County Council to deregister the land on the ground that it had been severed from the manor and thus had ceased to be waste land of a manor. The House of Lords overruled the decision of the Court of Appeal in *re Box Hill Common* [1979] and upheld the claim by the county council that the severance of the land from the manor did not result in the land ceasing to be common land. Lord Templeman, who gave the leading judgment, quoted the following words from the judgment of Slade J in *re Chewton Common* [1977] (which was overruled by the Box Hill case):

> the phrase 'waste land of a manor'... does not as a matter of legal language by any means necessarily import that the ownership of the land still rests with the lord of the relevant manor ... it is permissible to construe the phrase in this particular context of a post-1925 statute as meaning waste land which was once waste land of a manor in the days when copyhold tenure still existed.

2.123 It is no longer possible for land to become waste land of a manor. The manor as a legal entity ceased to have any significance when the tenure of land by copyhold was abolished by the Law of Property Act 1922.

2.124 It was recognised in the CLPS that applications to register waste land of a manor in 1967-70 failed because of the interpretation put on the phrase by commons commissioners and the courts before the House of Lords' decision in *Milburn*. Para 4 of sch2 to the 2006 act allows an application to be made to the registration authority, or for a proposal to be made by the authority without application (in both cases within the time limit laid down by regulations), to amend the register to add what is or was formerly waste land of a manor in the following limited circumstances:

(a) the land was provisionally registered as common land under s4 of the 1965 act;
(b) an objection was made to the registration; and

(c) the provisional registration was cancelled in the circumstances specified in subparas (3), (4) or (5).

These circumstances are:

Subpara(3):

(i) the provisional registration was referred to a commons commissioner;
(ii) the commissioner decided that, although the land was waste land of a manor at some time in the past, it was not so at the time of his decision because it was no longer connected with the manor; and
(iii) for that reason alone, the commissioner refused to confirm the provisional registration.

Subpara(4):

(i) the provisional registration was referred to a commons commissioner;
(ii) the commissioner determined that the land was not subject to rights of common and for that reason refused to confirm the provisional registration;
(iii) the commissioner did not consider whether the land was waste land of a manor.

Subpara(5): the applicant requested or agreed to the cancellation of the provisional registration, whether before or after its referral to a commons commissioner.

2.125 The registration authority must grant the application if satisfied the foregoing circumstances are met. Detailed regulations may be made under s24 of the 2006 act regarding the procedure to be followed in relation to applications, and regulations about the payment of costs may be made under para 6 of sch2.

D Town or village green wrongly registered as common land

2.126 Para 5 of sch2 enables an application to be made to the registration authority, or for a proposal to be made by the authority without application (in both cases within the time limit laid down by regulations), to amend the register to remove land from the register of common land and register that land in the register of town or village greens. This topic is dealt with in chapter VII.

2.127 Land so removed from the register under the foregoing provisions ceases to be access land for the purposes of the 2000 act (chapter V).

E Buildings registered as common land

2.128 Para 6 of sch2 to the 2006 act enables an application to be made to the registration authority, or for a proposal to be made by the authority without application (in both cases within the time limit laid down by regulations), to remove land from the register of common land in these circumstances:

(a) the land was provisionally registered as common land under s4 of the 1965 act;
(b) on the date of provisional registration the land was covered by a building or was within the curtilage of a building;
(c) the provisional registration became final; and
(d) since the date of the provisional registration the land has been, and still is, covered by a building or is within the curtilage of a building.

It is known that a considerable number of registrations erroneously included buildings, car parks, industrial areas, gardens and similar land. The Common Land (Rectification of Registers) Act 1989 (2.111-116) attempted a partial rectification of errors where the properties were dwellings and their gardens. These new provisions are much wider in scope.

F Other land wrongly registered as common land

2.129 Para 7 of sch2 to the 2006 act enables an application to be made to the registration authority, or for a proposal to be made by the authority without application (in both cases within the time limit laid down by regulations), to remove land from the register of common land in the following circumstances:

(a) the land was provisionally registered as common land under the 1965 act on the basis of information supplied in the application;
(b) the provisional registration was not referred to a commons commissioner;
(c) the provisional registration became final; and
(d) immediately before the provisional registration the land was not:
  (i) subject to rights of common;
  (ii) waste land of a manor (see 2.120-1255);
  (iii) a town or village green within the meaning of the 1965 act as originally enacted (7.2); or
  (iv) land specified in s11 of the Inclosure Act 1845 (page 118).

2.130 The registration authority must grant the application if satisfied the foregoing circumstances are met. Detailed regulations may be made under s24 of the 2006 act regarding the procedure to be followed in relations to applications, and regulations about the payment of costs may be made under para6 of sch2.

2.131 Land so removed from the register under the foregoing provisions ceases to be access land for the purposes of the 2000 act (chapter V).

Transitional provisions

2.132 Para 2 of sch3 to the 2006 act makes provision for regulations to be made to enable registration authorities to update their registers to take account of 'qualifying events' which have taken place since 2 January 1970 and which are not already recorded. Those events are:

- (a) the creation of a right of common by any means, including prescription, after 2 January 1970 (the final date for applying to register a right of common under the 1965 act) and before the commencement of para 2;
- (b) any 'relevant disposition' of, or extinguishment of, a right of common registered under the 1965 act after its registration and before the commencement of para 2;
- (c) a disposition of common land or a green prior to the commencement of para 2 by virtue of a 'relevant instrument';
- (d) an exchange of land effected by means of a relevant instrument.

2.133 A relevant disposition is:

- (a) the surrender of a right of common;
- (b) the variation of a right of common;
- (c) the apportionment or severance of a right of common attached to land;
- (d) the transfer of a right of common in gross.

2.134 A relevant instrument is:

- (a) an order or other disposition under the Acquisition of Land Act 1981;
- (b) a conveyance under the New Parishes Measure 1943 (no 1) (acquisition of land by the Church Commissioners);
- (c) any other instrument made under statutory powers.

2.135 The regulations may provide for registration authorities to carry out a review of the information they hold on the registers, to publicise the review and to invite applications to amend the registers.

2.136 Para 3 provides that at the end of the transitional period any unregistered right of common is extinguished, but para 4 enables regulations to be made to allow a registration authority to amend the registers after the end of the transitional period if justice would be served thereby.

2.137 Para 6 provides that the repeal of s1(2)(b) of the 1965 act (2.82 above) does not affect the extinguishment of rights of common by virtue of the subsection.

2.138 Para 7 provides that the repeal of s21(1) of the 1965 act does not affect the application of s193 of the 1925 act to any land (4.29 below).

2.139 Para 8 maintains the ownership section of the registers compiled under the 1965 act until regulations provide for details of ownership to be removed and for documentation relating to ownership to be kept and archived. Para 8(2) effectively re-enacts s12(b) of the 1965 act which provided for the removal of ownership details where the land in question was registered under the Land Registration Acts (2.31 above).

2.140 Para 9 provides that the repeal of s8 of the 1965 act does not affect the vesting of a green in a local authority (7.25 below).

Supplementary provisions

2.141 S24 of the 2006 act enables regulations to be made to supplement the provisions of the act with regard to procedure, forms, publicity and the like to enable the act to be properly implemented. In particular, s24(8) enables regulations to include provision for (a) the appropriate national authority to appoint persons eligible to carry out the functions of a registration authority in relation to applications made to, and proposals made by, the authority, and (b) to appoint such persons to carry out those functions in prescribed cases. These provisions appear to give statutory backing to the hitherto non-statutory practice of appointing an independent person (usually called an inspector) to consider, and often to hold an informal inquiry into, applications to register new village greens. Detailed guidance on the registration of new greens can be found in the society's publication *Getting Greens Registered*.

2.142 S24 of the 2006 also enables regulations to be made for the payment of fees for making applications.

2.143 S25 of the 2006 act enables regulations to be made to require or permit the compilation of the registers in electronic form.

CHAPTER III

Common Land — The Rights of the Parties

3.1 This section deals with the rights and interests of four parties: the freehold owner, the commoners, those with certain private rights or interests and the public.

1. The owner's rights

3.2 Common land is owned by some person or body in the same way as any other land. The owner holds it subject to the rights of the commoners (if any) and to the acts of parliament relating to common land (which are discussed in detail in chapter IV). He is also subject to the law affecting all landowners, such as the Town and Country Planning Acts.

3.3 In practice, the main rights of the owner are:

(a) minerals
(b) sporting rights
(c) balance of grazing
(d) timber: planting and cutting of trees
(e) granting of easements
(f) maintaining an action for trespass.

(a) Minerals

3.4 The owner's mineral rights were considered in the case of *Hall* v *Byron* [1877]. B was the lord of the manor of Coulsdon (then in Surrey, but now in the London Borough of Croydon) and as such the owner of a number of commons, including Riddlesdown, Farthing Down and Coulsdon Common. He excavated the commons for gravel and proposed to extend these excavations. H had a right of pasturage and sued on behalf of himself and other commoners to prevent further excavations. Hall VC gave an injunction against B to prevent further gravel working 'so as in any manner to prevent, disturb or interfere with the exercise by the plaintiffs of their said rights'. He said:

> The law I consider to be that the lord may take gravel, marl, loam and the like in the waste, so long as he does not infringe upon the commoners' rights.

(b) Sporting rights

3.5 The shooting and taking of game is often an important right of the owner, but again its exercise must not interfere with commoners' rights. He may also grant sporting rights to, or license, others to take or shoot game.

3.6 A right to take game is not usually capable of being a right of common. However in his decision, *In the Matter of Knowstone Inner Moor, Knowstone Outer Moor etc, Devon*, Mr Commissioner Baden Fuller concluded that a right to take rabbits could be a right of common if the rabbits were taken for the purpose of being eaten by the commoner, which was the ruling in *Samford and Havel's case* [1612]. (On the evidence, however, he rejected the claim because the rabbiting was not for the claimant's exclusive consumption.)

(c) Balance of grazing

3.7 The owner may turn out his own animals to graze, but subject to the rights of the commoners. *In the Matter of Pasture End, Murton, Cumbria* raised the question whether the owner of common land could register rights equivalent to rights of common over it. The contention put forward on behalf of the owners was that normally an owner could rely on the unlimited (ie unquantified) grazing rights implied by his ownership. In the present case the commoners had registered so many rights that there was no balance of grazing left for the owners who needed the grazing for their farm. Although it was conceded that the owners could not have a legal right of common over their own land, there should be some specific rights shown on the register so that the owners were not unfairly prejudiced. In fact, the predecessor in title to the owners had registered a claim to 'rights' of common. Mr Commissioner Baden Fuller held that the law recognised for some purposes a quasi-right of common for an owner, citing *Musgrave* v *Inclosure Commissioners* [1874], and the 1965 act did not exclude the possibility of recording such rights on the register. He therefore upheld the registration.

(d) Timber: planting and cutting of trees

3.8 This was considered in *Arlett* v *Ellis* [1827] where the judge said:

> The lord, as owner of the soil has *prima facie* a right to plant trees and the trees would not become wrongful unless it were ... by not leaving them (ie the commoners) a sufficiency of common for their cattle ... and it lies on the lord to shew that a sufficiency of common is left.

3.9 In that case the lord had, in the judge's view, planted too much and the commoners succeeded in preventing further planting.

3.10 There is apparently no common law restriction on what an owner may cut down, since this was thought to extend the amount of land under grass for the commoners. However, if the appropriate authority approves any restricted works on common land in accordance with s38 of the 2006 act (see chapter VI below) he may impose conditions in the interests of nature or landscape conservation which could require the retention of trees or areas of woodland. The planning authority may also make a tree preservation order under s198 of the Town and Country Planning Act 1990. The cutting or lopping of trees in a conservation area is also subject to control under the 1990 act. A felling licence may be required under s9 of the Forestry Act 1967.

(e) Granting of easements

3.11 The owner may (subject to the rights of the commoners and of the public, where these exist) grant private rights of way, private rights to lay pipes and similar private rights in, on or over common land. Where such private rights are claimed to exist they may have been noted on the register in accordance with regulation 24 of the Commons Registration (General) Regulations 1966 (SI 1471, as amended), but registration is not proof that the claims are well founded in law. If a grant of an easement involves the carrying out of works on the common, the consent of the appropriate national authority may be required under s194 of the 1925 act (until it is repealed) (chapter VI part 1 below) or, after that repeal, where 'restricted works' on the common are involved, under s38 of the 2006 act (chapter VI, part 3 below). It would normally be the responsibility of the person to whom the easement is granted (the grantee) to obtain the necessary consent.

3.12 Prior to the coming into force of s6(1) of the 2006 act (page 155) it was possible to create a right of common by prescription or lost modern grant. S1 of the Prescription Act 1832 (page 117) provides for two periods of 30 years and 60 years in respect of evidence of claims to rights of common. If there is evidence of 30 years' exercise of the claimed right, such claim shall not be defeated merely because evidence is brought that it came into existence later than 3 September 1189 (the date on which Richard I ascended the throne and the limit of legal memory). It can still be defeated, however, by evidence that it commenced by permission of the owner of the soil of the common prior to the 30 years. If 60 years' user as of right is shown, the claim can only be defeated by production of written evidence that it was exercised with the owner's consent.

3.13 The doctrine of lost modern grant is a convenient fiction invented by the courts to give a legal origin to long enjoyment of unchallenged rights. The theory is that the court will presume the existence of a lost grant if a landowner can show that he and his predecessors have used a right over someone else's land for at least 20 years without force, openly and without seeking or being granted permission (*'nec vi, nec clam, nec precario'*). The presumption is irrebuttable, even if there is evidence that no grant was actually made.

3.14 The House of Lords case *Bakewell Management Ltd* v *Brandwood and Others* [2004] has altered the previous law relating to the acquisition of easements by prescription or lost modern grant and rendered the legislation relating to the compulsory granting of easements in s68 of the 2000 act practically nugatory. As a result, s68 was repealed by ss51 and 53 of the 2006 act (3.41-44).

(f) Action for trespass

3.15 The public does not have a legal right of access to common land under the common law. Various acts of parliament have in the past granted a right of public access, but in piecemeal fashion and covering only about one fifth of the total area of registered common land. However, s2 of the 2000 act grants a public right of access on foot (a) to all registered common land, and (b) with two exceptions, to land which, after the passing of the act, has ceased to be registered common land. The 2000 act is discussed in detail in chapter V.

3.16 The provisions of the 2000 act represent the successful culmination of a campaign to secure public access to commons which the society began towards the end of the nineteenth century. They also give legislative effect to one of the main recommendations of both the Royal Commission on Common Land (1.11 above) and the CLF (appendix 2).

2. The rights of the commoners

(a) General

3.17 The basic right of a commoner is to the peaceful enjoyment of his rights of common. Thus if the owner puts up fencing to keep the commoner out, the latter may pull it down. This proposition was laid down in an anonymous case reported in the *Year Book 15 Hy* 7 [1499-1500].

> If I have a right of common and he who hath the land makes a hedge on the land, whence the right of common issues, I may break down the whole hedge.

3.18 This was confirmed in *Arlett* v *Ellis* [1827] where the judge said:

> The commoners ... are entitled to consider the whole of that fence so erected upon the common as a nuisance and to remove it accordingly.

However, in *The National Trust for Places of Historic Interest or Natural Beauty* v *Ashbrook and others* [1997] the judge said that this right was not unqualified, but depended on the nature and location of the fence and the extent to which the fence impeded the commoners' access.

3.19 In *R* v *Dyer* [1952] the owners of the soil erected a notice board on the common. The commoners took it down and were convicted at Quarter Sessions of wilfully damaging property. They appealed and were upheld by the Court of Criminal Appeal which held that it was not unlawful for commoners to remove things placed on a common.

3.20 Where any works are carried out in contravention of s38(1) of the 2006 act s41 of the act gives any person the right to apply to the county court. The court has power:

(a) to order removal of works carried out without consent and restoration of the land to its original state; or
(b) to require works for which consent has been given to be carried out in accordance with the terms of the consent.

While this is useful, there is no doubt that a commoner may still use the old common law remedy of abatement to secure the removal works etc on the common which interfere with the exercise of common rights. S26(2) of the Local Government Act 1894 empowers a district council, with the consent of the county council, to assist a commoner in maintaining rights of common where, in the opinion of the council, the extinction of such rights would be prejudicial to the inhabitants of the district.

3.21 A commoner may do anything which is necessarily incidental to the exercise of his rights. Thus he may put troughs on the common for his animals to drink from and may drive vehicles on to the common, but only for the purpose of collecting his animals, taking fodder to them etc (*White* v *Taylor* [1968]).

3.22 Should common land be acquired by compulsory purchase, the commoners are entitled to a share in the monetary compensation given (Compulsory Purchase Act 1965 s21 and schedule 4 (page 131)). Alternatively, if exchange land is given, they are entitled to require that such exchange land be equally advantageous to them for the exercise of their rights (1981 act, s19) (6.51).

(b) Quantification of grazing rights

3.23 S15 of the 1965 act provided that all grazing rights must be quantified. This obliged all those claiming such rights in the initial registration period to put a figure on the numbers of animals in respect of which the rights were claimed. In effect, s15 did away with the previous common law rules by which the extent of grazing rights should be measured. No equivalent provision appears in the 2006 act, but none is necessary. There are specific provisions in the act relating to the creation and variation of rights of common (see chapter II above) which in effect require grazing rights to be quantified.

3.24 Apart from the 2006 act, powers to control grazing are contained in the Commons Act 1908 (4.56-57; page 126). The Dartmoor Commons Act 1985 provides statutory controls over grazing on common land on Dartmoor. The Greenham and Crookham Commons Act 2002 provides for the management commission established by the act to make regulations for this purpose. Otherwise, control of grazing is normally a matter for agreement between commoners, commoners' associations or commons councils (where they exist—see 4.50-51), although in a few places manorial courts have powers (see 4.52-55). There are special laws relating to the New Forest and the Forest of Dean: these are outside the scope of this book.

3.25 To assist commoners and landowners, the former Department of the Environment, Transport and the Regions issued the *Good Practice Guide on Managing the Use of Common Land* in June 1998. (The responsibilities of that department in relation to commons and greens have been transferred to Defra.)

(c) Sufficiency of land

3.26 As noted above (3.7), the owner must exercise his rights so as to leave a sufficiency for the commoners. The meaning of 'sufficiency' was at issue in *Robertson* v *Hartopp* [1889]. H was the lord of the manor and owner of Banstead Downs and Heath, from which he excavated gravel. It was established as fact by expert witnesses:

(a) the common had grazing capacity for some 1,200 animals,
(b) all the commoners' rights totalled grazing for 1,440 animals,
(c) in practice an average of 600 animals were turned out.

3.27 It was held that the test of sufficiency was whether enough grazing would be left for all the animals that could be turned out, not for those that generally were. Thus any further excavation by H would limit the grazing for 1,440 animals (even though there would still be enough for the normal 600). R was successful. The judge said:

> The Lord is bound to leave pasture enough to satisfy the commoners' rights whether such rights are likely to be exercised or no.

3.28 It is not clear how the rule laid down in this case was affected by s15 of the 1965 act (3.23). It would seem, however, that the owner must leave sufficient land for grazing in respect of all animals for which rights have been registered (but he may have some quasi-rights of his own: 3.7).

(d) Quantification of other rights

3.29 It is more difficult to quantify other rights of common, but the general rule is that the amount of estovers etc that may be taken is measured by the needs of the property to which the rights are attached or, where the rights are held in gross (ie not attached to land), by local custom. Sometimes, the right is quantified in an inclosure award.

(e) Can all the inhabitants be commoners?

3.30 Sometimes it is claimed that 'all the inhabitants' have rights on a particular common. Generally, this is not so. Rights of common must normally attach to a particular property and cannot exist for the benefit of a shifting and uncertain group of people. This was established in *Gateward's case* [1607] where it was pointed out that a right of common given to a body of people which could increase in numbers might lead to the destruction of the subject matter.

3.31 There are, however, three recognised exceptions to the rule. The first is exemplified by the case of *Willingale* v *Maitland* [1866], where it was held that a lost Crown grant to the inhabitants of Epping to lop branches was valid because the Crown can create a corporation. The grant is therefore presumed to have incorporated the inhabitants so that it is the deemed corporation which becomes the commoner, holding the rights on trust for the inhabitants.

3.32 The second is where the 'inhabitants' were freehold or copyhold tenants of the manor, ie the owners of identifiable properties (see the decision of the chief commons commissioner *In the Matter of the Hudnalls, St Briavels, Gloucestershire* (no 1)).

3.33 The third is where there is a grant to a corporation on trust for a fluctuating body (*Goodman* v *Mayor and Corporation of Saltash* [1882]), applied by the chief commons commissioner in his decision *In the Matter of Northam Burrows, Northam, Devon* (no 1).

3.34 It is also possible for a corporation (including a local council) to hold rights of common in trust for all the inhabitants of a place—see the decision of the chief commons commissioner *In the Matter of Snettisham Beach Shingle Fields, Snettisham, Norfolk* and in the *Hudnalls* case (above, 3.32).

(f) Can non-commoners use common rights?

3.35 A commoner may license another to exercise his registered grazing rights so long as the rightful numbers are not exceeded (*Davies* v *Davies* [1974]). There seems no reason in principle why other rights of common should not be the subject of a licensing arrangement, but there appears to be no judicial authority on the point. Para 2 of sch1 to the 2006 act permits temporary severance of rights of common from the land to which they are attached (2.72).

3. Driveways across commons

3.36 As noted above (3.11), the owner of a common may grant easements over the common to other individuals or bodies. Since there is a power to grant easements, it follows that, as a general rule, these may be acquired by long use or prescription in accordance with the Prescription Act 1832 or under the common law.

3.37 The most widespread form of easement likely to be found is a private right of way from a road to a house across a common. Can this include a right of way for vehicles? *Prima facie* the answer is 'yes'. However, until the unanimous decision of the House of Lords in *Bakewell Management Ltd* v *Brandwood and Others* [2004] (3.39-45) case law had established that, on commons subject to a right of access for air and exercise under s193 of the 1925 act (4.20-30 and page 128), s193(4) and on other commons, s34 of the Road Traffic Act 1988 (page 147), placed an insurmountable hurdle in the way. S193(4) makes it an offence, without lawful authority, to draw or drive any vehicle on land to which s193 applies. S34 makes it an offence, without lawful authority, to drive a motor vehicle on common land, except where the vehicle is driven not more than 15 yards from a road or is driven on the land in an emergency. The rulings of the Court of Appeal in *Hanning* v *Top Deck Travel Group Ltd* [1993] and *Massey* v *Boulden* [2002] and of the divisional court in *Robinson* v *Adair* [1995] were to the effect that an easement of way could not be acquired by long use or prescription where the use of the way was illegal (in the criminal sense) under a statute (specifically s193(4) of the 1925 act (page 128) and s34 of the Road Traffic Act 1988 (page 147)).

3.38 In order to ameliorate the position of people who claimed prescriptive rights of way over common land but who, because of the ruling in *Hanning*, could not establish their claim in law, Parliament enacted s68 of the 2000 act, providing in effect a compulsory purchase procedure for acquiring a vehicular easement across land where driving thereon was an offence. Detailed regulations were made setting out the procedures for acquiring an easement. The section has now been repealed by ss51 and 53 of the 2006 act (3.43).

3.39 In *Bakewell*, the House of Lords specifically ruled that *Hanning* and the cases which followed it were wrongly decided. The facts in *Bakewell* were that the appellants (Brandwood and others, 47 in number) obtained vehicular access to their houses over Newtown Common in Hampshire. The common was registered under the 1965 act and was subject to a deed of declaration made in 1928 by the then owner under s193 of the 1925 act (page 128). As indicated in the previous paragraph, it is an offence under s193(4) to drive over the common without lawful authority. The respondent (Bakewell) purchased the common in 1997 and sought to charge the appellants for vehicular access to their houses. The appellants defended the case on the basis that they, and their predecessors in title, had driven over the common openly and without permission for periods in excess of 20 years and had thus acquired prescriptive rights. The defence was rejected both by the judge at first instance and by the Court of Appeal on the ground that, as ruled in *Hanning*, no right of way could be acquired by acts made illegal by statute. In the House of Lords, Lord Scott of Foscote gave the leading judgment, with which the other law lords agreed. Lord Scott analysed *Hanning*, *Robinson* and *Massey* and several other cases. He pointed out that s193 of the 1925 act and 34 of the 1988 act made driving over common land etc a criminal offence only because the landowner had not given lawful authority. In this respect, the use of the land made criminal by the legislation was more akin to use of land which was illegal because it was tortious (ie involving a breach of the civil law—in this case trespass—rather than the criminal law). Lord Scott concluded that the matter was one of public policy and that an easement of way based on user in breach of s193(4) of the 1925 act or of s34 of the 1988 act could be acquired by prescription, whether the use relied on was illegal in the sense of being tortious or whether that user was illegal in the sense of criminal.

3.40 *Bakewell* did not specifically rule on cases where common land is subject to by-laws which prohibit driving on the land without lawful authority. There is power for landowners to make by-laws under a provisional order under the Commons Act 1876 (4.9-12 and page 120), a regulation scheme under the Commons Act 1899 (4.13-19 and page 122), s24 of the National Trust Act 1971 (not printed in this book), private acts regulating particular commons and commons regulated by local authorities. Does *Bakewell* apply in these cases? It is hard to see that *Bakewell* does not apply, since the acts which are rendered criminal can be authorised by the landowner or regulatory body. If this is so, then it follows that a right of way for vehicles could be acquired over land subject to a by-law prohibiting vehicular traffic without lawful authority.

3.41 In *Bakewell* the House of Lords made it clear that the cases (stretching back to the eighteenth century) established the rule that an easement cannot be acquired to do something which is prohibited by a public statute. This rule was shown in *Neaverson* v *Peterborough Rural District Council* [1902], cited in *Bakewell*. It is submitted that the rule would also apply where the claimed easement would constitute a public nuisance, as in *Sheringham* v *Holsey* [1904], where a claim to a right to use a public footway for wheeled vehicles after 40 years' use was refused on the ground that the user had all along been a public nuisance (and thus a criminal offence at common law). On this point, Lord Scott in *Bakewell* agreed with the view of Stuart-Smith LJ in *Hereford and Worcester County Council* v *Pick* [1995] that it was not open to a landowner to dedicate a footpath as a public vehicular highway where the use by vehicles would be a public nuisance to pedestrians using the road; accordingly, no such use could be claimed by presumed dedication. He referred to s30 of the Commons Act 1876 which effectively outlaws any action by the landowner which unreasonably interferes with the rights of commoners. He also said in the course of his judgment that 'authority to too many people to drive too many cars or other vehicles over the tracks on the common might not be lawful. It would depend on the facts'. However, the remarks by Lord Scott on the point were not part of his actual ruling and the issue may come before the courts again.

3.42 *Bakewell* ruled only on the acquisition of easements by prescription. If a landowner grants an easement by formal deed or gives specific permission for vehicular access over a common, there is of course no infringement of s193(4) of the 1925 Act or s34 of the 1988 Act. However, mere permission (as opposed to the grant of an easement) negates any claim to a prescriptive right; the essence of such a right is that it is exercised without permission.

3.43 A person who can prove a prescriptive right of way might be better advised to seek a confirmatory grant of an easement from the owner of the land. This could be recorded on the titles of both parties where their land is registered at the Land Registry. If the titles were not registered, the deed of grant would be one of the title deeds of the properties in question.

3.44 As a result of the ruling in *Bakewell*, Parliament decided that s68 of the 2000 act was no longer necessary and it was repealed by ss51 and 53 of the 2006 Act, with effect from 1 October in England only by virtue of the Commons Act 2006 (Commencement No 1, Transitional Provisions and Savings) (England) Order 2006 (SI 2504).

3.45 The effect of *Bakewell* on vehicular access over town and village greens is considered below (7.48-53).

4. The rights of the public: summary

3.46 Contrary to popular belief, the public has no right at common law to wander at large over common land (or any other land) and cannot acquire such a right by long usage. This was laid down in *AG* v *Antrobus* [1905], the so-called Stonehenge case, where a public right of access to Stonehenge was rejected, and affirmed by the Court of Appeal in *re Ellenborough Park* [1956].

3.47 Since the middle of the nineteenth century a series of statutes, both general and local, have given the public a right of access for air and exercise over certain commons, or have provided that the statute can be applied to particular commons later. These statutes have culminated in the 2000 act, which gives a qualified public right of access on foot to all finally registered common land outside Inner London. (It should be noted that there are no commons within inner London where public access is not allowed, except in the very limited areas usual in a public open space.) However, the public right of access granted by the 2000 act does not apply to land which is accessible to the public under the following statutes:

(a) s193 of the 1925 act (chapter IV, part 4 below),
(b) a local or private act (including a provisional order confirmation act) (chapter IV, part 2),
(c) a scheme made under part I of the Commons Act 1899 (chapter IV, part 3),
(d) an access agreement under part V of the National Parks and Access to the Countryside Act 1949 (chapter IV, part 7).

3.48 Where a local or private act or a scheme under the 1899 act confers a right of access on the inhabitants of a particular district or neighbourhood (however described) for the purposes of open-air recreation (however described), the right of access is exercisable by the public generally as well as by those inhabitants (s15(2) of the 2000 act).

CHAPTER IV

Management and Control of Common Land

4.1 Where an act provides for public access it has inevitably to provide for some form of management and control at the same time. This chapter describes the management/control schemes for commons regulated under specific acts. Access under the general provisions in the 2000 act is discussed in chapter V. Guidance on the management of common land can be found in *A Common Purpose: A guide to agreeing management on common land*, a joint publication by the National Trust, Natural England and the society issued in September 2005. This can be viewed on the society's website, www.oss.org.uk.

1. Metropolitan commons

4.2 Shortly after the society was founded, it greatly influenced the passing of the Metropolitan Commons Act 1866. This prevented the enclosure of any common wholly or partly within the Metropolitan Police District—a radius of 15 miles from Charing Cross—a limit which remains for this purpose although the boundaries of that district are now those of the London boroughs only. The 1866 act also provided for the making of management schemes to be confirmed by supplemental acts. Twenty-nine of these were subsequently passed, covering a rather large number of commons.

4.3 The commons held or managed by the London boroughs are managed under the Ministry of Housing and Local Government Provisional Order Confirmation (Greater London Parks and Open Spaces) Act 1967. The powers under articles 7 and 8 in its schedule (page 132) largely replace the detailed provisions contained in the original schemes and acts and, theoretically, permit much more development even though it is mainly for recreational purposes. However, article 12 of the schedule (page 135) prohibits any building or permanent enclosure without the consent of the secretary of state who also deals with the similar requirements of s38 of the 2006 act.

4.4 Article 17 of the schedule (page 136) gives a London borough council power to construct, alter or widen streets over these open spaces subject to the consent of the secretary of state. The current definition of 'street' is in s48(1) of the New Roads and Street Works Act 1991. While this includes all highways it can also include paths, roads or ways which are only intended for users of the open space. The power has been used with the intention of converting footpaths over a common into cycle tracks as defined in the Highways Act 1980 (as amended). The society believes that to be a misuse of the power, and all paths over open spaces not legally accepted as public rights of way should remain subject to the open space by-laws.

4.5 Other commons within the area became regulated under their own special acts, such as the Wimbledon and Putney Commons Act 1871, the Hampstead Heath Act 1871 and the Epping Forest Acts 1878-80. The Wimbledon and Putney Commons still have their own board of eight conservators, five directly elected by local council taxpayers living within three quarters of a mile of the common, and three appointed by government departments. Most of the other commons are now in the ownership of local authorities, though some are managed by them while remaining in the original ownership. Examples are Blackheath in south-east London, still part of the Royal Manor of Greenwich, and the Chiswick commons in west London, which are still parts of an ancient manor now owned by the Church Commissioners.

4.6 Although the City of London Corporation is at the heart of London, it is not, legally, one of the London boroughs into which the rest of Greater London is divided, and it has its own body of legislation. This includes the Corporation of London (Open Spaces) Act 1878 which has enabled the city to acquire such delightful rural commons as Burnham Beeches, Buckinghamshire and Farthing Down and Coulsdon in Croydon. The Epping Forest Acts 1878-80 provide the corporation with the powers of management of that famous open space; and there have been a number of subsequent amending City of London Acts which give powers additional to those in the original acts.

4.7 By the London Government Reorganisation (Hampstead Heath) Order 1989 (SI 1989/ 304) that open space—really a conglomeration of open spaces not all originally common land but now mostly registered as such—was transferred to the City of London. Among the powers it has been given are those under the 1967 act mentioned above and these will include article 12 where appropriate.

4.8 Outside Greater London, metropolitan commons may be managed by the appropriate district council under the original scheme powers as amended by other local legislation affecting their area.

2. Commons Act 1876

4.9 The basis of regulation by provisional order in accordance with the Commons Act 1876 is that the various interests concerned, including local authorities, appoint nominees to a board of conservators; each order sets out which interests and how many conservators. An example is provided by Winton and Kaber Fell (Cumbria). The Commons Regulation (Winton and Kaber) Provisional Order Confirmation Act 1911 provides for seven conservators to be appointed: one by the Lord of the Manor of Brough, one by Winton Parish Meeting, one by Kaber Parish Council and four by the commoners. The act also specifies that a privilege of playing games shall be reserved to the inhabitants on the areas of the commons, allotted for that purpose by the conservators. By virtue of s15(2) of the 2000 act (page 150), this privilege extends to members of the general public. Many extensive commons in areas of high amenity value are regulated in this way. Apart from Winton and Kaber Fell, already mentioned, they include Therfield Heath, near Royston, Hertfordshire; Bexhill Down on the East Sussex coast and the Clent Hills, Worcestershire.

4.10 Each order is subject to confirmation by the secretary of state and by parliament. The conservators may make necessary by-laws and must prevent encroachment. An order may give conservators power to raise money by levying a rate or by selling a small or outlying portion of the common not exceeding one fortieth of the total area (s14).

4.11 The need for parliament to confirm the relevant order and the difficulty sometimes experienced in satisfying the rights of the parties has led to the 1876 act provisions falling into disuse. The last provisional order confirmation act was passed in 1919 and related to Coity Wallia Commons in South Wales. Amendments thereto were made in 1976, but a private act was secured rather than a confirmation act under the 1876 act procedure.

4.12 Where a commons council is established (4.50-51), s36(2)(b) of the 2006 act empowers the appropriate national authority to vary or revoke any regulations or arrangements made under the 1876 act where it appears desirable to do so as a consequence of the conferring of functions on the council.

3. Commons Act 1899

4.13 This act is intended to provide a simple and inexpensive means of enabling district councils (and national park authorities within national parks) to manage and improve commons in the public interest.

This is defined in s1(1A) of the 1899 act (added by s50 of the 2006 act) as including (a) nature conservation; (b) conservation of the landscape; (c) protection of public rights of access to any area of land; and (d) protection of archaeological remains and features of historic interest. The act is applied primarily where use of the common for exercise and recreation is the prime consideration, and where the owner and commoners do not require a direct voice in the management (as they have under 1876 act schemes). The act also applies to village greens.

4.14 Schemes do not require the consent of the secretary of state or of parliament. Nothing in the scheme may take away or adversely affect the rights of the owner or the commoners without compensation being paid. Either the owner or persons representing one third in value of the interests of the commoners may veto the scheme.

4.15 The scheme must be in a form, and must be made in the manner, prescribed by regulations, subject to any permitted exceptions or modifications. The current scheme is prescribed by the Commons (Schemes) Regulations 1982 (SI 209). It includes a power to provide temporary car-parking spaces on the common subject to the consent of the owner of the soil and of the secretary of state being first obtained. The considerations to be taken into account by him before so doing are the same as those which relate to the placing of buildings etc on common land in accordance with s194 of the 1925 act. However, s194 is repealed by s53 of the 2006 act, so that new regulations will be needed to substitute references to part 3 of the 2006 act (chapter VI) Consent from the owner and the secretary of state must also be obtained for the erection of buildings on the common in connection with the council's management of it for recreation. Buildings or permanent works for other purposes are prohibited and can only be lawfully erected if the relevant area of land is excluded from the scheme or construction is authorised under other statutes.

4.16 A scheme may be amended or revoked in the manner prescribed by the 1982 Regulations. The council may make by-laws under the scheme and may delegate powers of management to a local council (s101 of the Local Government Act 1972). Delegation must be by resolution and may be of all or some of the powers. By s5 of the 1899 act, a local council may contribute to the costs of the scheme.

4.17 Examples of regulated commons include Bucklebury Common (regulated by West Berkshire District Council directly) and Austenwood Common, Buckinghamshire (regulated by Chalfont St Peter Parish Council under delegated powers).

4.18 The 1899 act provides for access to be granted by a scheme to the 'inhabitants' but, by virtue of s15(2) of the 2000 act (page 150), the right of access extends to members of the public in general.

4.19 Where a commons council is established (4.50-51), s36(2)(b) of the 2006 act empowers the appropriate national authority to vary or revoke any regulations or arrangements made under the 1899 act where it appears desirable to do so as a consequence of the conferring of functions on the council.

4. Section 193 of the Law of Property Act 1925

4.20 This section applies to:

(a) commons situated wholly or partly within a former borough or urban district as it existed on 31 March 1974 (after which date such local authority areas were abolished under the provisions of the Local Government Act 1972) and which are not subject to any other act, scheme or provisional order for the regulation of the land and any by-law, regulation or order made thereunder;

(b) commons which are subject to a deed of declaration by the owner of the common bringing the common under the section. The power of an owner to make such a deed was repealed by s46(1)(a) of the 2000 act. S46(1)(a) was brought into force in Wales on 21 June 2004 by the Countryside and Rights of Way Act 2000 (Commencement No 5) (Wales) Order 2004 (SI 1489) but was never brought into force in England. S46(1) was repealed in England on 1 October 2006 by s50 and sch6 to the 2006 act brought into force by the Commons Act 2006 (Commencement No 1, Transitional Provisions and Savings) (England) Order 2006 (SI 2504). It thus remains possible for a deed of declaration to be made in England. S50 and sch6 have not been brought into force in Wales, so that there is no power to make a deed of declaration over land there. S16 of the 2000 act enables a landowner to dedicate land as access land under the 2000 act (5.15-17).

4.21 Under the section, members of the public have a legal right of access 'for air and exercise' subject to three basic prohibitions set out in subs 4, which provides that it shall be an offence to drive a vehicle (including a bicycle), to camp and to light a fire anywhere on a common to which the section applies. It should be noted in particular that while it is an offence to drive a vehicle anywhere beyond 15 yards from a road on any common (Road Traffic Act 1988 s34, page 147), in the case of a common subject to s193 of the 1925 act it is an offence to drive anywhere at all on the common. However, subs 5 provides that the

15-yard rule does not apply where by-laws affect the land (7.40).

4.22 The scope of the rights granted by s193 is not defined in the 1925 act, but it is submitted that the public may do no more than indulge in informal recreation. In *R* v *Secretary of the State for the Environment ex parte Billson* [1998] it was held by the High Court that the right includes a right of access on horseback. On commons subject to s193 owned by National Trust, the riding of horses can be regulated by by-laws, although there is always a presumption in favour of access on horseback.

4.23 In addition to the statutory restrictions, an owner of a common subject to s193 may apply to the secretary of state for an order of limitations (in effect by-laws) further to control public behaviour on the common. Although this procedure is not called a scheme of management, in reality it is precisely that. It is most suitable where the owner wishes to maintain control in his own hands and at the same time to prevent public abuse of the common.

4.24 The order of limitations may prohibit access altogether to a portion of the common: this is mostly done where naturalist interests are involved, eg Roydon Common, Norfolk.

4.25 Once a deed has been made it must be deposited with the secretary of state. Most of the deeds have now been transferred to the National Archives at Kew (www.nationalarchives.gov.uk) and may be inspected there.

4.26 A deed can be revocable or irrevocable (s193(2) of the 1925 act, page 129). Where a deed is revoked the land becomes subject to s15 of the 2000 act (chapter V). There may still be an advantage to a landowner to revoke a deed in these circumstances because the rights enjoyed by the public under the 2000 act may be more circumscribed than those enjoyed under s193 of the 1925 act. For example (a) the right of access under the 2000 act is on foot only, whereas that under s193 includes access on horseback (see the *Billson* case, 4.22 above); and (b) the right of access under the 2000 act is subject to a number of exclusions which are not replicated in s193 (5.13).

4.27 What is the effect of land falling within s193 not being registered? Proviso (d) of subs 1 states that the rights of access cease to apply, firstly, to land over which rights of common are extinguished by or under statute. Without further provision, this would have applied to any land over which no rights of common were registered, because failure to register a right resulted in its extinguishment by virtue of s1 (2)(b) of the 1965 act (as interpreted in the *Clwyd* case, see 2.82). However, s21(1) of the 1965 act provided that s1(2) did not affect the application to any land registered under the act of s193 and s194 of the 1925 act. With the repeal of the whole of the 1965 act, para 7 of sch3 to the 2006 act effectively makes identical provision to s21(1). Thus s193 continues to apply, despite the absence of registered rights, so long as the land is still registered.

4.28 The public rights of access cease to apply, secondly, where rights of common are extinguished otherwise than by statute (eg by surrender, see 2.80) if the relevant county council, county borough council or metropolitan district council resolves to exclude the land from the operation of the section and the resolution is approved by the secretary of state.

4.29 The effect of s21 of the 1965 act was considered by Mr Commissioner Baden Fuller in *In the Matter of Carn Brea, Redruth, Cornwall*. The land in question was within the former Camborne-Redruth urban district and, if common land, was subject to s193. The commissioner found that there were no rights of common, but that on 1 January 1926 the land was waste land of the Manor of Tehidy. A conveyance in 1935 severed the land from the manor and he refused to confirm the registration. He pointed out, however, that his decision left unresolved whether the public rights of access would continue to exist. This would, it is submitted, depend upon whether or not the rights of common were extinguished by or under statute. In the case of Carn Brea itself, there was no evidence that rights of common had ever existed over the land, so it would perhaps be reasonable to infer that they were extinguished by virtue of s1(2)(b) of the 1965 act. If, on the other hand, they were extinguished by a different method, s193 would continue to apply in the absence of a county council etc resolution. It is worth pointing out that it may be possible to register Carn Brea as common land under para 4 of sch2 to the 2006 act (2.124).

4.30 Land subject to a deed of declaration will normally have been registered under the 1965 act, but not necessarily so because the validity of the deed does not depend upon registration. If it is registered, such land was covered by s21(1) of the 1965 act and is now covered by para 7 of sch3 to the 2006 act (4.27). For a decision where registration of land subject to a deed was refused, see *In the Matter of Bryniau, Dyserth, Clwyd* (land not subject to rights of common and not manorial waste but subject to a deed made by the Crown in 1932). In such a case, the land is subject to s15 of the 2000 act (5.5-6 and page 150).

5. Commons subject to special acts

4.31 It is impossible to generalise about commons under this heading: the only rule is to look at the act itself. As an example, the Dartmoor Commons Act 1985 establishes a Dartmoor Commoners' Council with powers to regulate the exercise of common rights on Dartmoor and also a duty to maintain a register of grazing rights separate from the register of common rights maintained by the commons registration authority. In addition, the 1985 act grants a qualified public right of access on foot and on horseback to the Dartmoor commons. The New Forest is regulated by a series of local acts which provide for its own register of common rights, kept by the Forestry Commission. The New Forest is exempted from the operation of part 1 of the 2006 act (see 2.83).

4.32 In some cases an act was obtained by a progressive local authority to regulate a common for the public before that concept had been accepted in general legislation, eg Southampton Marsh Act 1844 (Southampton Common) or the Clifton and Durdham Downs (Bristol) Act 1861, which provides for joint control of the downs by the Corporation and the Society of Merchant Venturers, owners of part of the freehold. A local act may provide for the extinguishment of rights of common and the regulation of the common solely for the public, or it may maintain the rights and give commoners a share of the control. Many of the older acts have often been amended and it can be difficult to identify when and where changes have been made.

4.33 The society was deeply involved in the enactment of the Greenham and Crookham Commons Act 2002 which restores, over a modified area, rights of common extinguished or rendered incapable of exercise because the land was acquired for an airbase under the Defence Acts. The act provides for a register of commoners to be kept by West Berkshire District Council and for the management by a commission (made up of various interests) of the restored commons for grazing, public recreation and education and conservation of the SSSI.

4.34 Where a commons council is established (4.50-51), s36(2)(b) of the 2006 act empowers the appropriate national authority to vary or revoke any regulations or arrangements made under any local or personal act where it appears desirable to do so as a consequence of the conferring of functions on the council.

6. National Trust commons

4.35 National Trust commons must be kept unenclosed and unbuilt on as open spaces for the enjoyment of the public: National Trust Act 1907 s29(A) (page 126). The section gives the trust general powers of draining, planting or improving turf and trees. Good-behaviour by-laws have been made by the trust and cover all its commons.

4.36 Where the trust acquires commons subject to revocable deeds under s193 of the 1925 act, it revokes them to avoid conflict with its own powers. Where they cannot be revoked or the commons are subject to s193 as urban commons, the trust's own powers will take precedence when a declaration of inalienability is made, in accordance with proviso (a) to s193(1).

4.37 Until 1971, the trust was unable to put any building or fence on its commons, even with the secretary of state's consent, apart from a tool shed or temporary fencing to protect growing grass or plants. S23 of the National Trust Act 1971 (page 141) gives the trust the same power as any other owner or management authority of applying to the secretary of state for his consent under s194 of the 1925 act for the erection of building or other works. The same rules as to benefit of neighbourhood apply as with other such applications (6.20-28). The trust uses this power for purposes such as constructing public conveniences, setting out car parks etc, which are necessary on many of its commons.

4.38 In 1997, the National Trust and the society sought a declaration from the High Court as to the power of the trust to erect fences on common land in its ownership: *National Trust for Places of Historic Interest or Natural Beauty* v *Ashbrook and others* [1997]. The court declared that, upon the true construction of s29 of the 1907 act and s23 of the 1971 act, the trust had the power to carry out fencing, walling or similar works intended to stand for the long term on the whole or any part of any trust property to which s29 applied, whether or not the same enclosed such property. This was subject (1) to its appearing *bona fide* to the trust to be desirable for the purpose of providing or improving opportunities for the enjoyment of the property by the public and in the interests of the persons resorting thereto within the meaning of s23, and (2) to the consent of the secretary of state being duly obtained under s23(2) where access by the public to the property would be prevented or impeded.

4.39 The trust occasionally leases smaller isolated properties to local authorities to manage them on its behalf. A common may then be subject to the powers and restrictions of both.

4.40 It should be noted that the National Trust Acts only apply to commons where the trust owns the soil. In a number of cases the trust is a commoner in respect of a nearby farm it owns. In such cases the trust is in no different position from that of any other commoner and has no special statutory duties in respect of the common. The fact that the trust is a right holder does not give the public the access it enjoys under s29 of the 1907 act to commons which the trust owns.

7. Commons subject to an access agreement under the National Parks and Access to the Countryside Act 1949

4.41 S46(1)(b) of the 2000 act provides that no new access agreements or access orders under the 1949 act can be made after the subsection has been brought into force (on 1 April 2001 in England and 1 May 2001 in Wales).

4.42 Relatively few commons are managed by this means, because usually one of the management methods expressly intended for common land was more appropriate; but circumstances might have indicated this to be the best one. For example if the common was to be merely one part of a larger access area consisting of non-common open land, then an access agreement to cover the whole was more suitable than different schemes to cover different parts.

4.43 Again, in the case of commons of agricultural value where the owner of the common had been exercising manorial rights but was prepared to restrict his agricultural activities in the public interest in return for compensation, an access agreement was probably the best method of proceeding. Thus at Itchingwood Common, Surrey, there were hardly any commoners, but very many members of the public interested in the common for access. The soil was reasonable and the owner wished to take crops from the common. Legally he had only to leave sufficient grazing for the commoners, and could disregard the public. An access agreement was reached whereby the owner agreed, in return for compensation given by the planning authority, to restrict his crop to hay and to permit public access except for a short time every year when the hay crop was taken.

4.44 The access provisions of the 2000 act do not apply to land subject to an access agreement under the 1949 act so long as the agreement is in force.

8. Commons purchased by a local authority

4.45 All local authorities, including local councils, have power under the Open Spaces Act 1906 (page 124) to acquire any open space and set it out for public walks and recreation. S20 (page 125) of that act includes in the definition of open space land which 'lies waste and unoccupied'. This definition which, it will be noted, is a definition of open land which can be acquired for public open space, clearly includes many commons, and manorial waste not subject to rights of common. Common land is frequently excellent land to purchase for this purpose because it is usually, for historical reasons, the area of poorest soil in the district and this, together with the legal restrictions on its use, means that the market value is likely to be small. Thus in the 1960s Surrey County Council purchased several thousand acres of Chobham and adjoining commons in the Woking area from the Onslow family who had been lords of several manors in north-west Surrey for centuries.

4.46 While in the past a rural common could perhaps be left for the few visitors it would attract, in more recent years action has sometimes been needed if visitors are not to ruin the unfettered beauty they seek. Proper car parks and public conveniences may be required and arrangements should be made for activities like riding. If the common has no real economic value, a lord of the manor may be only too pleased to sell at a low price to a local authority who will assume the financial burden of properly caring for the common in the public interest. Sometimes, of course, an authority is able to buy common land when a lord of the manor dies and his estate is sold. Common land with no agricultural or mineral or shooting value usually sells at a low price because the cost of upkeep may well be higher than the income.

4.47 Where a common is such that the manorial rights have an economic value, commons change hands at a fairly high figure. A moorland common may be valuable for the lord of the manor's shooting rights, or a river-terrace common, such as those in the Avon valley in Hampshire, may have extensive gravel potential.

9. Countryside Act 1968

4.48 This act does not give direct management powers for the whole common, but s9 (page 138) empowers a local authority to provide car parks, public conveniences and appropriate recreational facilities so as to enhance public enjoyment of a common. The secretary of state's consent is necessary and there is provision for advertisement, objection and public inquiry.

4.49 The section applies to commons subject to (a) s193 of the 1925 act (4.20-30 and page 128), (b) an access order or an access agreement under the 1949 act (4.41-44), and (c) any other common land to which the public has access permanently or for an indefinite period. In practice, the 1968 act powers have been very little used in respect of commons.

10. Commons Act 2006—commons councils

4.50 Part 2 of the 2006 act (ss26-37) provides for the establishment of commons councils, thus implementing the chief unimplemented recommendation of the Royal Commission on Common Land (1958) and proposals in the CLPS to provide more effective ways to manage agricultural practices on common land.

4.51 The main provisions of part 2 of the 2006 act are as follows:

(a) the appropriate national authority has the power to establish commons councils for any registered common land and for any town or village green which is subject to rights of common (s26);
(b) a commons council is a body corporate (and thus has its own legal personality in the same way as a local authority) (s26);
(c) the procedure for establishing a commons council is laid down in s27;
(d) a commons council is not be regarded as a servant or agent of the Crown (and thus will not benefit from any form of Crown immunity) nor as an authority with responsibilities under s28G of the Wildlife and Countryside Act 1981 (s25);
(e) the appropriate national authority must make regulations to prescribe standard terms for the constitution of a commons council but has power to vary those terms in relation to a particular constitution (s29);
(f) various matters for inclusion in the constitution of a commons council are specified in s30;
(g) the functions of a commons council and its ancillary powers are specified in ss31 and 32;
(h) s33 sets out the circumstances in which the consent of the owner of the land, or of a commoner, is required for actions taken by a commons council;
(i) ss34 and 35 make provision for the enforcement of the rules of a commons council;
(j) s36 confers power on the appropriate national authority to take specified action consequent upon the establishment of a commons council, including the variation or revocation of schemes made under the Commons Act 1876 (4.9-12), the Commons Act 1899 (4.13-19) and the Commons Act 1908 4.56-57) and varying or abolishing the jurisdiction of a manorial court (4.52-55);

(k) s37 provides for the variation and revocation of establishment orders.

11. Manorial courts

4.52 From the Middle Ages right up to the last century many commons were managed and controlled by manorial courts. These regulated the times of the year for turning out animals, settled the extent of the various rights and fined any commoner who exceeded his right.

4.53 The Administration of Justice Act 1977, s23 and schedule 4, provides that, as from 17 October 1977, all courts baron, courts leet and similar courts shall cease to have jurisdiction to hear and determine legal proceedings but may continue to sit and transact such business, if any, as was customary immediately before the coming into force of the section. Certain specified courts (32 in number) are listed in part III of the schedule together with the customary business they may continue to transact. In a number of cases, eg Spitchwick Courts Leet and Baron on Dartmoor, and the Courts Leet and Baron of the Barony of Cemaes, on the Preseli hills in Pembrokeshire, the management of commons is part of the customary business of the courts.

4.54 Most courts baron etc fell into disuse after the abolition of copyhold tenure by the Law of Property Act 1922. The distinguishing feature of copyhold tenure was that the title to a copyhold estate was evidenced by a copy of the court roll of the manor in which the land was situated. The effect of s128 and schedule 12 of the 1922 act was to prevent the creation of any further copyhold estates. In addition, the 1922 act enfranchised all existing land held by copyhold tenure by converting all copyholds into freeholds. From then on, there was no need to prove title to land by the production of a copy of the manorial court roll.

4.55 The 1977 act did not actually abolish the obsolete courts but made their revival a practical impossibility. Where a commons council is established (4.50-51), the appropriate national authority may vary or abolish the jurisdiction of the court relating to land managed or controlled by the court (s36(2)(a) of the 2006 act).

12. Commons Act 1908

4.56 This act (page 126) provides that a majority of those with a right to turn out animals on any common may apply to the secretary of state to make regulations governing the way entire animals are turned out. The scope of the regulations which can be made is narrow and the procedure has not proved very helpful in practice. The main area where grazing is regulated under this act is Bodmin Moor in Cornwall.

4.57 The CLPS proposed that the requirement for the approval of the secretary of state should be removed in cases where a properly constituted commoners' association exists. Where there is no such association, the responsibility for giving approval should be transferred to commons registration authorities. S36(2)(b) of the 2006 act empowers the appropriate national authority to vary or revoke any regulations or arrangements made under the 1908 act.

13. The Crown commons

4.58 The Crown, Crown agencies, government departments and government agencies are owners of extensive areas of common land. In 1932 the Crown Estate Commissioners set a good example by granting access by a revocable deed under s193 of the 1925 act (page 128) to some 75,000 acres of Crown common land in the former Welsh counties of Cardigan, Caernarvon, Carmarthen, Denbigh, Flint, Merioneth, Monmouth and Radnor. Many of these commons are in the Snowdonia National Park and are extensively used for public recreation. In 1933 the commissioners also made a deed applying s193 to Torver Commons (2,100 acres) near Coniston in the Lake District.

4.59 The Dartmoor Commons Act 1985 gives public access on foot and on horseback to all registered common land on Dartmoor, including that owned by the Duchy of Cornwall.

4.60 Part I of the 2000 act (5.1 and page 148) gives public access to all registered common land owned by the Crown. S43 provides that part I binds the Crown.

14. Caravans

4.61 S23 of the Caravan Sites and Control of Development Act 1960 (page 130) empowers a district council (and a national park authority in a national park) to make an order prohibiting, either absolutely or in specified circumstances, the stationing of residential caravans on common land or on a town or village green in its area. Breach of the order is an offence. The section does not apply to land subject to s193 of the 1925 act (4.20-30; page 128), or to the Commons Act 1899 (4.13-19 and page 122), or where a caravan site licence is in force.

15. Removal of trespassers

4.62 S61 of the Criminal Justice and Public Order Act 1994 gives the police wide powers to remove trespassers from land, including common land as defined in part 1 of the 2006 act (page 153). Where the senior police officer present believes that two or more persons are trespassing on land with the common intention of residing there, he may direct them to leave, provided that (a) the occupier has asked them to leave, (b) any of them has damaged the land or property on the land, or has used threatening, abusive or insulting words or behaviour to the occupier, a member of his family or his employee or agent, and (c) they have between them six or more vehicles. He may also order them to remove their vehicles or other property. Failure to comply with the officer's direction is an offence.

4.63 In respect of common land, (a) trespassing includes infringing the rights of commoners, and (b) both a commoner and, in relation to common land to which the public has access, a local authority within s45 of the 2006 act (replacing s9 of the 1965 act) (2.51-54; page 180) are treated as occupiers. The phrase 'common land to which the public has access' is not defined in the 1994 act. It is submitted that the phrase encompasses all common land subject to a right of access by or under statute (see the previous sections of this part immediately above and chapter V). This would thus include 'ownerless' common land (see 2.50-57). Accordingly, a local authority can invoke s61 to secure the removal of trespassers from all types of common land to which the public has access.

4.64 Under s77 of the 1994 act, a local authority (London borough, the Common Council of the City of London, county and district council in England, county and county borough in Wales) may direct unauthorised persons living in vehicles on (a) land forming part of a highway, (b) any other unoccupied land, or (c) any occupied land without the consent of the occupier, to leave with their vehicle(s). Failure to comply with a direction is an offence. The local authority may apply to a magistrates' court for an order for the removal of any vehicle or other property on the land.

16 Unauthorised agricultural activities

4.65 S46 of the 2006 act enables the appropriate national authority to take action to control unauthorised agricultural activities on registered common land and on registered greens which are subject to rights of common where those activities are detrimental to those having rights over the land, or to occupiers of the land or to the public interest. The intention is to enable the appropriate national authority to deal with problems where the owner, the commoners or some other body has been unable to act. The most common agricultural activity to which this might apply is where one or more persons is depasturing livestock on the common without any right to do so, and the commoners may be powerless to stop this from occurring.

4.66 S46(2) specifies the nature of the notice to be served on the person causing the activity. The intention is to allow the notice to be served on the person actually carrying out the unauthorised activity or, if that person is a contractor hired by someone else, on the person who has hired him. In this way any damaging activity may be stopped quickly without having to wait while the person causing the activity to be carried out is tracked down.

4.67 S46(3) to (5) provide that, before using this power, the appropriate national authority must, where appropriate and practicable, notify those with interests in the common of their intention to act. The power is limited to requiring the person undertaking the unauthorised activity (or causing it to be carried out) to stop carrying out the activity, not to carry out any other unauthorised agricultural activities and to provide any information requested. Where that fails the authority can obtain a court order requiring the activity to cease (subs 7) and the court may then decide the best way to secure compliance with the notice served.

4.68 S46(6) requires the appropriate national authority first to have regard to any actions a commons association might have taken to deal with the problem, and any current court proceedings that have been initiated, before deciding to exercise the power.

4.69 S46(9) defines the public interest to include the public interest in:

(a) nature conservation;
(b) conservation of the landscape;
(c) protection of public rights of access to any area of land; and
(d) protection of archaeological remains and features of historical interest.

CHAPTER V

Countryside and Rights of Way Act 2000 — Access Provisions

1. Access land

5.1 Part I of the 2000 act provides for a right of public access on foot to 'access land', defined to include two categories of common land: (i) registered common land shown on a map in conclusive form (5.8) and (ii) registered common land in any area outside inner London for which no such map has been issued. (Inner London comprises the City of London, the Inner and Middle Temples and the London boroughs of the City of Westminster, Camden, Islington, Hackney, Tower Hamlets, Greenwich, Lewisham, Southwark, Lambeth, Wandsworth, Hammersmith & Fulham and Kensington & Chelsea.) There is already a public right of access to all the commons in the inner London area under the Metropolitan Commons Acts (4.2-8).

5.2 However, the right of access granted under the 2000 act does not extend to (a) 'excepted land' and (b) land subject to s15 of the act.

2. Registered common land

5.3 This is defined as land which is registered as common land in a register of common land kept under part 1 of the 2006 act (2.29-34). Where land is removed from the register after the commencement of the 2006 act it can no longer be access land within the meaning of the 2000 act. In the short term, this will affect land which is subject to a successful application to remove the land from the register on the grounds of mistake in accordance with the transitional provisions in sch3 to the 2006 act (2.132-140).

3. Excepted land

5.4 This is defined in part I of schedule 1 (page 151). The categories set out in the schedule are largely self-explanatory. It should be noted that there may be a right or privilege of public access to some land within them under other legislation. A considerable number of public-access commons are, for instance, used wholly or partly as golf courses (eg Minchinhampton Common, Glos, owned by the National Trust).

4. Section 15 land

5.5 As indicated in the previous chapter certain common land is excluded from the general right of access under the 2000 act because public access exists under other statutes. These statutes are:

(a) s193 of the 1925 act (4.20-30 and page 128),
(b) a local or private act, including a provisional order confirmation act (4.9-12, 4.31-34),
(c) part I of the Commons Act 1899 (4.13-19, page 122), and
(d) part V of the National Parks and Access to the Countryside Act 1949 (4.41-44).

5.6 The exclusion lasts only so long as the common land in question is subject to the foregoing acts. This means that if that land ceases to be subject to those acts, and remains registered common land, it will be covered by the general right of access under part I of the 2000 act.

5. Maps of access land

5.7 S4 of the 2000 act provides that the Countryside Agency (in England) and the Countryside Council for Wales (in Wales) must prepare maps showing all registered common land and all 'open country' (defined in s1(2) as land which consists wholly or predominantly of mountain, moor, heath or down and which is not registered common land). (The Countryside Agency has now been abolished and its functions under the 2000 act transferred to Natural England.)

5.8 The initial procedure, which has now been completed, was similar to that for the preparation of definitive maps of rights of way and resulted in the identification of all access land in England and Wales. The maps showing these areas can be viewed on the countryside access websites (www.countrysideaccess.gov.uk for England and www.ccw.gov.uk for Wales).

5.9 Maps must be reviewed regularly; the maximum period between reviews is ten years.

6. The right of access

5.10 This is defined in s2 (page 149) as an entitlement to enter and remain on any access land for the purpose of open-air recreation, but only so long as (a) no wall, fence, hedge, stile or gate is broken and damaged, and (b) the general restrictions in schedule 2 and any other restrictions imposed under chapter II of the act are observed. Furthermore, the entitlement does not apply where entry on the land contravenes any prohibition in or under an act, other than a private or local act.

5.11 A person who breaks the foregoing conditions becomes a trespasser and can be removed by the owner of the land in accordance with the ordinary laws of trespass. A farm business tenant and a tenant of an agricultural holding are treated as owners for the purposes of s2. The trespasser may not, within 72 hours of leaving the land, exercise his right to enter the land again or enter other land in the same ownership.

5.12 The general restrictions set out in schedule 2 are an updated version of the restrictions imposed on persons entering land subject to an access agreement or order under the National Parks and Access to the Countryside Act 1949. In broad terms, they outlaw criminal and anti-social behaviour, the driving or riding of vehicles (other than invalid carriages), the playing of organised games (including hang-gliding and para-gliding) and the use of metal detectors.

5.13 Chapter II allows for exclusion from access land and the imposition of further restrictions on access, eg to avoid fire risk, to preserve natural features, to preserve historic features or in the interests of proper management or of national security. There is also a limited power for an owner to exclude or restrict access for up to 28 days in a calendar year. Detailed provisions about exclusion and restriction are contained in the Access to the Countryside (Exclusions and Restrictions) (England) Regulations 2002 (SI 2713) and the Countryside Access (Exclusions or Restrictions of Access) (Wales) Regulations 2003 (SI 142).

5.14 The foregoing is necessarily a very brief summary of the law. A full treatment of the access provisions of the 2000 act is outside the scope of this book.

7. Dedication of land as access land

5.15 Under s16 of the 2000 act an owner (a freeholder or a leaseholder with a lease of which at least 90 years remain unexpired) may dedicate his land for the purposes of part I of the act. A leaseholder must obtain the consent of the freeholder or the dedication must be made jointly.

5.16 A dedication under s16 is irrevocable, but dedication does not prevent the land from becoming excepted land (5.4).

5.17 S16 came into force on 30 January 2001. The form of a dedication instrument and other detailed provisions are made by the Access to the Countryside (Dedication of Land) (England) Regulations 2003 (SI 2004) and the Countryside Access (Dedication of Land as Access Land) (Wales) Regulations 2003 (SI 135).

8. Management of registered common land

5.18 Guidance on the management of common land can be found in *A Common Purpose: A guide to agreeing management on common land*, a joint publication by the National Trust, Natural England and the society in September 2005. This can be viewed on the society's website, www.oss.org.uk.

CHAPTER VI

Statutory Protection of Common Land

6.1 By the end of the nineteenth century it was the clear policy of the legislature strictly to limit and control further enclosures of common land. Yet an absolute prohibition of all further enclosure or fencing is obviously impossible. New roads cannot make a massive detour because a common lies on their route; if the public is to enjoy some commons properly, a few buildings such as games pavilions or public conveniences are essential. Therefore the law generally prohibits enclosure and building on commons, but provides two basic statutory procedures, involving the consent of the appropriate national authority and containing safeguards for the interests of commoners and public, whereby enclosures etc may be made for certain purposes. The two current procedures are contained in s194 of the Law of Property Act 1925 (6.2-6.34) and s19 of the Acquisition of Land Act 1981 (6.35-62). Once part 3 of the Commons Act 2006 is brought into force, which is expected to be by the end of 2007, s194 of the Law of Property Act 1925 will be repealed and replaced by ss38-44 of the 2006 act (6.63-76). In addition, there is a procedure for the exchange of land in accordance with s147 of the Inclosure Act 1845 (6.77-82). This will be replaced by ss14, 16 and 17 of the 2006 act (chapter II, 2.86-94), probably by the end of 2007.

1. Section 194 of the Law of Property Act 1925

6.2 This section is the key to the high degree of protection common land enjoys under the law. It prohibits building, fencing or other works on most common land which prevent or impede access, without the secretary of state's prior consent.

(a) The scope of the section

6.3 The scope of the section is wide, but it does not apply to all common land. Subs 3 provides that the section applies to any land which at the commencement of the act (1 January 1926) was subject to rights of common.

6.4 In most cases, such land will be registered under the 1965 act, and if rights of common are also registered over the land, it will be very difficult to show that the land was not subject to some rights in 1925/6.

Even if no rights of common are registered, it will normally be reasonable to assume that rights existed on 1 January 1926, since, it is submitted, at that date 'common land' meant land subject to rights of common; the inclusion of manorial waste not so subject in the definition of common land in the 1965 act was an artificial one for the purposes of registration.

6.5 It should be noted, too, that land subject to rights of common on 1 January 1926 could be, and was, registered as a village green and is thus subject to s194; the mutually exclusive distinction between common land and a village green made by the 1965 act is, again, a purely statutory provision made for registration purposes and does not affect the operation of s194.

6.6 There are instances of land not registered under the 1965 act which were subject to rights of common on 1 January 1926: to these s194 still applies. The most obvious category of such land comprises the commons exempted from registration (listed above, 2.83-85), although not every exempted common is necessarily within the section. Other instances may be more difficult to identify, and will become increasingly so as 1 January 1926 recedes further into the past.

(b) When does the section cease to apply?

6.7 The section ceases to apply, first of all, to any land over which the rights of common are extinguished by statute. Without further provision this would have meant that land registered as common land, but where no rights had been registered, would have lost the protection of s194 because failure to register a right resulted in its extinguishment by virtue of s1(2)(b) of the 1965 act (2.82). However s21(1) of the 1965 act provided that s1(2) was not to affect the application to any land registered under the 1965 act of ss193 and 194 of the 1925 act. S21(1) is repealed by s53 of the 2006 act and replaced by para 7 of sch3 to that act (2.138 above). Thus s194 continues to protect land subject to rights of common on 1 January 1926 provided the land is registered under the 1965 act or the 2006 act.

6.8 The section ceases to apply, secondly, where rights of common are extinguished otherwise than by or under statute (eg surrender: see 2.80) if the relevant county or county borough council resolves to exclude the land from the section and the resolution is approved by the secretary of state. For example, in July 2004 the National Assembly for Wales approved a resolution by the Council of the City and County of Swansea to exclude 2.85 hectares (7 acres) from Stafford Common, Kingsbridge, Swansea from the operation of ss193 and 194, (a) so that part of the land could be used for new changing-facilities; (b) to prevent public access particularly on to football pitches; and (c) to enable suitable fencing to be erected around the whole of the land for safety and security purposes and to prevent animals straying thereon and fouling the land. (*Letter of 23 July 2004 from the National Assembly to Swansea council's solicitors, ref A-PP184-09-011.*) It should be noted that, once s13 of the 2006 act is in force, the surrender and extinguishment of common rights otherwise than in accordance with statutory procedures will be ineffective in law (2.80).

(c) What operations are covered by the section?

6.9 The section applies to the erection of any building or fence, or the construction of any other 'work' which prevents or impedes access to the land.

6.10 A 'work' includes a car park on a common; *AG* v *Southampton Corporation* [1969]. There, Southampton Corporation sought to construct a car park on Southampton common without obtaining the secretary of state's consent. The common was subject to a public right of access, but the corporation argued that a car park was no impediment to access. Mr Justice Foster ruled that it was. He said:

> It is true that if you consider car parks without any cars parked upon them a person can exercise upon them but when the car parks have cars upon them, it seem to me inevitable that the space so occupied cannot be used for exercise or for air. In my judgment therefore the proposed works will be unlawful unless the minister's consent is obtained.

6.11 It also includes a private right of way with a permanent surface which impedes access to grazing by a commoner's animals (*Eaton* v *Kurton* [1966]).

(d) The meaning of 'access'

6.12 'Access' is not defined in the section, but in the *Southampton* case (cited above, 6.10) the judge said: 'where the word "access" is used in s194(1) I think that it refers to the expression "access for air and exercise" in s193'. With respect, it is submitted that the word should be given a wider meaning. It should certainly be construed to include access by commoners or others with legal rights over the land (eg those with private rights of way), a construction which is supported by the existence in s194(2) of a power for any other person interested in the common to take legal action to secure the removal of buildings etc erected without the secretary of state's consent. However, since the purpose of the section is to control enclosures of common, it is submitted that 'access' includes access for any purpose.

6.13 In practice, most applications for consent are made in cases where the land is not subject to s193.

(e) What is excluded from the section?

6.14 The section does not apply to works (a) specially authorised by act of parliament (ie specifically authorised eg by a private act); or (b) constructed etc in pursuance of an act or order having the force of an act (ie where the act or order authorises work on land to which the section applies without requiring compliance with subs 1 eg under article 12 of the 1967 London etc Act (page 135) and s23 of the National Trust Act 1971 (page 141)); or (c) constructed etc in connection with mineral extraction; or (d) involving the installation of electronic-communication apparatus for the purpose of an electronic network.

(f) Procedure for applications

6.15 Applications for the secretary of state's consent usually relate to small works of a public or semi-public nature, such as bus shelters, games pavilions, car parks, public conveniences and the like, or, on commons where grazing rights are important, to fencing to protect commoners' animals.

6.16 A briefing note on procedures, an application form and a questionnaire are available from Defra at Common Land Branch, Countryside Division, Temple Quay House, 2 The Square, Temple Quay, Bristol BS1 6EB in relation to land in England and from the National Assembly for Wales at Crown Buildings, Cathays Park, Cardiff CF10 3NQ in relation to land in Wales.

6.17 The society is consulted on all applications and it receives copies of all decisions by the secretary of state.

6.18 The secretary of state will consider an application only to the extent that the proposals have been brought to the attention of the public. This means that the application should including any buildings, fences or works (including gates and stiles) ancillary to the main proposal. All should be shown on a map or plan of the common, preferably an Ordnance Survey map, with the scale clearly identified, also indicating the boundaries of the common as registered and the Ordnance Survey grid references.

6.19 The procedure is applied from s11 of the Commons Act 1876. The applicant must advertise his proposals in a local paper and by notices on or near the common. The secretary of state must allow 21 days for objections and if there are objections may cause a local public inquiry to be held. At least one session of such an inquiry must be between the hours of 7 pm and 10 pm. In *R (Ashbrook)* v *Secretary of State for Environment, Food and Rural Affairs* [2004] the society took the secretary of state to the High Court because she failed to hold a public inquiry into a controversial application under s194 of the 1925 act to erect fencing to enclose 259 acres of Wisley Common, Surrey. The society argued that the wording of the Commons Act 1876 should be construed so as to oblige the secretary of state to hold an inquiry into every application under s194. Collins J in the High Court rejected this construction of the 1876 act, holding that the secretary of state had a discretion as to whether or not to hold a public inquiry. During the court hearing, Defra submitted that it would hold an inquiry (a) when a significant number of objections to the proposed works have been received, or (b) where the issues appear complex, or (c) if it is considered that further information about the proposals is needed and that this could only be obtained by holding a local public inquiry.

6.20 In deciding whether or not to give consent under s194 the secretary of state must have regard to the considerations set out in subs 1. He can therefore only give consent if satisfied that it is expedient to do so, having regard to the 'benefit of the neighbourhood' as well as the private interests in the land. He must also take into account any other relevant factors, including any objections which have been made.

6.21 The 'benefit of the neighbourhood' is defined in the preamble to the Commons Act 1876 as '... the health, comfort, and convenience of the inhabitants of any cities, towns or villages or populous places in or near any parish in which the land ... may be situate.' In applying this definition the secretary of state rejected an application to build 24 wind turbines and subsidiary buildings, 14 kilometres of 15-metre-wide access tracks and various temporary structures related to the construction of the turbines on common land at Roundthwaite and Bretherdale, Whinash, near Tebay, Cumbria. He adopted the conclusions of the inspector who conducted an inquiry into the proposal, as follows:

(a) although the turbines would not present any material impediment to the ability to wander at will, the loss of the sense of openness and freedom would not be of benefit to the neighbourhood;

(b) the turbines and access tracks would cause visual intrusion which would affect the enjoyment of the landscape at Whinash, and to a much wider landscape, part of which is of national importance;
(c) the presence of a wind farm on the proposed scale would fundamentally change the panorámic and interconnecting views of the area, and would fail to conserve or enhance the natural beauty of the Lake District and Yorkshire Dales national parks, from which the wind turbines would be visible; and
(d) the proposals would have an adverse effect on the value of the landscape for recreation and public enjoyment.

6.22 The term is further described in s10(4) of the 1876 act (page 121). The 'private interests' are there defined as 'the advantage of the persons interested in the common' (ie the owner of the soil, the commoners (if any) and any other person with legal rights in, or over the common).

6.23 The secretary of state has been advised that he should not consider whether any application for consent will be for the future benefit of the neighbourhood, but whether it has regard to the need for protecting the existing benefit of the neighbourhood arising from the common in its present state. In assessing the expedience of giving consent, he will take into account any possible additional benefit that may result, but it would not be given priority as a consideration.

6.24 The 1876 act (page 120) clearly contemplates that any enclosure will involve some encroachment on the common and some interference with the private interests, and therefore the acts do not require him, before giving consent, to form the opinion that the proposed enclosure or work will enure for the benefit of the neighbourhood and the private interests. He merely has to take them into account in making his decision.

6.25 Where there is no apparent 'benefit of the neighbourhood' in an application, it is nevertheless likely to be turned down. An example would be the building of a private house on a common. Thus in 1999 an application to build a double garage on Coldharbour Common, Dorking, Surrey was turned down by the secretary of state in the following words:

> The secretary of state takes the view that the purpose of the development is to provide private benefit. He accepts that this would enable ... vehicles to be parked other than in open space, but he attaches little weight to that aspect. Any benefit to the neighbourhood and to the private interests in the land is, in his view, outweighed by the desirability of protecting the

> common from development such as that proposed which he considers to be inappropriate. Accordingly, the secretary of state concludes that consent should not be granted for your application.

(Department of the Environment, Transport and the Regions' (DETR) decision letter dated 18 June 1999, ref CYF 1077/1056)

6.26 As a general rule, car parks, sports pavilions, children's playgrounds and other public facilities of a recreational/social nature are acceptable. Applications based on conservation or environmental considerations will often be acceptable as well, provided that adequate safeguards for the public are included in the consent. With fencing applications rights of way must not be obstructed, which may involve the provision of gates and/or stiles (which also need the consent of the highway authority under section 147 of the Highways Act 1980). Since all commons have a public right of access under the 2000 act, there must be a reasonable number of gates and, if necessary, stiles to facilitate access. All gates and stiles should be to the British Standard 5709:2006. In 1999 the secretary of state gave consent for the erection of fencing to enclose 34.9 hectares (86 acres) of land on Stedham Common, West Sussex, to enable grazing management to be restored to heathland on the common. Fourteen gates were provided (eight bridle-gates for walkers and riders, two kissing-gates for walkers and four vehicle-gates). The secretary of state took the view that the fencing and the low-density grazing would not significantly affect the general accessibility of the common or the freedom of the public to roam at will, the common not then being subject to a public right of access (*DETR letter of 20 May 1999 ref CYD 1077/1084*).

6.27 By contrast, in a slightly earlier decision in October 1998, the secretary of state refused an application to provide 4,205 metres of fencing, with appropriate access points, for a period of seven years on Chobham Common, Surrey. As at Stedham, the fencing was to allow grazing in order to restore the lowland heath habitat. The secretary of state took the view that, while the proposed fences and gates would not materially reduce the general accessibility of the common, as most people used the customary access points, it was the unfenced and ungated nature of the common which distinguished it from most of the countryside. The extensive grazing would be an additional benefit to the neighbourhood which should be taken into account, but this did not outweigh the harmful effect on the existing benefit of the neighbourhood in relation to the appearance and accessibility of the common (*DETR letter of 21 October 1998, ref CYD 1077/1104*).

6.28 Internal fencing can rarely be for the benefit of the neighbourhood and may have the effect of wholly or partially dividing the common into fields. This was the issue in relation to an application to retain a one-metre-high fence around 13.74 hectares of Llanbister and Moelfre Hill Common, Beguildy, Powys. The fence had been erected without consent under s194 but the applicant had a licence from the Crown Estate (the freeholder) for the erection of the fence. The officer appointed by the National Assembly for Wales to decide the application refused consent. The fence effectively prevented animals (belonging to other commoners) from gaining access to the fenced area and was a barrier to members of the public and other commoners gaining access to the land. She rejected the submission by the applicant that people could easily step over a one-metre-high fence; the fence was a hindrance to access. While access to the land could be obtained from a gate along the adjacent bridleway, this was not sufficient to mitigate the adverse effect the fence had on the availability of access to the enclosed land (*letter from National Assembly of Wales dated 23 January 2002, ref A-PP106-09-020*).

6.29 It is interesting to note that the fence was erected without permission under s194 (see 6.32 below).

(g) What conditions can the secretary of state impose?

6.30 S7 of the Commons Act 1876 (page 120) provides that the inclosure commissioners (whose statutory successor is the secretary of state) could insert in a provisional order any or all of five terms and conditions (referred to as statutory provisions) for the benefit of the neighbourhood, namely:

(a) free access to particular points of view,
(b) trees or objects of historical interest which are to be preserved,
(c) a privilege of playing games to be reserved on parts of the common,
(d) roads, bridleways and footpaths are to be set out as appears commodious,
(e) any other specified thing is to be done which may be thought equitable for the benefit of the neighbourhood.

6.31 S194 of the 1925 act obliges the secretary of state to have regard to the same considerations as are directed by the Commons Act 1876. Clearly, in many applications for small enclosures, the s7 conditions are not relevant. But consider a case where the owner applies to fence a part of a common so as to improve it for agriculture. It may be reasonable for this to be done if, say, the local inhabitants can be sure they will have access to the rest of the common. The secretary of state takes the view that he cannot impose Commons Act 1876 conditions on an applicant, but if the applicant includes them in his proposals, then clearly that is a factor affecting the benefit of the neighbourhood which the secretary of state may take into account in reaching his decision. It is therefore good for the applicant to consult the society and others before submitting proposals for approval.

(h) Unlawful buildings, fences or works

6.32 S194(2) (page 130) makes it unlawful to erect a building or fence, or construct any other work, whereby access to the common is prevented or impeded unless the secretary of state's consent is obtained. In respect of works etc erected or constructed before 28 June 2005 (the date on which the Commons Bill was introduced into parliament) the county, county borough or district council, the lord of the manor or any other person interested in the common may apply to the county court for an order to remove the work and to restore the common to its previous state (1876 act, s30). A person 'interested' in the common must have a legal interest, such as the freehold, a lease, a right of common or an easement (eg a private right of way or of drainage). A member of the public has no power to take legal action under the subsection in respect of works etc undertaken before 28 June 2005, even if the common is subject to a public right of access under s193 (page 128).

6.33 Under para 6 of sch4 to the 2006 act, that restriction on members of the public taking action under s194(2) of the 1925 act is removed. This provision was brought into force, in England only, on 1 October 2006 by the Commons Act 2006 (Commencement No 1, Transitional Provisions and Savings) (England) Order 2006 (SI 2504) with effect from 28 June 2005. This enables the public to apply to the county court for an order to remove any works etc erected after 28 June 2005.

6.34 Where public access is impeded by unlawful works, pressure should be brought on the relevant county or district council to take action in the interests of the general public, even where the unlawful works were undertaken after 28 June 2005. An example where such action might have been possible was at Bowden and Liddaton Downs, Brentor, West Devon, where fencing and earth banks were erected without the secretary of state's consent. A retrospective application was opposed by both Devon County Council and West Devon Borough Council and was turned down by the secretary of state (*DETR letter of 31 May 2000, ref CYD 1077/1127*). The councils threatened legal action, and eventually the fence and earth banks were removed.

2. Section 19 of the Acquisition of Land Act 1981

6.35 S 19 of the Acquisition of Land Act 1981 (page 144) provides that if common land is the subject of a compulsory purchase order by a public authority, the authority must give to the common, in exchange, land which is not less in area and 'equally advantageous' to commoners and public, or submit the order to parliament under special parliamentary procedure. This system is usually applied by an act authorising compulsory purchase of land eg Highways Act 1980, Housing Act 1985, Transport and Works Act 1992, and has also been applied by s229 of the Town and Country Planning Act 1990 (page 148) to cases where an authority already owns a common for one purpose, eg public open space, but wishes to appropriate it and use it for another purpose, eg highways.

6.36 This section lays down the procedure to be followed by bodies having and needing compulsory powers to acquire a common (which includes a town or village green) to carry out or facilitate development which would not otherwise be permissible under the laws governing this type of land.

6.37 The bodies concerned include government departments, local authorities, transport and utility undertakings and the Welsh and regional development agencies. A local or development authority may not require the land for its own proposals but to facilitate private development which it wishes to encourage.

6.38 S19 is applied by other legislation which gives these bodies the powers to carry out or facilitate the particular development concerned, such as for education, housing, railways, airfields, power stations etc or under the Forestry Act 1967. The application will be made to the appropriate national authority for an order under those powers. The common may already be owned by the local authority wishing to use it for other purposes. In that case, an order for appropriation must be applied for under s229 of the 1990 act, which also incorporates s19.

6.39 Planning permission will also be required, and that may be sought first, but it is quite often dealt with concurrently so that there is only one public inquiry. A proposal considered important enough to require the taking of a common or a town or village green is likely also to require the preparation by the applicant of an environmental impact assessment (EIA) which should provide much more information about its alleged advantages and disadvantages. It is not necessary here to consider these aspects, but those concerned with the protection of the common or green should be aware of them and be prepared to examine the EIA with care in the few weeks within which objections must be lodged.

6.40 If the developing body intends to give land in exchange it must specify this in the draft order (and it might need to be acquired compulsorily under the main powers sought) and obtain a certificate from (in England) the secretary of state for Defra (not from the department responsible for development) or the National Assembly for Wales that the exchange land is 'not less in area and equally advantageous to the public'. The secretary of state must advertise his intention to give the certificate and allow a period of 28 days for public objection. If he is not satisfied that the alternative land is equally advantageous he must refuse his certificate and the work cannot take place unless the order is approved by parliament under Special Parliamentary Procedure (SPP).

6.41 The only exceptions to the rule are where the common or green (a) is being purchased or appropriated in order to secure its preservation or improve its management, or (b) the area does not exceed 250 square yards in extent or is needed for the widening or drainage of an existing highway. The secretary of state has power in such cases to certify that no exchange land is necessary, but even here, if he thinks it necessary in any particular case, he can require exchange land to be given.

6.42 In all other cases where the authority does not offer alternative land, the order appropriating the land is subject to SPP.

6.43 It is the secretary of state's duty to determine whether the alternative land is really 'equally advantageous' to that to be taken. Decisions indicate that the land offered must be a genuine exchange. For example in 1969 the City and County of Bristol (Durdham Down) Appropriation Order was submitted to the Minister of Housing and Local Government. The order sought to appropriate 2.5 acres of Durdham Downs for the purpose of constructing a roundabout. In exchange the council offered 2.5 acres of land adjoining another part of the downs formerly owned by the university. This proposed exchange land was not separated from the downs and had been used as public open space for many years. The minister refused his certificate and thus the appropriation order failed. To quote from the decision: 'Whatever may be the legal status of the land, it is not acceptable for exchange purposes as it will not increase the actual area of the open space on the downs' (*MHLG letter of 15 September 1969, ref P8/903/11/33*).

6.44 A similar case occurred a year later at Bedford. There Bedford Corporation sought to appropriate one acre of Langholme meadow, an attractive riverside open space in the centre of the town, for an inner ring road. In exchange the corporation offered three possible sites, A, B or C. All of them had been used by the public for 15 years although they were held under general private act powers and not public open space powers. The minister refused his consent. The inspector concluded that sites A and C would not be equally advantageous to the public since both were separated from the main riverside area. The inspector found as a fact 'that the public have used sites A, B and C for 15 years as public open space. He feels bound to say that in the above circumstances none of the three sites A, B and C would be acceptable as exchange land for the purpose of a certificate' (*MHLG letter of 29 June 1970, ref PF3/831/11/1*).

6.45 The decision is interesting for the inspector's conclusion supports the view that the exchange of land must also be of a similar character (in the Bedford case, riverside) to the land appropriated.

6.46 However, a different conclusion was reached by the secretary of state in the case of the Wisley, Surrey, interchange for the M25 motorway. Parts of Wisley Common, Chatley Heath and Ockham Common were to be taken for the interchange and some of the exchange land offered had been used by the public *de facto* as open space. The secretary of state considered that such land was equally advantageous to the public because there was no evidence that the public use of the land was with lawful authority; nor was there any indication of how long such use might be allowed to continue. It would thus be advantageous to acquire the land specifically to preserve it for the benefit of the public (*letter of South-East Region of Department of Environment and Transport of 19 June 1979, ref SE2/5076/12/13*).

6.47 Furthermore, the position of the land to be acquired in relation to the common as a whole is relevant. At Esher, Surrey, the Department of the Environment sought to acquire by compulsory purchase some 55 acres of Esher and neighbouring commons for a bypass. The 55 acres were, broadly, across the middle of the commons. The exchange land offered would be added to the edges. Esher Urban District Council and the society argued that 55 acres taken from the middle of a common were particularly valuable and should be compensated by about 90 acres of exchange land added to one side of the common. The department, while strongly arguing the details, apparently accepted the broad principle of this argument for it offered some 66 acres in exchange for the 55. At the subsequent inquiry the inspector accepted the argument of Esher UDC and the society and recommended that consent be refused on the ground that the land the department was offering was not 'equally advantageous'. The secretary of state accepted the inspector's recommendations (*DoE letter of 10 November 1972, ref PC2/692/304/1*).

6.48 This is an interesting example of the secretary of state, in his capacity as consenting authority to the appropriation of common land, ruling against himself in his capacity as highway authority for a proposed new road. The Department of the Environment later made new proposals whereby some 89 acres of exchange land were offered for the 55 acres to be appropriated. Furthermore, part of the 89 acres would link up two separate commons to make one large one. This is more or less what the society asked for at the original inquiry. The Esher case thus provides guidelines for the quantity and quality of exchange land an authority should offer.

6.49 Those guidelines were followed in the case of Fordham Heath, Eight Ash Green, Colchester, Essex. Here, the parish council wished to appropriate 427.5 square metres of Fordham Heath, a registered village green over which rights of common of grazing and turbary were registered, for a children's play area. The area to be appropriated was roughly in the middle of the heath. The land offered in exchange was 500 square metres in area and lay immediately to the north of the heath. It was an area of pasture land already belonging to the parish council. The main objections to the appropriation were that the exchange land was inferior because of its location, remoteness, boggy nature and poor conservation interest.

6.50 The secretary of state's conclusions were as follows:

> 8. The secretary of state notes that the common land proposed to be taken is a grassed area and part of a copse, forming 427.5 square metres of Fordham Heath, lying west of a cricket pavilion and east of a track leading due south from Heath Road to Huxtables Lane. She notes that the area to be given in exchange is 500 square metres in area, and that it is part of a sloping grassed field with woodland lying to its west and south.
>
> 9. The secretary of state notes that the land to be given in exchange for the common land is greater in extent. She accepts that the exchange land would be as advantageous as the common land for grazing or taking turves, and that the registered rights of common would not, therefore, be prejudiced by the exchange. She notes that the exchange land has better views than the common land to be taken, though she also recognises that the exchange land has no identified

nature conservation interest.

10. The secretary of state acknowledges that the exchange land is more isolated and harder to access than the present common land because it is on the periphery of the heath and hidden from the public view beyond woodland. She accepts that this could lead to some apprehension by potential users who might feel less secure using this area. She also notes that the accesses to the exchange land are enclosed and could become muddy and slippery in wet weather, potentially making access hazardous in winter, whereas the present common land is of a drier nature. She accepts the inspector's view that the advantages of the exchange land would, on balance, be insufficient to outweigh its disadvantages in terms of location, access and other amenity.

11. The secretary of state notes and accepts the inspector's overall conclusion. She considers that the land to be given in exchange for the common land to be taken, although greater in area, would not be equally advantageous to the persons, if any, entitled to rights of common or other rights, and to the public. She therefore concludes that the certificate should not be given.

(Defra letter of 4 February 2002, ref CYD/1077/1196)

6.51 To sum up therefore, the following criteria for equally advantageous exchange land are suggested:

(a) it should be of the same nature as the land taken eg riverside, woodland,
(b) it should not if possible be *de facto* public open space,
(c) it should serve approximately the same purpose,
(d) if common rights are exercised then the quality of the soil and the grazing should be as good,
(e) minor disadvantages on the above may be compensated by offering a greater area in exchange.

6.52 Some of the above examples are taken from the secretary of state's decisions made before 1980 on public open spaces which were not commons or greens. Since then, applications to appropriate or dispose of such land do not have to go to the secretary of state but under amended ss122 and 123 (subs 2A in both cases) of the Local Government Act 1972 (page 142), the local authority merely has to advertise its intentions and consider any objections received. There is no compulsion to offer exchange land.

6.53 However, applications under s229 of the Town and Country Planning Act 1990 (page 148) and s122 of the Local Government Act 1972 as amended (page 142) for the intended appropriation of common land or town or village greens exceeding 250 square yards remains subject to the approval of the secretary of state.

6.54 Curiously, under s123 of the Local Government Act 1972 (page 142) the disposal of common land or greens by agreement is not subject to the secretary of state's approval if it is sold for not less than the best consideration reasonably obtainable. The safeguard is that the land remains with the same status as common or green and the new owner has to consider his own powers to obtain an alternative use, for instance by way of compulsory purchase (3.22) or exchange (6.77-82).

6.55 If the developer agrees to provide exchange land but does not in fact do so, the law does not prescribe any specific penalty or sanction. This means that a person aggrieved by the omission would have to seek judicial review in the High Court: an expensive and uncertain course of action. Specialist advice should be taken before seeking judicial review.

6.56 What happens if no land is offered in exchange? The compulsory purchase order then becomes subject to the Statutory Orders (Special Procedure) Acts 1945 and 1965. The order must be advertised in the *London Gazette* and in a local newspaper and 28 days allowed for objections. If any such objection is duly made and is not withdrawn the authority empowered to make or confirm the order must take the objection into consideration and 'shall cause a local public inquiry to be held unless they are satisfied that in the special circumstances of the case the holding of such an inquiry is unnecessary' (Statutory Orders (Special Procedure) Act 1945, first schedule, para 3).

6.57 If, after holding the inquiry, the secretary of state confirms the order, he must then lay it before parliament and advertise his intention of doing so in the *London Gazette*. Objectors have 21 days to petition parliament. Where a petition is lodged the order goes before a joint committee of both Houses (usually two peers and two MPs). The order-making authority and the objectors then each present their case. The committee can approve the order, reject it or amend it. The committee's decision is reported to each House. It is usual for the Houses to endorse the committee's findings.

6.58 If no petition against the order is lodged, a prayer may be moved in either House to annul it.

6.59 One example of a successful petition was the High Wycombe (Inner Relief Road) Appropriation Order 1964. High Wycombe

Borough Council had obtained planning permission to construct an inner relief road and in 1964 the minister confirmed an appropriation order to authorise the appropriation of 2.5 acres of Wycombe Rye for the road. No exchange land was offered and the order was submitted to parliament. A local amenity body—the Rye Protection Society—petitioned on the ground that the Rye was an attractive and valuable open space, in the centre of the town, which would be ruined if a portion of it were taken for a road. The petitioners could not afford counsel and their case was argued before the joint committee by their secretary, a local schoolmaster. Parliament accepted the petitioners' case, the order was not approved and the Rye remains intact to this day.

6.60 Another example was provided by the County of Dorset (Lytchett Minster and Upton Bypass) Compulsory Purchase Order 1970. By this order Dorset County Council sought to acquire some 20 acres of fuel allotment land for a new road. The land was near Poole and was physically open heathland, although technically the public had no legal right of access. The county offered no land in exchange and the order thus became subject to special parliamentary procedure. A local member of the society objected and was heard by a joint parliamentary committee, which held that Dorset should provide 20 acres of public open space to replace the fuel allotment land. This was subsequently done. (*Report of Joint Parliamentary Committee into the County of Dorset (Lytchett Minster and Upton Bypass) Compulsory Purchase Order 1970 held on Tuesday 25 April 1972. Chairman: Sir John Langford-Holt MP*)

6.61 The SPP procedure has not been transferred to the National Assembly for Wales in relation to land in Wales Accordingly, any compulsory purchase order made by the Assembly where exchange land is not offered is subject to final determination by parliament.

6.62 The National Trust has its own protection from compulsory purchase under s18 of the 1981 act. SPP will apply if the trust objects to the order. However, even if it does not object, any member of the public can do so and require the s19 powers to be applied.

3. Sections 38-44 of the Commons Act 2006

6.63 S38-44 of the 2006 act (replacing with modifications s194 of the 1925 act) (page 175) controls the carrying out of works on common land.

6.64 S38(1) prohibits the carrying out of 'restricted works' (ie works which prevent or impede access to the land in respect of which consent is sought or which are resurfacing works) on:

(a) registered common land;
(b) land which is not registered common land but is regulated by a provisional order confirmation act made under the Commons Act 1876 (chapter IV, 4.9-12) or a scheme under the Commons Act 1899 (chapter IV, 4.13-19); and
(c) land within the New Forest which is subject to rights of common but not within (a) or (b)

unless the consent of the appropriate national authority is obtained.

6.65 The word 'access' is not defined in the 2006 act (nor is it under s194 of the 1925 act). It is submitted that the word should be construed as access for any purpose. The criteria laid down in s39 (6.69 below) to be taken into account by the appropriate national authority when determining an application for consent are widely drawn. More significantly, s41 (6.73 below) allows anyone to bring proceedings to secure the removal of unlawful works or to secure compliance with the terms of a consent.

6.66 Works include, in particular, fencing, the erection of buildings and other structures, the digging of trenches and the building of embankments (s38(3)). Resurfacing consists of the laying of concrete, tarmacadam, coated roadstone or the like, but not the repair of an existing surface made of such material (s38(4)).

6.67 The prohibition in s38(1) does not apply in the following cases:

(a) where the works are authorised under another enactment, eg under a local act or a management scheme (chapter IV above);
(b) where the works are authorised by an enactment applying to common land (which phrase is to be interpreted to apply generally to registered common land, common land, commons, commonable land, land subject to inclosure under statute, or other land of a similar description);
(c) where the works are authorised under a scheme under the Metropolitan Commons Act 1866 or the Commons Act 1899 without the requirement for the appropriate national authority to give consent to the works (chapter IV above);
(d) where the works are for the installation of electronic-communications apparatus.

6.68 The grant of planning permission for works covered by (a) above does not constitute permission under s38; nor does the conferral of functions on a commons council (chapter IV above) (s38(7)). Generally speaking, consent given under s38 does not obviate any requirement to obtain consent from someone else (eg the owner of the land or the local planning authority).

6.69 S39 lays down the matters to which the appropriate national authority must have regard when considering an application for consent. These are:

(a) the interests of the occupiers and those having rights on or over the land and in particular the rights of commoners;
(b) the interests of the neighbourhood;
(c) the public interest;
(d) any other matter considered to be relevant.

6.70 The public interest includes interest in:

(a) nature conservation;
(b) landscape conservation;
(c) protection of public rights of access to any area of land (not just the application area);
(d) protection of archaeological remains and features of historic interest.

6.71 S38(3)–(6) give greater flexibility to the appropriate national authority in considering whether or not to give consent than was possible under s194 of the 1925 act. The authority may:

(a) give consent to all or part of the proposed works, with or without modifications;
(b) take into consideration any previous consent given under s38(1) or under s194 of the 1925 act;
(c) on the application of the person to whom the consent was given, vary or revoke any modification or condition attached to a consent;
(d) give consent to works which have been started or completed, with the consent running from the date on which the works began.

6.72 S40 provides for regulations to be made to set out in detail the steps to be taken in making and determining applications under ss38 and 39. The regulations may include provision for the payment of fees for making applications.

6.73 Where works are carried out in contravention of s38(1), s41 empowers any person to apply to the county court. The court may:

(a) in any case, order the removal of the works and restoration of the land to its previous condition;
(b) where works have not been carried out in accordance with a consent granted under s38(1), order that the works are carried

out in such manner and subject to such conditions as the order may specify.

6.74 S42 is intended to clarify the situation in relation to the carrying out of works on land which is subject to a scheme of management under the Metropolitan Commons Act 1866 or the Commons Act 1899. Where such a scheme contains a provision which prohibits the carrying out of works and the scheme does not allow for any person to consent to the works, those works are not in breach of s38(1) if carried out in accordance with a consent given by the appropriate national authority. Where the scheme provides for consent to be given for works by the appropriate national authority then consent must be obtained under s38(1) and not under the provisions of the scheme.

6.75 S43 gives the appropriate national authority power to exempt some kinds of work from the necessity to obtain consent under s38(1). The power may only be exercised where the works are necessary or expedient for one or more of the following purposes:

- (a) use of the land by members of the public for open-air recreation in exercise of a right of access (eg under the 2000 act (chapter V));
- (b) exercise of common rights;
- (c) nature conservation;
- (d) protection of archaeological remains and features of historic interest;
- (e) use of the land for sporting or recreational purposes.

The power may also be exercised where the land is subject to a resolution made by a county council or a metropolitan district council to exclude the land from the operation of s193 of the 1925 act (4.20-30).

6.76 S44 and sch4 make supplementary provision. The main provisions are:

- (a) the appropriate national authority may amend any local or personal act or any provisional order confirmation act passed before the 2006 act (4.31-34; 4.9-12) in order to make provision about works on common land to which the act relates;
- (b) detailed amendments to the legislation relating to metropolitan commons and to the National Trust and to new Church of England parishes;
- (c) s194(2) of the 1925 act (6.32) is amended so as to enable any person to take action in the county court to secure the removal of unlawful works carried out on or after 28 June 2005. This provision came into force on 1 October 2006, in England only, by virtue of the Commons Act 2006 (Commencement No 1,

Transitional Provisions and Savings) (England) Order 2006 (SI 2504).

4. Exchange-land procedures

6.77 The 1981 act code (6.35-62) requires that an acquiring authority must, as a general rule, provide land in exchange where common land (or village green land) is taken by compulsory purchase.

Inclosure Act 1845

6.78 There is also a voluntary procedure under s147 of the Inclosure Act 1845 (page 118), whereby an order by the secretary of state effects an exchange of a piece of common or green for other land. The legal effect is that the other land becomes part of the common or green in place of the original part. In consequence, an amendment to the register should be made (see 2.86-87).

6.79 The procedure is useful chiefly in cases where a landowner wishes to acquire a small area of a common or green and is willing to add a piece of his own land to the common or green. A recent example was at Beam Heath Estate, Cheshire, where 0.65 ha was exchanged for 4.26 ha in order to provide a cemetery extension. The society objected on the grounds that (a) the exchange land was some distance from the common land and this was not compensated by the larger area; and (b) the exchange land might not be available for public access under the 2000 act because crops might be grown on the land (the area to be exchanged was planted with crops). Consent was given for the exchange. The cemetery extension was urgently needed; access to the exchange land was likely to be maintained all year round, whereas access to the original land was restricted by crops; and there was no detrimental effect on anyone with an interest in the land or on the general public. (*Defra, ref CLI 202, dated 13 December 2005*) By contrast, at Mynydd Lliw common, Grovesend, Swansea, an application to exchange land in order to regularise the inadvertent construction of part of a new dwelling on part of the common was refused. While the authorised officer of the National Assembly for Wales was satisfied that the exchange would benefit the applicant, she did not accept that the exchange would be just and reasonable for the commoners and members of the public. The land on offer was in poor condition. While the land could be brought into a suitable condition to meet the needs of the commoners and the public, the assembly had no power to attach any requirement to that effect to a consent under s147. Accordingly, consent was refused. (*NAW letter of 23 August 2004, ref A-PP-184-09-009*)

6.80 A contrasting case concerned Scout Moor, Turf Moor and Knowl Moor in the districts of Rossendale in Lancashire, and Rochdale. The application was made to exchange 8.69 hectares common for 9.3 hectares of other land so that a wind farm could be constructed on the common. The society was among 15 objectors, the others including Rochdale Metropolitan Borough Council, Rossendale Borough Council and Lancashire County Council. Following a public inquiry, the inspector recommended that the exchange be made and the secretary of state agreed. The secretary of state took the inspector's view that the quality of grazing for commoners' animals would only be marginally affected. So far as the general public was concerned, from a recreational perspective the wind farm would not prevent continuing public access to Scout and Knowl Moors; while it would be a different recreational experience for many, for the less agile the tracks might increase accessibility and make the moors more inclusive. Furthermore, the public's right to roam would be substantially unaffected and there would be a slight gain as the public would have unfettered access to the additional land which would slightly widen their choice of routes. The exchange order included an agreed provision, granting licence to the commoners, and to members of the public who previously had a right of access under s193 of the 1925 act (see 4.20-30 above), to cross on foot those parts of the former common land not required for the purposes of the wind turbines, subject to limited restrictions. (*Defra letter of 5 May 2006, ref GW1/TH1/342722.1*)

6.81 The procedure can also be used if a landowner wishes to replace an existing track over a common with another which is both better for access and advantageous from the public point of view, even if it is only an exchange of a private right of way.

6.82 As from 1 April 2006 Defra charges an administration fee of £370 for handling applications under s147 and requires reimbursement of the actual cost of having the two pieces of land valued. This latter amount is likely to be in the region of £500 to £1,000, and will relate to the time taken to undertake the valuations. So far, the National Assembly for Wales does not charge a fee.

Commons Act 2006

6.83 Ss14, 16 and 17 of the 2006 act provide the voluntary exchange of common land or town or village green land for other land. This topic is covered in chapter II, 2.86-94.

CHAPTER VII

Town and Village Greens

7.1 The origin of town and village greens (which are legally identical) is to be found in customary law. They were originally small areas, usually forming part of the waste land of a manor, over which local inhabitants indulged in lawful sports and pastimes. What must originally have been technically a trespass, or at most carried on with the permission of the lord of the manor, ultimately matured into a customary right enforceable through the courts. In many instances, village greens were also common land and it was only the 1965 act which made the two categories of land mutually exclusive for the purposes of registration.

1. Registration of greens during the initial registration period

7.2 The 1965 act provided for the registration of village greens in exactly the same way as for common land (see chapter II for a description of the procedures). For the purposes of registration, s22 of the 1965 act (as originally enacted) defined a village green as:

> land which has been allotted by or under any act for the exercise or recreation of the inhabitants of any locality or on which the inhabitants of any locality have a customary right to indulge in lawful sports and pastimes or on which the inhabitants of any locality have indulged in such sports and pastimes as of right for not less than twenty years.

7.3 It was decided in the *Clwyd* case (2.82) that a failure to register common land and common rights during the initial registration period resulted in the loss of status of the land as common and the extinguishment of the rights. In *Oxfordshire County Council* v *Oxford City Council and another* [2006] (the Trap Grounds case), the House of Lords ruled that the non-registration of land subject to customary or statutory rights of recreation as a town or village green in accordance with the 1965 act resulted in the extinguishment of those rights.

(a) Recreation allotments

7.4 The first limb of the definition set out above refers to allotments 'for the exercise and recreation' of the inhabitants of places where the open commons were enclosed by act of parliament. Such allotments became usual after about 1830. A good example is provided by the inclosure award of 10 August 1859 for Stourpaine in Dorset. The award allotted 'unto the Church wardens and Overseers of the Poor of the said Parish of Stourpaine all that piece or parcel of land numbered 21 on the said map containing four acres, to be held by them and their successors in trust as a place of exercise and recreation for the inhabitants of the said Parish and neighbourhood ...'.

7.5 Almost all awards made under inclosure acts passed after 1840 or under provisional orders confirmed under the Inclosure Act 1845 made provision for recreation allotments. This was the result of the standing orders of the House of Commons or of s30 of the Inclosure Act 1845, which provided that if no recreation allotment was made in an award, the inclosure commissioners had to state their reasons in a report to parliament. A recreation allotment could be made either to public officers (usually the Churchwardens and Overseers) under s73 of the 1845 act or to a private person under s74. In both cases the allottees could enjoy or let the herbage (1845 act, s74) but held the land itself as trustees and could not do anything to interfere with the rights of the inhabitants. After 1876 recreation allotments could no longer be made to private persons. The importance of the two types today is that recreation allotments made to the Churchwardens and Overseers should have passed to the local council (or sometimes the district council in England or the county or county borough council in Wales) by s6 of the Local Government Act 1894. Recreation allotments made to private persons may still be in private hands.

7.6 The word 'allot' refers to a distribution or setting aside of land by or under an inclosure act. It was so held in *re the Rye, High Wycombe, Bucks* [1977], where the High Court upheld the refusal by a commons commissioner to confirm the registration of land set aside by a private act of parliament as a public park. In his decision, *In the Matter of the Downs, Herne Bay, Kent*, the chief commons commissioner held that the acquisition of land as public pleasure grounds under s164 of the Public Health Act 1875 was not an allotment within the meaning of the 1965 act.

7.7 By s19 of the Commons Act 1876 (page 121) it is made unlawful to authorise the use of, or to use, a recreational allotment (wholly or in part) for any purpose other than that set out in the relevant act or award. Subsequent legislation has modified this prohibition so that such land can be acquired under compulsory powers (6.35-62) or exchanged for other land (see 6.77-82), or sold under an order of the Charity

Commissioners, or made subject to a scheme of regulation under the Commons Act 1899 (4.13-19).

7.8 As well as being registrable as greens, recreational allotments are charities and come under the jurisdiction of the Charity Commissioners by virtue of s18 of the Commons Act 1899. The general powers of the commissioners are contained in the Charities Act 1993 and include a power to authorise a sale or exchange of an allotment. A recreational allotment may be the subject of an application to register the allotment as a village green in accordance with para 3 of sch2 to the 2006 act (7.55 below).

(b) Customary right to indulge in lawful sports or pastimes

7.9 For centuries the courts have recognised that the inhabitants of a locality may acquire a customary right of recreation over a particular piece of land. One of the early cases was *Abbot* v *Weekly* [1665]. There, a field owned by A had been used by the villagers for many years for dancing. The court held that A could not stop W entering it for open air dancing: 'This is a good custom and it is necessary for Inhabitants to have their recreation.'

7.10 The doctrine was propounded more fully in *Fitch* v *Rawling* [1795] where an old custom of playing cricket in a field was held enforceable at law and again in *Hall* v *Nottingham* [1875] where maypole dancing was upheld.

7.11 To establish a valid custom in law, the courts have ruled that the custom must be certain, reasonable and have continued without interruption for the necessary period.

(i) Type of activity

7.12 The old cases appeared to show that the sport or pastime had to be something definite; a mere strolling round for pleasure was not enough. In *AG* v *Antrobus* [1905] the plaintiff claimed that there was a general right to wander around Stonehenge (then in private ownership). The court ruled there was not, and the judge stated clearly:

> The public cannot prescribe nor is *jus spatiandi* (a right to wander) known to our law as a possible subject matter of grant or prescription.

But in *Abercromby* v *Town Commissioners of Fermoy* [1900] the judge said: 'legal principle does not require that rights of this nature should be limited to certain ancient pastimes'.

7.13 The commons commissioners took the view in many cases arising out of the registration of greens under the 1965 act that the sport or pastime did not have to be organised. Children playing cowboys and indians and informal cricket and football was held to be good evidence that the land was a green: *In the Matter of Bridge Green, Hargrave, West Suffolk*.

7.14 The commissioners' view was upheld by the courts, and in the *Oxfordshire County Council* case (7.3) Lord Hoffmann, giving the leading judgment, stated that land registered as a town or village green can be used generally for sports and pastimes.

7.15 For the registration of a new green see below, 7.63-72.

(ii) Inhabitants of a locality

7.16 It was a clear rule that a valid custom could only be enjoyed by the inhabitants of a locality and not by the public at large. This appears from Cockburn CJ's judgment in *Earl of Coventry* v *Willes* [1863] (claim of an alleged public right to look at horse races) where he said:

> A customary right can only be applicable to certain inhabitants of the district where the custom is alleged to exist and cannot be claimed in respect of the public at large.

7.17 This was followed in *Hammerton* v *Honey* [1876] (alleged rights for Londoners to play football on Stockwell Green failed) and reached its almost absurd limit in *Edwards* v *Jenkins* [1896]. In that case the claim was that the inhabitants of the then three parishes of Beddington, Mitcham and Carshalton in Surrey had the right to play games on a piece of land in Beddington. The judge held that three parishes were wider than the term 'the district' to which a custom must apply and implied that a custom can only attach to the smallest unit of local government, ie a parish or, where there are no parishes, presumably a borough or district. The correctness of this decision was doubted by the Court of Appeal in the *New Windsor* case (7.20).

7.18 The definition of a village green in s22 of the 1965 act was amended by s98 of the 2000 act with the intention of making it easier to identify the locality in relation to which a claim for a new green is made. The whole of the 1965 act will be repealed by s53 of the 2006 act and the amended definition is re-enacted in substance in s15(2) of the 2006 act (7.63-64).

(iii) No consent

7.19 A custom, like a right of common, had to be established 'as of right', ie without consent. The House of Lords confirmed the law on this point in *R* v *Oxfordshire County Council and another ex parte Sunningwell Parish Council* [1999] (7.69).

7.20 A customary right of recreation, once it validly exists, cannot be lost by abandonment: *New Windsor Corporation* v *Mellor* [1975]. There it was shown that a valid custom of archery had existed in the nineteenth century. The chief commons commissioner held that non-exercise since 1875 had not destroyed the right and his decision was upheld by the Court of Appeal.

(iv) Right must be of recreation

7.21 Other customary rights can exist but the right on a green must be of recreation. For example in *Mercer* v *Denne* [1905] it was held that a traditional use of land for drying nets near the seashore was a valid legal custom. Such land would not however be a green, for the fishing in that case was the men's livelihood. Again in *Tyson* v *Smith* [1838] a right was upheld for victuallers to pitch stalls at a fair. Here the fair appeared to be one for the buying and selling of goods and so hardly recreational.

(v) Extent

7.22 The use of the land is looked at as a whole: it is not necessary for games to have been played on every square yard. Thus where part of an area of land had been a swamp, but games had been played on the remainder, it was held by a commons commissioner that the whole of the land was properly a green: *In the Matter of Gleaston Green, Aldingham, Lancs.*

(c) 20 years' use as of right

7.23 The third limb of the definition in s22 of the 1965 act was presumably intended to ensure registration of land which had been used as if a customary right existed, but where no such right could be established under the common-law rules. It was the view of all the judges in the *New Windsor* case (7.20) that the relevant period of use was 20 years immediately before 5 August 1965, the date on which the 1965 act came into force. Their view was not part of the actual decision in the case (which concerned a customary right) but it was accepted by the commons commissioners as a correct interpretation of s22. Of course, the relevance of that date was significant only in relation to applications to register land as a green in the initial registration period. In relation to new greens, see 7.63-72.

7.24 It was confirmed in the *Oxfordshire County Council case* (7.3) that land registered as a green on the basis of 20 years' use as of right is subject to s12 of the Inclosure Act 1857 and s29 of the Commons Act 1876 (7.35-39 and pages 119 and 122).

2. The ownership of greens

7.25 The procedure in the 1965 act for claiming and determining the ownership of common land (2.36-42) applied equally to greens. However, s8 of the 1965 act provided that, where a commons commissioner was unable to discover the owner of a registered green, the green vested in the local council or, if there was no such council, in the district council (in Wales, the county or county borough council) or the London borough council. The authority acquiring the green was to manage it under the Open Spaces Act 1906 (page 124).

7.26 The owner of a green cannot do anything which interferes with the lawful recreational activities of the local inhabitants. He is not obliged, however, to maintain the green in a suitable state for recreation, although he could not prevent appropriate maintenance (grass cutting etc) by local inhabitants.

7.27 Where the owner is a local authority or other body with statutory powers of management, by-laws may be made to regulate recreational activities (7.29-30).

7.28 The CLPS proposed that (a) land which was vested in a local authority can be restored to its former owner on proof of title and within a specified period from the date of legislation and (b) that a procedure similar to s8 of the 1965 act (7.25) will be applied to new greens where the owner is unknown.

3. The management of greens

7.29 There are various public general acts of parliament which give statutory powers of management. Local or private acts may give similar or additional powers. The public general acts are:

(a) ***Commons Act 1899*** (page 122): a district council may make a scheme of regulation for a green under the 1899 act. The procedure is described in detail above (4.13-19).

(b) ***S 193 of the Law of Property Act 1925*** (page 128): the owner of land subject to s193 may apply for an order of limitation to control public behaviour (4.23-24). Normally, only a private person or body would seek to obtain an order, since local authorities and certain other bodies have other statutory powers to make by-laws etc.

(c) ***Open Spaces Act 1906*** (page 124): this is the principal act which empowers local authorities (ie county, county borough, district and local councils) to manage village greens. By-laws to control public behaviour may be made and areas may be set aside for cricket, football or similar organised games.

7.30 Where the owner of a green is a private person or body, a local authority has no power to manage the land without the owner's agreement. The CLF recommended that local councils should be given powers to manage or acquire greens in private ownership where irreconcilable disputes have arisen.

4. Rights of common over greens

7.31 Rights of common may exist over a green if registered, although such registrations are rare. Where they do exist, it seems that normally they take precedence to customary rights of recreation in the case of any conflict between the two, the reason being that a legal right of property is higher than a customary right. In *Fitch* v *Fitch* [1797] (a sequel to *Fitch* v *Rawling* (7.10)) it was held not to be a lawful exercise of a custom to enter upon the land when the grass had been allowed to grow and had been cut for hay, and to throw the hay about and mix it with gravel and spoil it. Since the customary right in this case was to play cricket, it would seem, however, that the inhabitants could lawfully have prevented the crop from growing by exercising their right.

5. Greens and highways

7.32 Under the 1965 act, land could not for the purposes of registration be both common land and a highway, ie a public highway (s22(1), 1965 act). This was not the case with village greens and there is no reason in law why land cannot be both a highway and subject to a customary right of recreation. A full discussion of the matter is to be found in the decision of Mr Commissioner Baden Fuller *In the Matter of Medstead Village Green, Medstead, Hampshire*.

7.33 For the position with regard to the registration of new greens, see 7.63-72.

6. Damage to and encroachment on a green

7.34 It is an offence under s12 of the Inclosure Act 1857 (page 119) and s29 of the Commons Act 1876 (page 122) to damage or encroach upon a town or village green. Neither section includes a definition of a green and in the past doubt has been expressed as to whether or not the sections apply to all registered greens. That doubt has been stilled by the clear decision of the House of Lords in the *Oxfordshire County Council* v *Oxford City Council and another* [2006] (the Trap Grounds case) —see paragraphs 54-6, 116 and 129 of the judgment—that registration of land as a town or village green under the 1965 act is conclusive in accordance with s10 of that act (2.95-96).

(a) S 12 of the Inclosure Act 1857

7.35 The terms of the section are very wide and cover any act which injures the green or interrupts its use as a place for exercise and recreation. Certain acts are offences only if done 'wilfully', ie deliberately, even if there was no intention to injure etc the green: an act is wilful if its effect is to cause the injury, whatever the motive of the doer. However, the phrase 'do any other act whatsoever' is not qualified by 'wilfully', so that an accidental act, or an act done in ignorance of the status of the land, would be an offence. In practice, of course, it is unlikely that a person would be prosecuted in these circumstances.

7.36 It is submitted that 'any act whatsoever' includes the driving and parking of motor vehicles where this causes injury to the green or interrupts its use for recreation, even though motor vehicles did not exist when the 1857 act was passed.

(b) S 29 of the Commons Act 1876

7.37 This section overlaps with s12 of the 1857 act to some extent, but it also covers permanent encroachment or enclosures (eg fencing off part of a green so as to incorporate it in a private garden, or erecting a building on a green, or laying down a private driveway across a green). It should be noted that an offence is committed only where the encroachment etc is made 'otherwise than with a view to the better enjoyment of the green'. Thus the provision of facilities to assist in the enjoyment of recreation is not in breach of the section. Examples include tennis-courts, cricket nets, goalposts, children's playground equipment, seats and shelters. The provision of more substantial buildings, such as sports pavilions, which are directly beneficial to recreational use, would also be permitted under the section. However it is doubtful whether a village hall or community centre would be lawful, since its use would not be directly linked to use of the green.

7.38 The CLF recommended that s12 of the Inclosure Act 1857 and s29 of the Commons Act 1876 should be combined and redrafted in contemporary language.

7.39 The CLPS proposed that there should be some relaxation of the restrictions of the sections to enable facilities of public benefit to be established on a green.

7. Car parking

7.40 Driving vehicles on a green is normally in breach of s12 of the Inclosure Act 1857 (page 119) or s29 of the Commons Act 1876 (page 122) or both. It is also an offence under s34 of the Road Traffic Act 1988 (page 147) to drive anywhere off the road (except within 15 yards of a road solely in order to park) without 'lawful authority' (ie the consent of the owner of the land, or under a legal right or with statutory authority). However, subs 5 specifically provides that the 15-yard rule does not apply, *inter alia*, where by-laws affect the land; thus parking on a village green within the 15-yards limit would still be an offence under a by-law which prohibited parking anywhere on a green. The provisions in the 1857 and 1876 acts are also unaffected because s34(2) provides that it is not an offence under the section to drive on land within 15 yards of a road for the purpose only of parking: it can thus be an offence under other statutory provisions to do so. It is also possible that driving and parking on a village green is an offence under s1 of the Criminal Damage Act 1971 (destroying or damaging property recklessly or without lawful excuse).

7.41 How can parking best be curbed or controlled? The erection of a suitable barrier (eg whitened stones, dragon's teeth, bollards or a low fence) is often the most effective deterrent, but is not always possible. Control is usually best exercised by providing alternative parking facilities, but these cannot be provided on the green itself because to do so would involve breach of the 1857 and 1876 acts. If the owner of a green puts up a 'no parking' notice on the edge of the road, a person ignoring the notice would be trespassing by parking on the green (if there were no by-laws in force to control parking).

7.42 Under s57 of the Road Traffic Regulation Act 1984 a local council may provide off-street parking places for bicycles and motorcycles without consent, but if it wishes to provide parking for other vehicles the consent of the county or county borough council or metropolitan district council must first be obtained. The district council must be informed of any application for consent. In all cases, the local council may, 'notwithstanding anything in any other enactment', appropriate for the purpose—

(a) any part of a recreation ground provided or maintained under s8 of the Local Government Act 1894;
(b) any part of an open space controlled or maintained under the Open Spaces Act 1906, other than a part which has been consecrated as a burial ground or in which burials have taken place;
(c) any part of any land provided as a playing field or for any other purpose under s19 of the Local Government (Miscellaneous Provisions) Act 1976;

provided that the area appropriated does not exceed one eighth of the total area of the land concerned, or 800 square feet, whichever is the less.

7.43 It is possible that land falling within these categories has been registered as a village green, particularly in category (b). However, it is submitted that the special legal character of a village green overrides the provisions of s57 because they cannot be construed as empowering a local council to interfere with the legal rights of the inhabitants to indulge in lawful sports and pastimes. The phrase 'notwithstanding anything in any other enactment' is intended to free the appropriated area from the requirements of s10(a) of the 1906 act (page 124) and s229 of the Town and Country Planning Act 1990 (page 148) and nothing more.

7.44 The CLF recommended that (1) temporary use of a limited area of a green for informal car-parking in connection with recreational activities should be allowed, and (2) it should be lawful to grant vehicular access over and allow the erection of certain public facilities on a green with the consent of the secretary of state.

7.45 The CLPS proposed that landowners and management bodies should be allowed to grant permission for temporary parking in connection with an event on a green.

8. Appropriation and exchange of greens for other purposes

7.46 A town or village green is included in the definition of a common in the 1981 act (6.35-62 and page 144) and the procedures described in chapter VI in relation to common land apply equally to greens. It would be necessary to use these procedures to appropriate land for a car park on a village green.

7.47 The deregistration and exchange procedures in ss16 and 17 of the 2006 act (2.88-94) apply to greens.

9. Driveways across greens

7.48 As noted above (3.11-12) the owner of a common may generally grant private rights of way over it, but not in circumstances that would amount to a public nuisance (see the words of Lord Scott in *Bakewell Management Ltd* v *Brandwood and Others* [2004] noted above at 3.41). In many cases this has been done to provide vehicular access to properties fronting a common. Following the decision in *Bakewell*, it is possible also to acquire a right of way by prescription across a common, notwithstanding the general prohibition of driving on common land in s34 of the Road Traffic Act 1988 (3.36-45).

7.49 There is no specific provision which prohibits the owner of a green from granting a right of way over it, and where this is one which does not interfere with the inhabitants' right of recreation or with any other established rights (eg rights of common) it is lawful. For example, the grant of a right of way on foot only would not interfere with other rights. Prior to the decision in *Bakewell* (3.36-45), it was generally thought that the grant of a vehicular right of way over a green was legally ineffective where exercise of the right would amount to a breach of s12 of the Inclosure Act 1857 (7.35-36 and page 119) or of s29 of the Commons Act 1876 (7.37-39 and page 122), on the basis that it was impossible to establish by prescription a right the exercise of which involved the commission of an offence. However, *Bakewell* has ruled that it is possible to acquire a prescriptive right of way in breach of s193(4) of the 1925 act and of s34 of the Road Traffic Act 1988 (see 3.36-45 and pages 129 and 147 respectively for the text of the statutory provisions). Does this ruling mean that a right of way for vehicles can be acquired by prescription over a village green in breach of the 1857 and 1876 acts?

7.50 In *Massey and Drew* v *Boulden and Boulden* [2002], following *Hanning* (3.37), the Court of Appeal ruled that s34 of the Road Traffic Act 1988 (page 147) prevented the acquisition of a prescriptive right of way over a village green. However, in the course of his judgment, Simon Brown LJ stated that the grant of vehicular rights over a green was not in breach of s12 of the Inclosure Act 1857 (page 119) because 'there was no sufficient reason to regard the existence and use of the track as injuring the green or interrupting its use or enjoyment by others'. He also expressed disagreement with the view of counsel for the appellants (the Bouldens) that driving over the green was in breach of s29 of the Commons Act 1876. He accepted the judge's finding of fact that the use of the way in question had been for a long enough period prior to the registration of the green (part in 1972 and the remainder in 1994) for a prescriptive right of way to be established. In *Bakewell*, Lord Scott made the point that none of the members of the Court of Appeal in *Massey* addressed the critical issue of whether or not public policy should preclude the obtaining by prescription, or by presumed grant, of an easement or right over land that would have been lawful for the landowner to grant notwithstanding that the user was, in the absence of a grant, unlawful and criminal. This seems to indicate that Lord Scott was in favour of treating a breach of s12 of the Inclosure Act 1857 (and by implication s29 of the Commons Act 1876) in the same way as a breach of s193(4) of the 1925 act and s34 of the Road Traffic Act 1988. However, as confirmed by the House of Lords in *Oxfordshire County Council* v *Oxford City Council and another* (the Trap Grounds case)—see paragraphs 45-53, 114 and 124 of the judgment—local inhabitants have a right to indulge in lawful sports and pastimes on registered greens. Interference with that right is an offence under s12 of the Inclosure Act 1857 and s29 of the Commons Act 1876 and there is no provision in the sections (as there is in the case of s34 of the Road Traffic Act 1988) for the giving of lawful authority to allow what would otherwise be a criminal act. The ruling in *Bakewell* (3.36-45) can thus be said not to be directly applicable to the acquisition of vehicular rights over a green. It is submitted that the issue of whether a prescriptive right of way for vehicles can be acquired over a village green in breach of the 1857 and 1876 acts remains undetermined and may come before the courts again, notwithstanding the view of the government on the point (7.53).

7.51 A further, unresolved, point arising out of *Massey* is whether or not driving across a green constitutes a public nuisance. The remarks of Lord Scott in *Bakewell* referred to in 3.41 above are equally applicable to the grant or acquisition of vehicular rights of way over a green as they are to the acquisition of rights of way over a common.

7.52 Whether or not s12 of the Inclosure Act 1857 and s29 of the Commons Act 1876 preclude the acquisition of prescriptive rights of way over a green, those sections are not retrospective and cannot therefore take away any rights acquired before their enactment.

7.53 The provisions of s68 of the 2000 act and the regulations made thereunder (3.44) applied to greens as well as to commons. With the repeal of s68, a person seeking to claim a prescriptive right of way for vehicles over a town or village green will have to rely on the common law as interpreted in the *Bakewell* case. The view of the government on this point was expressed by the Parliamentary Under-Secretary of State at Defra, Barry Gardiner MP, when introducing the amendment to the Commons Bill to repeal s68 (*Hansard*, 29 June 2006, col 414). He said:

> Even on village greens, where a residual role for section 68 was initially alleged following *Bakewell*, we have concluded that there is no circumstance in which the section can help a householder to regularise his use of a vehicular track to his house over common or other land. If the particular driving does not cause injury to the green and the owner of the land could lawfully give permission to drive over the land in the way that the householder has done in past, such use will have been capable of creating a prescriptive right under the *Bakewell* principle. We do not consider that any special provisions are needed for greens. Section 12 of the Inclosure Act 1857 and section 29 of the Commons Act 1876 are both concerned with injury to the green. In our view, whether or not driving across a green in a particular way contravenes those provisions would be a matter of fact and of degree to be decided on the circumstances of individual cases. If driving does cause injury to the green, section 68 does not reduce the strict protection greens enjoy, which would prevent an easement from being granted at all.

7.54 S42 of the Dyfed Act 1987 (page 149) (which applies only in the area of the former county of Dyfed, now the counties of Carmarthenshire, Ceredigion and Pembrokeshire) authorises the county council to permit the creation of a vehicular or other access across a registered green, subject to the consent of the National Assembly for Wales. An example of the use of s42 was at Trefin, Pembrokeshire. The owner of a property with vehicular access across the village green applied for consent to retain the tarmac, which had been used without objection for 30 years. There was no practical alternative access to the property. The society did not object on being assured that villagers' recreational rights over the access were not being suspended. Consent was given. (*NAW letter dated 4 November 2004 ref A-PP127-09-014*)

10. Non-registration of greens

7.55 Para 3 of sch2 to the 2006 act enables an application to be made to the registration authority, or for a proposal to be made by the authority without application (in both cases within the time limit laid down by regulations), to register land as a town or village green in these circumstances:

(a) on 31 July 1970 (the final date for registering land as a town or village green at the end of the initial registration period) the land was a recreational allotment (7.4-7.8);
(b) the land was not at any time finally registered as a town or village green or as common land under the 1965 act;
(c) the land continues to be a recreational allotment;
(d) the land is land to which part 1 of the 2006 act applies (ie all land in England and Wales except the New Forest, Epping Forest and the Forest of Dean);
(e) the land satisfies any conditions specified in regulations.

Under these provisions, it will be possible to seek registration of recreational allotments which were not registered during the initial registration period (2.18-19).

11. Greens wrongly registered as common land

7.56 Para 5 of sch2 to the 2006 act enables an application to be made to the registration authority, or for a proposal to be made by the authority without application (in both cases within the time limit laid down by regulations), to transfer land registered as common land to the register of town or village greens. An application will have to show that, at the time of registration as common land, the land was in law a village green. This could be done, for example, by showing that the land had been allotted for recreational purposes under an inclosure award or similar legislation or that it had been used as of right for lawful sports and pastimes for 20 years prior to the registration as common land.

12. Buildings registered as town or village green

7.57 Para 8 of sch2 to the 2006 act enables an application to be made to the registration authority, or for a proposal to be made by the authority without application (in both cases within the time limit laid down by regulations), to remove land from the register of town or village greens in these circumstances:

(a) the land was provisionally registered as town or village green under s4 of the 1965 act;
(b) on the date of provisional registration the land was covered by a building or was within the curtilage of a building:
(c) the provisional registration became final; and
(d) since the date of the provisional registration the land has been, and still is, covered by a building or is within the curtilage of a building.

7.58 It is known that a considerable number of registrations erroneously included buildings, car parks, industrial areas, gardens and similar land. The Common Land (Rectification of Registers) Act 1989 (2.111-116) attempted a partial rectification of errors where the properties were dwellings and their gardens. These new provisions are much wider in scope.

13. Removal of other land from the registers of town or village greens

7.59 Para 9 of sch2 to the 2006 act allows an application to be made to the registration authority, or for a proposal to be made by the authority without application (in both cases within the time limit laid down by regulations) to amend the register of town or village greens to remove the land from the register in the following circumstances:

(a) the land was provisionally registered as a town or village green under the 1965 act on the basis of information supplied in the application;
(b) the provisional registration was not referred to a commons commissioner;
(c) the provisional registration became final; and
(d) immediately before the provisional registration the land was not:
  (i) common land within the meaning of the 1965 act; or
  (ii) a town or village green.

7.60 Para 5(3) provides that land is not a town or village green:

(a) if (and only if) throughout the 20 years prior to the date of provisional registration the land was physically unusable by members of the public for lawful sports or pastimes; and
(b) at the time of provisional registration and at the time of application the land was not a recreational allotment (7.4-8).

7.61 In relation to applications and proposals under paras 10-13 above, para 10 of sch2 to the 2006 act enables regulations to be made about the payment of costs.

7.62 Land removed from the register under the foregoing provisions ceases to be access land for the purposes of the 2000 act (chapter V).

14. New greens

7.63 S15 of the 2006 act (page 160) enables any person to apply to register land as a town or village green, so long as one of the following conditions set out in s15(2) of the 2006 act are met:

(a) a significant number of the inhabitants of any locality, or of any neighbourhood within a locality, have indulged as of right in lawful sports and pastimes on the land for a period of at least 20 years and they continue to do so until the time of application; or
(b) they have so indulged for at least 20 years, ceased to do so before the time of application but after the coming into operation of s15 and an application is made within two years after the activity has ceased; or
(c) they have so indulged for at least 20 years, but ceased to do so before the coming into operation of s15 and an application is made within five years after the activity ceased.

7.64 In relation to (c) only, an application cannot be made where:

(a) planning permission was granted before 23 June 2006;
(b) construction work began before that date in accordance with the planning permission on the land or any other land covered by the same permission; and
(c) the land has, or will, become permanently unusable by members of the public for lawful sports and pastimes.

7.65 In determining the 20-year period, any time during which access to the land is prohibited to members of the public under an enactment is disregarded. This could happen, for example, where public access is curtailed under statutory powers to control foot-and-mouth disease.

7.66 Where persons have indulged as of right in lawful sports and pastimes for 20 years, but have ceased to do so before an application is made to register the land as a green, the use of the land for those purposes with permission during the period between the cessation and the application is disregarded. This would be relevant where, the 20-year period of use as of right having been completed, the landowner fenced the land but allowed its use for recreation to continue as permissive. Provided that the period of permissive use did not exceed two years or five years (as the case may be—see para 7.63), then an application could be made to register the land as a town or village green on the basis of the 20 years' unchallenged use.

7.67 The interpretation of the word 'significant' in the revised wording of s22 of the 1965 act as amended by the 2000 act (which is effectively the same in s15 of the 2006 act) was considered by the High Court in *R (on the application of Alfred McAlpine Homes Ltd)* v *Staffordshire County Council* [2002]. The brief facts were that planning permission was granted for 58 houses on an area of land at Leek, Staffs, popularly known as Ladydale Meadow. An application to register the land as a village green was made in order to frustrate the intended development. A non-statutory inquiry was held, following which the inspector recommended that the registration be confirmed. He found that a significant number of local inhabitants had used the land for the requisite minimum period of 20 years preceding the application. In dealing with the word 'significant', he said:

> 'Significant' is rather an imprecise word but it is an ordinary word of the English language and there is little help to be gained from trying to define it in other language. It seems to me that it is really a matter of impression. In my view, the evidence shows that the recreational use of the application land has been by a significant number of the inhabitants of Leek.

The county council confirmed the registration and McAlpine sought judicial review in the High Court. In effect, the judge adopted the inspector's interpretation of 'significant', and emphasised that the word in the context of s22 did not mean a considerable or substantial number. The registration was upheld.

7.68 The phrase 'as of right' means that the use of the land for recreation must not have been with the permission of the landowner. The phrase has been considered by the House of Lords twice in recent years. In *R (on the application of Pamela Beresford)* v *City of Sunderland* [2001], the Washington First Forum applied to register as a new green a grassed area surrounded on three sides by a double row of wooden benches. In 1973 the site had been designated as 'parkland/open space/major playing field'. A non-turf wicket was constructed in 1979 and, throughout the 20-year application period up to 18 November 1999, the grass was cut by the owners from time to time. The application was refused on the basis that the use of the area had been by implied licence from the owners. The applicants appealed to the High Court, which rejected their appeal, and a further appeal was made the Court of Appeal. The Court ruled that the use of the land had been with the implied licence or permission of the owners. This was reversed by the House of Lords in *R* v *City of Sunderland (Respondents) ex parte Beresford (FC) Appellant* [2003]. The fact that the land was publicly owned was of particular significance because it was the responsibility of the local authority to discharge their functions for the benefit of the public. The encouragement of the use of the land by the provision of benches and regular cutting of the grass reinforced, rather than undermined, the impression that members of the public were using the area as of right.

7.69 The second case was *R* v *Oxfordshire County Council and another ex parte Sunningwell Parish Council* [1999]. In that case, the parish council sought to register an area of glebe land as a new green. Following a public inquiry, the county council refused the application on the basis that the land could not have been used as of right since the villagers were not aware that that they were using the land 'as of right'. The applicant appealed, ultimately to the House of Lords, which rejected the county council's view and allowed the appeal. The House ruled that the term 'as of right' was derived from past authority and earlier legislation on the acquisition of rights by prescription. To require an inquiry into the subjective state of mind of a user was contrary to the whole English theory of prescription, which depended on acquiescence by the landowner giving rise to an inference or presumption of an earlier grant or dedication. Neighbourly toleration by the landowner would not defeat an application for a new green unless there was strong evidence that the use as of right was not consistent with any toleration.

7.70 The *Sunningwell* case also confirmed that lawful sports and pastimes do not have to be organised or have a communal element. Activities such as dog walking, kite flying, solitary or family activities are sufficient to justify registration so long as there is an established practice of use which is not trivial or sporadic.

7.71 In the *Staffordshire County Council* case (7.67) the High Court ruled that an application for a new green could be amended to exclude part of the area for which registration had been applied, so long as the interests of the landowner, tenant or occupier of the land were not prejudiced. This ruling was confirmed by the House of Lords in the *Oxfordshire County Council* case (7.3).

7.72 Detailed guidance on the registration of new greens is given in the society's publication *Getting Greens Registered*.

7.73 S15(8) of the 2006 act enables a landowner to make a voluntary application to register land as a town or village green but must get the consent of any 'relevant leaseholder' (ie a leaseholder whose lease is for more than seven years from the date of grant) and any person with a 'relevant charge' over the land. In the case of land with a registered title this means a registered charge. For land without a registered title, a relevant charge is a charge registered under the Land Charges Act 1972 or a legal mortgage within the meaning of the Law of Property Act 1925 which is not registered under the 1972 act.

CHAPTER VIII

The Future of Common Land and Village Greens

8.1 The final chapter of the fourth edition of this book deplored the failure of successive governments to implement the main recommendations of the Royal Commission on Common Land relating to access and management and drew attention to the deficiencies in the 1965 act with regard to the registration of commons and greens

8.2 In 1986, the Common Land Forum issued its report, which made a number of sensible recommendations. Many of these have now been implemented by the 2006 act, if not always in the form the forum recommended. Those which have not been implemented either in substance or in form are noted at the appropriate place in the text and are set out in appendix 1.

8.3 Further progress has been made in completing the unfinished business of the Royal Commission with the enactment of a statutory public right of access on foot to all registered common land in the 2000 act (chapter V).

8.4 In July 2002, Defra and the National Assembly for Wales published their conclusions in their *Common Land Policy Statement 2002*. Many of its recommendations have been enacted in the 2006 act or by judicial action in court cases. Those which remain unimplemented are noted where appropriate in the text and are set out in appendix 2.

8.5 In view of the enactment of the 2006 act, it is unlikely that further legislation on common land or village greens will be brought forward in the foreseeable future. Only if the reforms enacted in the 2006 act fail to work as intended might legislation be contemplated.

8.6 A great deal of the detailed implementation of the 2006 act is left to regulations to be made by the appropriate national authority. So far as England is concerned, these are not expected to be made until the spring of 2007 and are unlikely to come into effect until the end of 2007. In the case of the registration provisions (see chapter II), Defra has indicated that implementation is likely to be spread over several years on a regional basis, beginning in 2008 and ending in 2013. The timetable for implementation of the act in Wales is not yet known.

APPENDIX 1

The Common Land Forum

Summary of unimplemented recommendations

Common land - vesting of unclaimed land

At present unclaimed common land is placed in the 'protection' of the local authorities which may only 'take such steps for the protection of the land against unlawful interference as could be taken by an owner in possession of the land' (1965 act, s9). Such land will be vested in the local council and failing that the district council.

Town and village greens

Local councils will be given powers to manage or acquire greens where irreconcilable disputes have arisen.

S12 of the Inclosure Act 1857 and s29 of the Commons Act 1876, which make it an offence to damage or encroach upon a green, will be combined and redrafted in contemporary language.

Temporary use of a limited area of green for informal car-parking in connection with recreational activities will be allowed. The grant of vehicular access across and the erection of certain public facilities on a green will be subject to the consent of the secretary of state.

Signatories of the report

Associations of County and District Councils and of Metropolitan Authorities, British Horse Society/Byways and Bridleways Trust, Councils for British Archaeology, National Parks, the Protection of Rural England and of Wales, Country Landowners' Association, Countryside Commission, Crown Estate Commissioners, National Association of Local Councils, National Farmers' Union, National Trust, Nature Conservancy Council, Open Spaces Society, Ramblers' Association, Sports Council, Association of Welsh Commoners, John Ellis (an English commoner), Ian Mercer (Dartmoor National Park Officer).

APPENDIX 2

Common Land Policy Statement 2002

Summary of unimplemented recommendations

Common land

Ownership issues

All unclaimed common land to be vested in an appropriate body with a range of powers to help ensure effective management (paragraph 12).

Provision to be made for unknown owners to come forward within a reasonable time period to re-claim such vested land (paragraph 15).

The period for reclaiming title should be the normal limitation period—12 years (paragraph 16).

In the absence of conclusive evidence of title at the Land Registry, the commons commissioners will be able to inquire into cases where disputed ownership is detrimental to effective management. For the purposes of commons legislation, where neither party produces satisfactory evidence, the commissioners will find in favour of the claimant currently registered in the commons registers (paragraph 17).

Bodies vested with unclaimed land will be placed under duties and responsibilities that reflect the diversity of commons and the different interests in them (paragraph 18).

Works and fencing on common land

We will consider the need and scope for an urgent s194 procedure in certain circumstances (paragraph 39).

Grazing rights

We do not propose to undertake a wholesale review of registered rights but will enable individual commoners or associations to refer cases of wrongly registered rights to the commons commissioners for investigation (paragraphs 96 to 98).

Town and village greens

Registration issues

Provision will be made for landowners to give notification that any further use of land for recreation has ceased to qualify for registration purposes (paragraph 50).

Ownership and related issues

Provision will be made for unknown owners to come forward and re-claim title to town and village green land vested in local authorities. As with the vesting of common land, a time limit will be imposed (paragraph 54).

Reflecting arrangements for greens registered before 1970, and subject to the reclamation of title safeguard above, provision will be made for greens registered after 1970 with no known owner to be vested in local authorities (paragraph 54).

Subject to appropriate controls, provision will be made for landowners to give consent for temporary vehicle-parking on town and village greens (paragraph 67).

Local planning authorities will be able to issue enforcement notices in respect of s12 of the Inclosure Act 1857 and 29 of the Commons Act 1876 as a preliminary step before proceeding to prosecution in the courts (paragraph 61).

Subject to safeguards, provision will be made to create strictly limited scope for establishing facilities on greens that would add comfort or convenience for users (paragraph 63).

The protection of s194 of the Law of Property Act 1925 [now part 3 of the 2006 act] will be extended to all registered town and village greens on a qualified basis. Consent will be required in all cases where rights of common remain registered over the green. If there are no registered commoners, consent will not be required for proposed works that are permissible under ss12 and 29. Consent will be required in all cases of proposals concerning facilities to add comfort and convenience whether there are registered commoners or not (paragraph 65).

Vehicular access ways and greens

S68 of the Countryside and Rights of Way Act 2000 enables the acquisition of easements in certain circumstances and we will ensure that in those circumstances, an exemption from the effects of ss12 and

29 will apply (paragraph 69).

Unless it is in the interests of the green's users and the secretary of state or National Assembly for Wales has given consent, we will reinforce the existing position that new vehicular access ways should not be created over land that remains registered as a town or village green (paragraph 70).

In respect of existing access ways that do not qualify for an easement under s68, no easement granted by the landowner will be lawful without the consent of the secretary of state or National Assembly for Wales (paragraph 71).

Consent from the secretary of state or National Assembly for Wales will be required for any improvement to existing access ways and there will be provision to impose conditions (paragraph 72).

[Note: the above proposals relating to access ways over village greens have been effectively overtaken by the repeal of s68 of the 2000 act—see 7.53.]

* Bracketed paragraph numbers refer to the policy statement.

Extracts from Acts of Parliament and Statutory Instruments

Note: (1) The acts are printed as amended by subsequent legislation and show the position as at September 2006. Amendments are shown in square brackets.

(2) 'The Secretary of State' means, for England, the Secretary of State for the Environment, Food and Rural Affairs and, for Wales, the national assembly.

(3) Crown Copyright legislation is reproduced under the terms of Crown Copyright Policy Guidance issued by Her Majesty's Stationery Office.

(4) The number given at the beginning of each extract is that of the section quoted. Subsections, if any, are bracketed ( ).

(5) The functions of the Inclosure Commissioners, the Board of Agriculture, the Minister of Land and Natural Resources and the Minister of Agriculture are now exercised by the secretary of state in England and the national assembly in Wales.

PRESCRIPTION ACT 1832 (2 & 3 Will 4 c 71)

1. No claim which may be lawfully made at the common law, by custom, prescription, or grant, to any right of common or other profit or benefit to be taken and enjoyed from or upon any land of our sovereign lord the King ... or any land being parcel of the Duchy of Lancaster or of the Duchy of Cornwall, or of any ecclesiastical or lay person, or body corporate, except such matters and things as are herein specially provided for, and except tithes, rent, and services, shall, where such right, profit, or benefit shall have been actually taken and enjoyed by any person claiming right thereto without interruption for the full period of thirty years, be defeated or destroyed by showing only that such right, profit, or benefit was first taken or enjoyed at any time prior to such period of thirty years, but nevertheless such claim may be defeated in any other way by which the same is now liable to be defeated; and when such right, profit, or benefit shall have been so taken and enjoyed as aforesaid for the full period of sixty years, the right thereto shall be deemed absolute and indefeasible, unless it shall appear that the same was taken and enjoyed by some consent or agreement expressly made or give for that purpose.

4. Each of the respective periods of years herein-before mentioned shall be deemed and taken to be the period next before some suit or action wherein the claim or matter to which such period may relate shall have been or shall be brought into question; and ... no act or other matter shall be deemed to be an interruption, within the meaning of this statute, unless the same shall have been or shall be

submitted to or acquiesced in for one year after the party interrupted shall have had or shall have notice thereof, and of the person making or authorising the same to be made.

(Text 3.12, 3.36)

INCLOSURE ACT 1845 (8 & 9 Vict c 118)

11. All such lands as are herein-after mentioned, (that is to say), all lands subject to any rights of common whatsoever, and whether such rights may be exercised or enjoyed at all times, or may be exercised or enjoyed only during limited times, seasons, or periods, or be subject to any suspension or restriction whatsoever in the time of enjoyment thereof; all gated and stinted pastures in which the property of the soil or some part thereof is in the owners of the cattle gates or other gates or stints, or any of them; and also all gated and stinted pastures in which no part of the property of the soil is in the owners of the cattle gates or other gates or stints, or any of them; all land held, occupied, or used in common, either at all times or during any time or season, or periodically, and either for all purposes or for any limited purpose, and whether the separate parcels of the several owners of the soil shall or shall not be known by metes or bounds or otherwise distinguishable; all land in which the property or right of or to the vesture or herbage, or any part thereof, during the whole or any part of the year, or the property or right of or to the wood or under-wood growing and to grow thereon, is separated from the property of the soil; and all lot meadows, and other lands the occupation or enjoyment of the separate lots or parcels of which is subject to interchange among the respective owners in any known course of rotation or otherwise, shall be land subject to be inclosed under this Act.

(Text 1.7, 2.129)

147. It shall be lawful for the commissioners, upon the application in writing of the persons interested, according to the definition herein before contained, in lands not subject to be inclosed under this Act, or in lands subject to be inclosed under this Act as to which no proceedings for an enclosure shall be pending, and who shall desire to effect an exchange of lands in which they respectively shall be so interested, to direct inquiries whether such proposed exchange would be beneficial to the owners of such respective lands; and in case the commissioners shall be of opinion that such exchange would be beneficial, and that the terms of the proposed exchange are just and reasonable, they shall, unless notice of dissent to the proposed exchange shall be given under the provision hereinafter contained, cause to be framed, and confirmed under the hand and seal of the commissioners, an order of exchange, with a map or plan thereunto annexed, in which order shall be specified and shown the lands given and taken in exchange by each person so interested respectively; and a copy of such order, under the seal of the commissioners, shall be delivered to each of the parties on whose application the exchange shall have been made; and such order of exchange shall be good, valid and effectual in the law to all intents and purposes whatsoever, and shall be in nowise liable to be impeached by reason of any infirmity of estate or defect of title of the persons on whose application the same shall have been made; and the land taken upon every such exchange shall be and enure to, for, and upon the same uses, trusts, intents, and purposes, and subject to the same conditions, charges, and encumbrances, as the lands given on such exchange would have stood limited or been subject to in case such order had not been made; and all expenses with reference to such order and exchange, or the inquiries in relation thereto, or to any proposed exchange, shall be borne by the persons on whose application such order shall have been made or such inquiries undertaken: Provided always, that no exchange shall be made of any land held in right of any church or chapel or other ecclesiastical benefice, without the consent, testified in writing, of the bishop of the diocese and the patron of such benefice.

(Text 6.78-81)

167. In the construction and for the purposes of this Act... 'land ' shall mean and include all messuages, lands and corporeal tenements and hereditaments ....

INCLOSURE ACT 1857 (20 & 21 Vict c 31)

12. And whereas it is expedient to provide summary means of preventing nuisances in town greens and village greens, and on land allotted and awarded upon any enclosure under the said Acts as a place for exercise and recreation: If any person wilfully cause any injury or damage to any fence of any such town or village green or land, or wilfully and without lawful authority lead or drive any cattle or animal thereon, or wilfully lay any manure, soil, ashes, or rubbish or other matter or thing thereon, or do any other act whatsoever to the injury of such town or village green or land, or to the interruption of the use or enjoyment thereof as a place for exercise and recreation, such person shall for every such offence, upon a summary conviction thereof before two justices, upon the information of any churchwarden or overseer of the parish in which such town or village green or land is situate, or of the person in whom the soil of such town or village green or land may be vested, forfeit and pay, in any of the cases aforesaid, and for each such offence, over and above the damages occasioned thereby, any sum not exceeding [level 1 on the standard scale] and it shall be lawful for any such churchwarden or overseer or other person as aforesaid to sell and dispose of any such manure, soil, ashes, and rubbish, or other matter or thing as aforesaid; and the proceeds arising from the sale thereof, and every such penalty as aforesaid shall, as regards any such town, or village green not awarded under the said Acts or any of them to be used as a place for exercise and recreation, be applied in aid of the rates for the repair of the public highways in the parish, and shall, as regards the land so awarded, be applied by the persons or person in whom the soil thereof may be vested in the due maintenance of such land as a place for exercise and recreation; and if any manure, soil, ashes, or rubbish be not of sufficient value to defray the expense of removing the same, the person who laid or deposited such manure, soil, ashes, or rubbish shall repay to such churchwarden or overseer or other person as aforesaid the money necessarily expended in the removal thereof; and every such penalty as aforesaid shall be recovered in manner provided by the Summary Jurisdiction Act 1848, and the amount of damage occasioned by any such offence as aforesaid shall, in case of dispute, be determined by the justices by whom the offender is convicted:

and the payment of the amount of such damage, and the repayments of the money necessarily expended in the removal of any manure, soil, ashes, or rubbish, shall be enforced in like manner as any such penalty.

(Text 7.24, 7.35-36, 7.38, 7.40, 7.49, 7.50, 7.52, 7.53, App1)

See also, s189(3) of the Local Government Act 1972 below.

METROPOLITAN COMMONS ACT 1866 (29 & 30 Vict c 122)

3. In this Act—

The term 'common' means land subject at the passing of this Act to any right of common, and any land subject to be included under the provisions of the Inclosure Act 1845; the term 'commoner' means a person having any such right of common; the term 'manor' includes reputed manor; and those terms used in this Act respectively refer to any particular common to which this Act applies, and to any person having a right of common in, over, or affecting that common, and to the manor of the wastes thereof that common is part;

The term 'the Commissioners' means the Inclosure Commissioners for England and Wales; and the term 'assistant commissioner' means the assistant commissioner appointed by the Inclosure Commissioners [note: the functions of the Inclosure Commissioners are now vested in the Secretary of State].

4. This Act shall apply to any common the whole of part whereof is situate within the Metropolitan Police District as defined at the passing of this Act (referred to in this Act as a metropolitan common).

5. ...The Commissioners shall not entertain an application for the inclosure of a metropolitan common [which is under the control and management of a London borough council].

(Text 1.8, 2.83, 2.94, 2.118, 4.2, 6.67, 6.74)

COMMONS ACT 1876 (39 & 40 Vict c 56)

7. In any provisional order in relation to a common, the Inclosure Commissioners shall, in considering the expediency of the application, take into consideration the question whether such application will be for the benefit of the neighbourhood, and shall, with a view to such benefit, insert in any such order such of the following terms and conditions (in this Act referred to as statutory provisions for the benefit of the neighbourhood) as applicable to the case; that is to say,

(1) That free access is to be secured to any particular points of view; and
(2) That particular trees or objects of historical interest are to be preserved; and
(3) That there is to be reserved, where a recreation ground is not set out, a privilege of playing games or of enjoying other species of recreation at such times and in such manner and on such parts of the common as may be thought suitable, care being taken to cause the least possible injury to the persons interested in the common; and

(4) That carriage roads, bridle paths, and footpaths over such common are to be set out in such directions as may appear most commodious; and
(5) That any other specified thing is to be done which may be thought equitable and expedient, regard being had to the benefit of the neighbourhood.

(Text 6.30-31)

10. (4) Evidence in relation to benefit of neighbourhood. The information to be furnished as bearing on the expediency of the application, considered in relation to the benefit of the neighbourhood, shall comprise statements as to the particulars following; that is to say, as to the number and occupation of the inhabitants of the parish or place in which the common is situate; as to the population of the neighbourhood, and the distance of the common from any neighbouring towns and villages; as to the intention of the applicants to propose the adoption of all or any of the statutory provisions as defined by this Act for the benefit of the neighbourhood; as to the circumstances of any ground other than the common to which application relates being available for the recreation of the neighbourhood; and in the case of a common being waste land of a manor, as to the site, extent, and suitableness of the allotments, if any, proposed to be made for recreation grounds and field gardens, or for either of such purposes; and as to any other matter which in the judgment of the [Secretary of State] may assist them in forming an opinion as to whether such application ought to be acceded to, having regard to the benefit of the neighbourhood, and if acceded to, as to what statutory provisions as defined by this Act ought to be inserted in the provisional order for the benefit of the neighbourhood:

The Inclosure Commissioners shall also require, in the case of an application for inclosure, special information as to the advantages the applicants anticipate to be derivable from the inclosure of a common as compared with the regulation of a common, also the reasons why an inclosure is expedient when viewed in relation to the benefit of the neighbourhood.

(Text 6.22)

19. Whereas by several awards made under the authority of Inclosure Acts prior to the year 1845 fuel allotments for the poor have been set out and awarded, and vested in divers persons and bodies of persons as trustees of such allotments:
And whereas under the provisions of the Inclosure Acts 1845 to 1868, and the several Acts of Parliament and awards made thereunder, allotments for recreation grounds and field gardens have been set out and awarded to the churchwardens and overseers of parishes and other persons:
And whereas power exists or is claimed under divers Acts of Parliament, to divert such allotments from the uses declared by Parliament respecting the same:
Be it enacted, that after the passing of this Act, notwithstanding anything in any other Act contained, it shall not be lawful (save as herein-after mentioned) to authorise the use of or to use any such allotment, or any part thereof, for any other purpose than those declared concerning the same by the Act of Parliament and award, or either of them, under which the same has been set out;...

(Text 7.7)

29. An encroachment on or inclosure of a town or village green, also any erection thereon or disturbance or interference with or occupation of the soil thereof which is made otherwise than with a view to the better enjoyment of such town or village green or recreation ground, shall be deemed to be a public nuisance, and if any person does any act in respect of which he is liable to pay damages or a penalty under section 12 of the Inclosure Act 1857, he may be summarily convicted thereof upon the information of any inhabitant of the parish in which such town or village green or recreation ground is situate, as well as upon the information of such persons as in the said section mentioned.

This section shall apply only in cases where a town or village green or recreation ground has a known and defined boundary.

(Text 7.24, 7.37-40, 7.49-50, 7.52-53)

37. In this Act, unless the context otherwise requires: 'A common' means any land subject to be inclosed under the Inclosure Acts 1845 to 1868. 'Waste land of a manor' means and includes any land consisting of waste land of any manor on which the tenants of such manor have rights of common or of any land subject to any rights of common which may be exercised at all times of the year for cattle levant and couchant, or to any land subject to any rights of common which may be exercised at all times of the year, and are not limited by number or stints; 'person' includes a body corporate.

COMMONS ACT 1899 (62 & 63 Vict c 30)

1. (1) The council of an urban ... district may make a scheme for the regulation and management of any common within their district [in the public interest].

[(1A) In subsection (1), the reference to the public interest includes the public interest –

(a) nature conservation;
(b) the conservation of the landscape;
(c) the protection of public rights of access to any area of land; and
(d) the protection of archaeological remains and features of historical interest.]

(2) The scheme may contain any of the statutory provisions for the benefit of the neighbourhood mentioned in section 7 of the Commons Act 1876.

(3) The scheme shall be in the prescribed form, and shall identify by reference to a plan the common to be thereby regulated.

(4) Regulations under subsection (3) may –

(a) prescribe alternative forms;
(b) permit exceptions or modifications to be made to any prescribed forms.]

2. (1) [A council is to make and approve a scheme under this Part of this Act in the prescribed manner.]

(2) Provided that if, at any time before the council have approved of the scheme, they receive a written notice of dissent either—

(a) from the person entitled as lord of the manor or otherwise to the soil of the common; or

(b) from persons representing at least one-third in value of such interests in the common as are affected by the scheme,

(c) and such notice is not subsequently withdrawn, the council shall not proceed further in the matter.

3. The management of any common regulated by a scheme made by a district council under this part of this Act shall be vested in the district council.

5. A parish council may agree to contribute the whole or any portion of the expenses of and incidental to the preparation and execution of a scheme for the regulation and management of any common within their parish (including any compensation paid under this Act).

6. No estate, interest, or right of a profitable or beneficial nature in, over, or affecting any common shall, except with the consent of the person entitled thereto be taken away or injuriously affected by any scheme under this part of this Act without compensation being made or provided for the same by the council making the scheme, and such compensation shall, in case of difference, be ascertained and provided in the same manner as if it were for the compulsory purchase and taking, or the injurious affecting, of lands under the Lands Clauses Acts.

7. A district council may acquire the fee simple or any estate in or any rights in or over any common regulated by a scheme under this part of this Act by gift or by purchase by agreement, and hold the same for the purposes of the scheme.

[9. (1) A scheme under this Part of this Act for any common may, in prescribed circumstances, be amended in the prescribed manner.

(2) A scheme under this Part of this Act for any common may, where a new scheme is made under this Part of this Act for the whole of that common, be revoked in the prescribed manner.]

[10. (1) A council which has made a scheme under this Part of this Act in relation to any common may make byelaws for the prevention of nuisances and preservation of order on the common.

(2) Sections 236 to 238 of the Local Government Act 1972 (which relate to the procedure for making byelaws, authorise byelaws to impose fines not exceeding level 2 on the standard scale, and provide for proof of byelaws in legal proceedings) apply to all byelaws under this section.]

11. All expenses of and incidental to the preparation and execution of a scheme under this part of this Act shall be paid by the district council.

12. The council of any [district] may, with a view to the benefit of the inhabitants of their district, enter into an undertaking with any other council making or having made a scheme under this part of this Act to contribute any portion of the expenses incurred by that council in executing the scheme.

14. A scheme under this part of this Act shall not apply to any common which is or might be the subject of a scheme made under the Metropolitan Commons Acts 1866 to 1878 or is regulated by a provisional order under the Inclosure Acts 1845 to 1882, or has been acquired, or managed as an open space, under the powers of the Corporation of London (Open Spaces) Act 1878, or any Act therein referred to, or is the subject of any private or local and personal Act of Parliament having for its object the preservation of the common as an open space, or is subject to by-laws made by a parish council under section 8 of the Local Government Act 1894.

15. In this part of this Act, unless the context otherwise requires,—

The expression 'common' shall include any land subject to be inclosed under the Inclosure Acts 1845 to 1882, and any town or village green;

The expression 'prescribed' shall mean prescribed by regulations made by the Board of Agriculture.

18. Any provisions with respect to allotments for recreation grounds, field gardens or other public or parochial purposes contained in any Act relating to inclosure or in any award or order made in pursuance thereof, and any provisions with respect to the management of any such allotments contained in any such Act, order, or award, may, on the application of any district or parish council interested in any such allotment, be dealt with by a scheme of the Charity Commissioners in the exercise of their ordinary jurisdiction, as if those provisions had been established by the founder in the case of a charity having a founder.

(Text 2.83, 2.94, 2.118, 3.40, 3.47, 4.13-19, 4.51, 4.61, 5.5, 6.64, 6.67, 6.74, 7.7-8, 7.29)

OPEN SPACES ACT 1906 (6 Edw 7 c 25)

9. A local authority may, subject to the provisions of this Act—

(a) acquire by agreement and for valuable or nominal consideration by way of payment in gross, or of rent, or otherwise, or without any consideration, the freehold of, or any term of years or other limited estate or interest in, or any right or easement in or over, any open space or burial ground, whether situate within the district of the local authority or not; and

(b) undertake the entire or partial care, management, and control of any such open space or burial ground, whether any interest in the soil is transferred to the local authority or not; and

(c) for the purposes aforesaid, make any agreement with any person authorised by this Act or otherwise to convey or to agree with reference to any open space or burial ground, or with any other persons interested therein.

10. A local authority who have acquired any estate or interest in or control over any open space or burial ground under this Act shall, subject to any conditions under which the estate, interest, or control was so acquired—

(a) hold and administer the open space or burial ground in trust to allow, and with a view to, the enjoyment thereof by the public as an open space within the meaning of this Act and under proper control and regulation and for no other purpose; and

(b) maintain and keep the open space or burial ground in a good and decent state;

and may inclose it or keep it inclosed with proper railings and gates, and may drain, level, lay out, turf, plant, ornament, light, provide with seats and otherwise improve it, and do all such work and things and employ such officers and servants as may be requisite for the purposes aforesaid or any of them.

14. A county council may ... support or contribute to the support of public walks or pleasure grounds provided by any person whomsoever.

15. (1) A local authority may, with reference to any open space or burial ground in or over which they have acquired any estate, interest, or control under this Act, make by-laws for the regulation thereof, and of the days and times of admission thereto, and for the preservation of order and prevention of nuisances therein, and may by such by-laws impose penalties recoverable summarily for the infringement thereof, and provide for the removal of any person infringing any by-law by any officer of the local authority or police constable.

(2) All by-laws made under this Act by any local authority shall be made—
(e) in the case of a ... district or parish council, subject and according to the provisions with respect to by-laws contained in sections 182 to 186 of the Public Health Act 1875, and those sections shall apply to a parish council in like manner as if they were a local authority within the meaning of that Act, except that by-laws made by a parish council need not be under common seal.

(3) The trustees or other persons having the care and management of any open space, who in pursuance of this Act admit to the enjoyment of the open space any persons not owning, occupying, or residing in any house fronting thereon, shall have the same powers of making bylaws as are conferred on a committee of the inhabitants of a square by section 4 of the Town Gardens Protection Act 1863, and that section shall apply accordingly.

16. Any two or more local authorities may jointly carry out the provisions of this Act and may make any agreement on such terms as may be arranged between them for so doing and for defraying the expenses of the execution of this Act, and any local authority may defray the whole or any part of the expenses incurred by any other local authority in the execution of this Act.

20. In this Act, unless the context otherwise requires—
The expression 'open space' means any land, whether inclosed or not, on which there are no buildings or of which not more than one-twentieth part is covered with buildings, and the whole or the remainder of which is laid out as a garden or is used for purposes of recreation, or lies waste and unoccupied.

(Text 4.45, 7.25, 7.29, 7.42)

NATIONAL TRUST ACT 1907 (7 Edw 7 c xxxvi)

4. (1) The National Trust shall be established for the purposes of promoting the permanent preservation for the benefit of the nation lands and tenements (including buildings) of beauty or historic interest and as regards lands for the preservation (so far as practicable) of their natural aspect features and animal and plant life.

29. [(1)] By virtue of this Act there shall be imposed upon the National Trust with respect of any of the Trust property which [is land to which this section applies] the following duties and the National Trust shall (subject to the provisions of this Act) have with respect to the same property the following powers (namely):

(A) Except as in this Act otherwise provided they shall at all times keep such property unenclosed and unbuilt on as open spaces for the recreation and enjoyment of the public;

(B) They may plant drain level and otherwise improve and alter any part or parts of such property so far as they may deem necessary or desirable and they may make temporary enclosures for the purposes of this subsection and for the purpose of protecting or renovating turf and for protecting trees and plantations:

(C) They may make and maintain roads footpaths and ways over such property and may make and maintain ornamental ponds and waters on such property:

(D) They may on such property erect sheds for tools and materials and may maintain and repair such sheds:

(E) They shall by all lawful means prevent resist and abate all enclosures and encroachments upon and all attempts to enclose or encroach upon such property or any part thereof or to appropriate or use the same or the soil timber or roads thereof or any part thereof for any purpose inconsistent with this Act:

(F) They may set apart from time to time parts of such property upon which persons may play games or hold meetings or gatherings for athletic sports.

[(2) This section applies to –

(a) any land registered as common land;

(b) any land not so registered which is:

  (i) regulated under an Act under the Commons Act 1876 confirming a provisional order of the Inclosure Commissioners; or

  (ii) subject to a scheme under the Metropolitan Commons Act 1866 or the Commons Act 1899.

(c) land not falling within paragraph (a) or (b) which is in the New Forest and is subject to rights of common.]

(Text 4.35-40)

COMMONS ACT 1908 (8 Edw 7 c 44)

1. (1) The persons for the time being entitled to turn out animals on a common at a meeting convened in manner provided by this Act may, by a resolution passed by a majority in value of interest of the persons present by themselves or by their proxy or attorney,—

(a) Make, alter, or revoke regulations for determining the times, if any, at which and the conditions under which entire animals or entire animals of any class or description or age specified in the regulation may be upon the common, and for authorising the removal by an officer appointed to enforce the regulations of any animal found upon the common in contravention of the regulations, and the detention and disposal of any animal so removed, and for raising such sums as may be necessary for defraying expenses incurred in making, publishing, or enforcing the regulations, either by annual contributions payable by the person for the time being entitled to turn out animals on the common, or by way of an annual payment in respect of each animal turned out on the common, and for prescribing the person to receive or sue for such payments;

(b) Appoint and remove, or provide for the appointment and removal of, officers to enforce any such regulations;

(c) Constitute and regulate the constitution of a committee consisting of persons entitled to turn out animals on the common, and delegate to the committee such of the powers exercisable by resolution under this Act as may be specified in the resolution;

but no such regulations and no alteration or revocation thereof shall take effect unless and until they have been confirmed by the Board of Agriculture and Fisheries, and the Board may confirm them either without modification or subject to such modifications as the Board, after considering any objections by persons appearing to the Board to be interested, considers desirable.

(2) The owner of any animal which is found on any common in contravention of a regulation made under this Act, and any person who obstructs any officer appointed under this Act in the execution or enforcement of a regulation, shall be liable on summary conviction to a fine not exceeding [level 1 on the standard scale], or in the case of a continuing offence not exceeding [50 pence] for every day during which the offence continues.

(3) A meeting for the purposes of this Act may be convened in respect of any common by the Board of Agriculture and Fisheries upon the application of any three persons claiming to be entitled to turn out animals upon the common or of the council of the county [, county borough or metropolitan district] in which any part of the common is situate.

(4) The value of the interest of any person for the time being entitled to turn out animals on a common shall be ascertained, and a meeting for the purposes of this Act shall be convened and held, and proxies and attorneys shall be appointed, in accordance with rules made by the Board of Agriculture and Fisheries.

(5) If any question arises as to whether a resolution has been passed by the required majority, the question shall be settled by the Board of Agriculture and Fisheries, whose decision shall be final for the purposes of this Act, but such decision shall not otherwise affect or prejudice any right or claim in respect of the common.

(6) No regulation approved by the Board of Agriculture and Fisheries shall be questioned on the ground of informality, and the Documentary Evidence Acts 1868 to 1895 shall apply to regulations so approved as if they were regulations issued by the Board.

(7) For the purposes of this Act two or more adjoining commons may, by order of the Board of Agriculture and Fisheries, be declared to be one common, and shall be treated as such accordingly.

(8) This Act shall apply to a common notwithstanding that the soil of the common is vested in His Majesty by the right of His Crown or His Duchy of Lancaster or forms part of the possessions of the Duchy of Cornwall, but shall not apply to the New Forest or to any common in respect of which the conservators or other body appointed by or under any Act of Parliament to regulate the common have powers of making by-laws in respect of matters for which regulations may be made under this Act.

(9) In this Act the expression 'animals' means horses, asses, cattle, sheep, goats, and swine, and the expression 'common' includes any commonable land.

2. The powers by this Act conferred on the persons for the time being entitled to turn out animals on a common (except the power to raise money) may in the case of the forest or chase of Dartmoor be exercised by the Duke of Cornwall, but so that a regulation shall not be submitted for confirmation until it has been approved by a resolution passed by a majority in value of interest of the persons for the time being entitled to turn out animals on the forest or chase, present by themselves or by their proxy or attorney at a meeting of such persons convened in manner provided by this Act, and the provisions of this Act shall apply to the forest or chase accordingly.

(Text 2.95, 4.51, 4.56-57)

LAW OF PROPERTY ACT 1925 (15 & 16 Geo 5 c 20)

193. (1) Members of the public shall, subject as hereinafter provided, have rights of access for air and exercise to any land which is a metropolitan common within the meaning of the Metropolitan Commons Acts, 1866 to 1898, or manorial waste, or a common, which is wholly or partly situated within [an area which immediately before lst April 1974 was] a borough or urban district, and to any land which at the commencement of this Act is subject to rights of common and to which this section may from time to time be applied in manner, hereinafter provided:
Provided that—

(a) such rights of access shall be subject to any Act, scheme, or provisional order for the regulation of the land, and to any by-law, regulation or order made thereunder or under any other statutory authority; and

(b) the Minister shall, on the application of any person entitled as lord of the manor or otherwise to the soil of the land, or entitled to any commonable rights affecting the land, impose such limitations on and conditions as to the exercise of the rights of access or as to the extent of the land to be affected as, in the opinion of the Minister, are necessary or desirable for preventing any estate, right or interest of a profitable or beneficial nature in, over, or affecting the land from being injuriously affected, for conserving flora, fauna or geological or physiographical features of the land, or for protecting any object of historical interest and, where any such limitations or conditions are so imposed, the rights of access shall be subject thereto; and

(c) such rights of access shall not include any right to draw or drive upon the land a carriage, cart, caravan, truck, or other vehicle, or to camp or light any fire thereon; and

(d) the rights of access shall cease to apply (i) to any land over which the commonable rights are extinguished under any statutory provision; (ii) to any land over which the commonable rights are otherwise extinguished if the council of the county in which the land is situated by resolution assent to its exclusion from the operation of this section, and the resolution is approved by the Minister.

(2) The lord of the manor or other person entitled to the soil of any land subject to rights of common may by deed, revocable or irrevocable, declare that this section shall apply to the land, and upon such deed being deposited with the Minister the land shall, so long as the deed remains operative, be land to which this section applies.

(3) Where limitations or conditions are imposed by the Minister under this section, they shall be published by such person and in such manner as the Minister may direct.

(4) Any person who, without lawful authority, draws or drives upon any land to which this section applies any carriage, cart, caravan, truck, or other vehicle, or camps or lights any fire thereon, or who fails to observe any limitation or condition imposed by the Minister under this section in respect of any such land, shall be liable on summary conviction to a fine [not exceeding level 1 on the standard scale] for each offence.

(5) Nothing in this section shall prejudice or affect the right of any person to get and remove mines or minerals or to let down the surface of the manorial waste or common.

(6) This section does not apply to any common or manorial waste which is for the time being held for Naval, Military or Air Force purposes and in respect of which rights of common have been extinguished or cannot be exercised.

(Text 1.10, 2.93-94, 2.138, 3.37, 3.39, 3.42, 3.47, 4.20-30, 4.36, 4.49, 4.58, 4.61, 5.5, 6.12, 6.32, 6.75, 6.80, 7.29, 7.49-50)

194. (1) The erection of any building or fence, or the construction of any other work, whereby access to land to which this section applies is prevented or impeded, shall not be lawful unless the consent of the Minister thereto is obtained, and in giving or withholding his consent the Minister shall have regard to the same considerations and shall, if necessary, hold the same inquiries as are directed by the Commons Act 1876, to be taken into consideration and held by the Minister before forming an opinion whether an application under the Inclosure Acts 1845 to 1882, shall be acceded to or not.

(2) Where any building or fence is erected, or any other work constructed without such consent as is required by this section, the county court within whose jurisdiction the land is situated, shall, on an application being made by the council of any county [or county borough] or district concerned, or by the lord of the manor or any other person interested in the common, have power to make an order for the removal of the work, and the restoration of the land to the condition in which it was before the work was erected or constructed, but any such order shall be subject to the like appeal as an order made under section 30 of the Commons Act 1876.

(3) This section applies to any land which at the commencement of this Act is subject to rights of common:

Provided that this section shall cease to apply (a) to any land over which the rights of common are extinguished under any statutory provision; (b) to any land over which the rights of common are otherwise extinguished, if the council of the county, county borough or metropolitan district in which the land is situated by resolution assent to its exclusion from the operation of this section and the resolution is approved by the Minister.

(4) This section does not apply to any building or fence erected or work constructed if specially authorised by Act of Parliament, or in pursuance of an Act of Parliament or order having the force of an Act, or if lawfully erected or constructed in connection with the taking or working of minerals in or under any land to which the section is otherwise applicable, or to any [electronic communications apparatus installed for the purposes of an electronic communications network].

(Text 1.10, 3.11, 4.15, 4.27, 4.37, 6.2-34, 6.65, 6.71, 6.76)

CARAVAN SITES AND CONTROL OF DEVELOPMENT ACT 1960 (8 & 9 Eliz 2 c 62)

23. (1) This section applies to any land in the area of a [district council] which is or forms part of a common, not being land falling within any of the following descriptions, that is to say—

(a) land to which section 193 of the Law of Property Act 1925 (which relates to the rights of the public over certain commons and waste lands), for the time being applies;

(b) land which is subject to a scheme under Part I of the Commons Act 1899 (under which schemes may be made for the regulation and management of certain commons);

(c) land as respects which a site licence is for the time being in force.

(2) The [council of a district] may make with respect to any land in their area to which this section applies an order prohibiting, either absolutely or except in such circumstances as may be specified in the order, the stationing of

caravans on the land for the purposes of human habitation.

(3) Without prejudice to the provisions of section 1 of this Act, any person who stations a caravan on any land in contravention of an order under this section for the time being in force with respect to the land shall be guilty of an offence and liable on summary conviction to a fine [not exceeding level 1 on the standard scale].

(4) It shall be the duty of a [district council] to take all reasonable steps to secure that copies of any order under this section which is for the time being in force with respect to any land in their area are so displayed on the land as to give to persons entering thereon adequate warning of the existence of the order, and the council shall have the right to place on the land such notices as they consider necessary for the performance of their duty under this subsection.

(5) An order under this section may be revoked at any time by a subsequent order made thereunder by the [district council], or may be so varied either so as to exclude any land from the operation of the order or so as to introduce any exception, or further exception, from the prohibition imposed by the order.

(6) Where the whole or a part of any land with respect to which an order under this section is in force ceases to be land to which this section applies, the said order shall thereupon cease to have effect with respect to the said land or part; and where an order ceases under this subsection to have effect with respect to a part only of any land, the [district council] shall cause any copy of the order which is displayed on that part of the land with respect to which the order continues in force to be amended accordingly.

(8) In this section the word 'common' includes any land subject to be inclosed under the Inclosure Acts 1845 to 1882, and any town or village green.

(Text 4.61)

COMPULSORY PURCHASE ACT 1965 (c 56)

SCHEDULE 4—COMMON LAND

1. (1) The compensation in respect of the right in the soil of any of the land subject to compulsory purchase and subject to any rights of common shall be paid to the lord of the manor, in case he is entitled thereto, or to such party, other than the commoners, as is entitled to the right in the soil.

(2) The compensation in respect of all other commonable and other rights in or over such land, including therein any commonable or other rights to which the lord of the manor may be entitled, other than his right in the soil of the land, shall be determined and paid and applied in the manner provided in the following provisions of this schedule with respect to common land the right in the soil of which belongs to the commoners; and upon payment of the compensation so determined either to the persons entitled thereto or into court all such commonable and other rights shall cease and be extinguished.

(Text 3.22)

MINISTRY OF HOUSING AND LOCAL GOVERNMENT (GREATER LONDON PARKS AND OPEN SPACES) ACT 1967 (c xxix)

1. The order of the Minister of Housing and Local Government which, as amended, is as set out in the schedule to this Act is hereby confirmed and shall have full validity and force.

SCHEDULE

7. (1) A local authority may in any open space—

(a) provide and maintain—

(i) swimming baths and bathing places whether open air or indoor;

(ii) golf courses and grounds, tracks, lawns, courts, greens and such other open air facilities as the local authority think fit for any form of recreation whatsoever (being facilities which the local authority are not otherwise specifically authorised to provide under this or any other enactment);

(iii) gymnasia;

(iv) rifle ranges;

(v) indoor facilities for any form of recreation whatsoever;

(vi) centres and other facilities (whether indoor or open air) for the use of clubs, societies or organisations whose objects or activities are wholly or mainly of a recreational, social or educational character;

(b) provide amusement fairs and entertainments including bands of music, concerts, dramatic performances, cinematograph exhibitions and pageants;

[(bb) without prejudice to the generality of the powers in the last foregoing subparagraph, provide exhibitions and trade fairs for the purpose of promoting education, the conservation of the environment, recreation, industry, commerce, crafts or the arts;]

(c) provide and maintain in time of frost facilities for skating and flood any part of the open space in order to provide ice for skating;

(d) provide meals and refreshments of all kinds to sell to the public;

(e) provide and maintain swings, platforms, screens, chairs, seats, lockers, towels, costumes and any apparatus, appliances, equipment or conveniences necessary or desirable for persons resorting to the open space;

(f) erect and maintain for or in connection with any purpose relating to the open space such buildings or structures as they consider necessary or desirable including (without prejudice to the generality of this paragraph) buildings for the accommodation of keepers and other persons employed in connection with the open space; and

(g) set apart or enclose in connection with any of the matters referred to in this article any part of the open space and preclude any person from entering that part so set apart or enclosed other than a person to whom access is permitted by the local authority or (where the right of so setting apart or enclosing is granted to any person by the local authority under the powers of this Part of this order) by such person:

Provided that -

(i) where any part of an open space is set apart or enclosed under the foregoing provisions of this article for the playing of games and that part is not specially laid out and maintained for that purpose, the power under this article to preclude any person from entering that part shall not apply while the part is not in actual use for games;

(ii) the part of any open space set apart or enclosed for the use of persons listening to or viewing an entertainment (including a band concert, dramatic performance, cinematograph exhibition or pageant) shall not exceed in any open space one acre or one-tenth of the open space, whichever is the greater;...

((iii) – (vi) omitted)

[(vii) a local authority shall not exercise their powers under subparagraph (bb) of this paragraph in any open space which is a common; and

(viii) a local authority shall not exercise their powers under subparagraph (bb) of this paragraph in an open space on more than 8 Sundays in any year;]

(2) A local authority may employ such persons (including instructors or organisers in connection with the use or enjoyment of any of the facilities in an open space provided and maintained by the local authority under subparagraph (a) of paragraph (1) or under any other enactment), do such acts and make and enforce such restrictions or conditions necessary or desirable in connection with the exercise of their powers any of the matters referred to in this article.

8. (1) A local authority may, subject to such terms and conditions as to payment or otherwise as they may consider desirable, grant to any person the right of exercising any of the powers conferred upon the local authority by article 7 and let to any person, for any of the purposes mentioned in that article, any building or structure erected or maintained, and any part of an open space set apart or enclosed, pursuant thereto.

(2) The terms and conditions subject to which a right may be granted or letting effected under this article may include a term that the local authority shall contribute either directly or pursuant to a guarantee given by them towards the expenses to be incurred by any person in the provision of any entertainment or otherwise in pursuance of such grant or letting.

[(3)(a) Without prejudice to any power exercisable by a local authority, or by a person to whom the right of exercising that power has been granted by a local authority, to sell, hire or demonstrate goods or services in an open space, where a local authority exercise their powers under subparagraph (b) or (bb) of article 7 or grant under this article the right of exercising the powers conferred on the local authority by the said subparagraph (b) or (bb), they may (subject to such terms and conditions as they may consider desirable) permit persons to sell, hire or demonstrate goods or services of any kind:

Provided that -

(i) the sale, hire or demonstration of goods or services by virtue of this paragraph shall be for the purposes, and as part, of the function in question;

(ii) the area occupied by shops or stands from which is carried on the sale, hire or demonstration by virtue of this paragraph of goods or services which are not related to any form of recreation or education shall not exceed one-tenth of the area of that part of the open space occupied by the function of which those shops or stands form part; and

(iii) the sale, hire or demonstration of goods or services by virtue of this paragraph shall not be permitted in an open space on more than 35 days, or on more than 8 Sundays, in any year.

((b) omitted)

(c) In this paragraph, 'stand' includes any platform, stall, structure, space or other area.]

9. A local authority may enclose during such periods and subject to such conditions as they may deem necessary or expedient any part of any open space—

(a) for the purpose of or in connection with the cultivation or preservation of vegetation in the interests of the public; or

(b) in the interests of the safety of the public;

and may preclude any person from entering any part so enclosed.

10. A local authority may—

(a) make such reasonable charges as they think fit for—

(i) the use or enjoyment of anything provided by them under subparagraphs (a) to (e) of paragraph (l) of article 7; or

(ii) the use of any building or structure erected or maintained by them under subparagraph (f) of the said paragraph (1); or

(iii) admission to, or the use of, any part of any open space set apart or enclosed by them under subparagraph (g) of that paragraph; and

(b) authorise any person to whom any right is granted or any building or structure is let under article 8 to make reasonable charges in respect of the purposes for which the local authority themselves may make charges under subparagraph (a) of this article:

11. (1) Subject to the provisions of this article and of article 12, the powers conferred on the local authority by articles 7 to 10 may be exercised notwithstanding the provisions of any enactment or any scheme made under, or confirmed by, any enactment but shall not be exercised in such a manner as to—

(a) contravene any right which any person may have otherwise than as a member of the public; or

(b) prejudice or affect any provision contained in any enactment or scheme for the protection of any specified person;

without the consent of that person which consent he is hereby empowered to give notwithstanding any disability which may otherwise exist. Nor shall the said powers be exercised in such a manner as to prejudice or affect the operation of the proviso to section 10 of the Paddington Recreation Ground Act 1893 or to prevent the free use and enjoyment by the public of the portion of the recreation ground reserved pursuant to the said proviso.

(2) Subject to the provisions of so much of article 9 as relates to the enclosure of any part of an open space in the interests of public safety, the powers of articles 7, 8 and 10 shall not be exercised in respect of any open space in such a manner that members of the public are by reason only of the exercise of such powers unable to obtain access without charge to some part of such open space.

(3) No power conferred upon a local authority under articles 7 to 10 shall be exercised with respect to any open space in such manner as to be at variance with any trust for the time being affecting such open space (not being a trust existing by virtue of section 10 of the Open Spaces Act 1906) without an order of the High Court of Justice or of the Charity Commissioners or (where the trust instrument reserves to the donor or any other person the power to vary the trust) without the consent of such donor or other person.

(4) Nothing in articles 7 to 10 shall prejudice or affect the operation of, or derogate from, any of the provisions of—

(a) the relevant provisions of the London Building Acts within the meaning of section 43(5) of the London Government Act 1963 or any by-law or regulation for the time being in force thereunder; or

(b) any enactment relating to building control and to buildings and structures which is applied to Greater London by section 40 of the said Act of 1963 or any instrument for the time being in force under any such enactment; or

(c) the Town and Country Planning Act 1962 or any agreement, scheme or order for the time being in force under, or by virtue of, that Act.

(5) Nothing in articles 7 to 10 shall exempt any building or structure erected under the said articles in an open space outside Greater London from any relevant enactment or by-law relating to the erection, construction, alteration or elevation of buildings or restricting the provision of means of access to any street or road for the time being in force in the district in which the open space is situate.

12. (1) In the exercise of powers conferred by articles 7 and 8 the authority shall not, without the consent of the Minister, erect, or permit to be erected any building or other structure on, or enclose permanently, or permit to be enclosed permanently, any part of a common.

(2) Nothing in this article shall be deemed to require the consent of the Minister to—

(a) the maintaining or re-erecting by, or with the permission of, a local authority of any building or other structure erected on a common before the date of operation of this order; or

(b) the continuing by, or with the permission of, a local authority of any permanent enclosure of part of a common made before that date;

and any such building or structure, or permanent enclosure, shall be deemed to

have been lawfully erected or made (as the case may be).
[(2A) Sections 39 and 40 of the Commons Act 2006 apply in relation to an application for consent under paragraph (1) as they apply in relation to an application for consent under section 38(1) of that Act.

(2B) Section 41 of that Act applies in relation to the carrying out of works in contravention of paragraph (1) as it applies to works carried out in contravention of section 38(1) of that Act as if references to consent under that provision were to consent under paragraph (1).]

17. (1) Notwithstanding anything contained in any enactment, a local authority, upon such terms and conditions as they think fit (whether as to payment or otherwise) for the purpose of the construction, widening or alteration of any street (whether carried out by a local authority or by any other person), may—

(a) utilise, alienate or exchange for other land any part of any open space;
(b) in a case where land is utilised under this article, debit the account relating to the construction, widening or alteration of the street with an amount

representing the whole or a portion of the value of the land so utilised.

(2) No land shall be utilised, alienated or exchanged under this article except with the consent of the Minister.

[(2A) Where an application is made for consent under paragraph (2) in the case of any common, section 40 of the Commons Act 2006 applies in relation to the application as it applies in relation to an application for consent under section 38(1) of that Act.

(2B) Where an application is made for consent under paragraph (2) in any other case, the Minister before giving his consent shall have regard to any representations made to him in the manner specified in paragraph (3).]

(3) As soon as practicable after making an application for the consent of the Minister under paragraph (2) [in a case to which paragraph (2B) applies], the local authority shall fix on, or in the vicinity of, the open space a placard in a conspicuous position

(a) giving notice of the making of such application;
(b) specifying the powers proposed to be exercised;
(c) stating at which office of the local authority a plan relating to the proposal may be inspected; and
(d) stating that representations as to the proposal may be made twenty-eight days from the date of such notice to the Minister;

and the placard shall be retained until the last date for making representations has expired.

(4) Where under paragraph (1) a local authority utilise, alienate or exchange for any other land any part of any open space they shall expend on capital account for or in the acquisition of lands to be used as, or to be added to, an open space payment of any compensation payable by them under this article or under article

15(2) sums not less than any moneys which—

(a) in the case of such utilisation, they may have debited to the account relating to the construction, widening or alteration of the street under paragraph (1); or

(b) in the case of such alienation, they may receive as consideration for the land alienated by them; or

(c) in the case of such exchange, they may receive for equality of exchange.

(5) Where a part of an open space is utilised, alienated or exchanged for other land that part shall cease for all purposes to form part of such open space and all rights of common, public rights of way and other public rights in, over or affecting the same be extinguished.

(6) Any land acquired under this article by a local authority in exchange for, or for the purpose of the provision of, an open space shall as from the date on which the authority receive vacant possession thereof, (if adjacent to an open space and acquired for addition thereto) be subject to the like rights, trusts and incidents as attached to, and to the provisions of any enactment, by-laws or scheme specially relating to, the said open space.

(7) Any land acquired under this article by a local authority in exchange for an open space otherwise than for addition to an existing open space shall be deemed to have been acquired under the Open Spaces Act 1906.

(8) All private rights in, over or affecting land acquired by a local authority under paragraph (6) or (7) shall be extinguished unless and except so far as the local authority otherwise determine and, in any case in which they so determine, they shall give notice in writing of their determination to the persons entitled to the private rights to which the determination relates:

Provided that in the event of such extinction—

(i) where the lands are acquired by way of exchange under private rights paragraph (1), the authority or other person constructing, widening or altering the street; or

(ii) where the lands are acquired by expenditure of money under paragraph (4), the local authority;

shall make full compensation to all parties interested in respect of any private rights extinguished by virtue of this paragraph and the compensation shall be settled in the manner provided by the Land Compensation Act 1961.

(9) Except with the consent in writing of the owner of any protected square within the meaning of the London Squares Preservation Act 1931 (not being a protected square vested in a local authority) nothing in this article shall confer upon a local authority any greater or other powers of dealing with such protected square than they would have possessed otherwise than by virtue of this article.

(Text 4.3-4, 6.14)

COUNTRYSIDE ACT 1968 (c 41)

9. (1) This section has effect as respects any common land to which the public have rights of access, and the powers conferred by this section are to be exercised in the interests of persons resorting to the common land for open-air recreation.

(2) Subject to the provisions of section 6 above, a local authority may exercise the powers conferred by this section on land taken out of the common land in accordance with this section and Schedule 2 to this Act, or on other land in the neighbourhood of the common land.

(3) A local authority shall have power to do anything appearing to the local authority to be desirable for the purpose set out in section 6(l) above, and in the interests of persons resorting to the common land, and in particular—

(a) to provide facilities and services for the enjoyment or convenience of the public, including meals and refreshments, parking places for vehicles, shelters and lavatory accommodation,

(b) to erect buildings and carry out works:

Provided that a local authority shall not under this section provide accommodation, meals or refreshments except in so far as it appears to them that the facilities therefor in the neighbourhood of the common land are inadequate or unsatisfactory, either generally or as respects any description of accommodation, meals or refreshments, as the case may be.

(4) Schedule 2 to this Act shall have effect for the purposes of this section, and in that Schedule 'the principal section' means this section.

(5) A local authority shall have power to acquire compulsorily any land in the neighbourhood of the common land which is required by them for the purposes of their functions under this section and which is not common land.

(6) In this section—
'common land' means –

(a) [land registered as common land in a register of common land kept under Part 1 of the Commons Act 2006;

(b) land to which Part 1 of that Act does not apply and which is subject to rights of common within the meaning of that Act.]

SCHEDULE 2

PROCEDURE FOR TAKING COMMON LAND

1. (l) For the purpose of enabling a local authority to exercise their powers under the principal section on land taken out of the common land the Minister may in accordance with this schedule authorise a local authority to acquire any part of the common land, including all commonable and other rights in or over the land, and, where the local authority already hold the land, to appropriate that land for the purposes of the principal section.

(2) Where the local authority already hold the land, but subject to any

commonable or other rights in or over the land, they shall not appropriate the land until they have, under subparagraph (1) above, acquired all those rights.

(3) Land acquired or appropriated as authorised under this paragraph shall be held by the local authority free from the public right of access, but shall be used for the benefit of public resorting to the common land.

(4) The Minister shall not give his authority under this paragraph unless he is satisfied—

(a) that there has been or will be given in exchange for the land other land, not being less in area and being equally advantageous to the persons, if any, entitled to commonable and other rights, and to the public, and that the land given in exchange has been or will be vested in the persons in whom the land taken was vested, and subject to the like rights, trusts and incidents as attached to the land taken, or

(b) that the giving in exchange of such other land is unnecessary, whether in the interests of the persons, if any, entitled to commonable or other rights or in the interests of the public.

Preliminary notices

2. (1) Before a local authority apply to the Minister for authority under paragraph 1 above as respects any part of the common land, they shall in two successive weeks publish in one or more newspapers circulating in the locality of the land a notice—

(a) stating that the local authority propose to make the application;

(b) giving particulars of the land which it is proposed to take out of the common land;

(c) stating whether land has been or is to be given in exchange, and, if so, giving particulars of that land, and stating the respective areas of the land to be taken and of the land given or to be given in exchange.

(2) If all or any part of the land to be taken is in a parish, the local authority shall, not later than the time of first publication of the notice, serve a copy of the notice on the parish council or, in the case of a parish not having a parish council, on the chairman of the parish meeting.

(3) The notice shall name a place within the locality where a map showing the said land, and any land given or to be given in exchange, may be inspected, and shall specify the time (not being less than twenty-eight days from first publication of the notice) within which and the manner in which representations with respect to the proposals in the notice may be made to the Minister.

(4) The Minister shall before giving his decision on the application take into consideration every representation which has been duly made and which has not been withdrawn, and may if he thinks fit either afford to each person making such a representation an opportunity of appearing before and being heard by a person appointed by the Minister for the purpose, or cause a public inquiry to be held.

Compulsory purchase

3. (l) A local authority shall have power to acquire compulsorily any land which is required by them for the purposes of their functions under the principal section, and which is part of the common land (or any commonable or other rights in or over that land), but the Minister shall not confirm a compulsory purchase order made in pursuance of this section except after giving his authority under paragraph 1 above as respects the land.

(2) Any notice which relates to a compulsory purchase order made in pursuance of this paragraph and which is published or served under [section 11 or 12 of the Acquisition of Land Act 1981] shall refer to the provisions of this schedule and shall state whether land has been, or is to be, given in exchange.

(3) The notice to be published under paragraph 2 of this schedule may be combined with a notice to be published [under the said section 11 of the said Act of 1981] in the same newspaper and relating to the same land.

(4) If land has been, or is to be, given in exchange—

(a) the notice to be published and served under [section 11 or 12 of the said Act of 1981] shall give particulars of that land and state the respective areas of the land to be taken and of the land given or to be given in exchange,

(b) the map in the compulsory purchase order shall show that land,

(c) the compulsory purchase order may provide for vesting any land to be given in exchange in the persons, and subject to the rights, trusts and incidents, mentioned in paragraph 1(4) above.

(5) A compulsory purchase order made in pursuance of this paragraph may provide for discharging the land purchased from all rights, trusts and incidents to which it was previously subject.

(6) [Section 19 of the Acquisition of Land Act 1981] (special provisions for acquisition of common land) shall not apply to a compulsory purchase order made in pursuance of this paragraph, and section 22 of the Commons Act 1899 (consent of Minister required for purchase of common land) shall not apply to the acquisition of land in pursuance of such a compulsory purchase order.

Acquisition by agreement and appropriation

4. (l) A local authority shall not acquire by agreement, or appropriate, any common land for the purposes of the principal section except as authorised under paragraph 1 of this schedule.

(2) Subject to subparagraph (1) above, a local authority may appropriate any common land for the purposes of the principal section without compliance with the provisions of section 163 of the Local Government Act 1933 or section 104 of the act of 1949 as amended by section 23 of the Town and Country Planning Act 1959 (under which the approval of the Minister is required).

(3) On an appropriation of land under this paragraph such adjustment shall be made in the accounts of the local authority as the Minister may direct.

Power to override restrictions affecting common land

5. No restrictions applying to commons generally, or to any particular common, contained in or having effect under any enactment, and no trust subject to which the common land is held, shall prevent a local authority from taking part of common land in accordance with the Schedule.

Protection for statutory undertakers

6. References in this Schedule to commonable and other rights in or over common land shall not be taken as including references to any right vested in statutory undertakers for the purpose of the carrying on of their undertaking [or to any right conferred by or in accordance with the telecommunications code on the operator of a telecommunications code system].

Interpretation

7. In this Schedule 'common land' has the meaning given by the principal section.

(Text 4.48-49)

NATIONAL TRUST ACT 1971 (c vi)

23. (1) Subject to the provisions of this section, in addition to the powers conferred on the National Trust by section 29 (Powers exercisable over certain Trust property) of the Act of 1907, the National Trust shall have power with respect to any Trust property to which that section applies to do anything appearing to the National Trust to be desirable for the purpose of providing, or improving, opportunities for the enjoyment of the property by the public, and in the interests of persons resorting thereto, and in particular—

(a) to provide or arrange for the provision of facilities and services for the enjoyment or convenience of the public, including meals and refreshments, parking places for vehicles, shelters and lavatory accommodation;

(b) to erect buildings and carry out works.

(2) The erection of any building (other than a shed for tools and materials), or the construction of any other work, whereby access by the public to any Trust property to which the said section 29 applies is prevented or impeded, shall not be lawful unless the consent of the Secretary of State is obtained.

[(2A) Sections 39 and 40 of the Commons Act 2006 apply in relation to an application for consent under subsection (2) of this section as they apply in relation to an application fro consent under section 38(1) of that Act.

(2B) Section 41 of that Act applies in relation to the carrying out of works in contravention of subsection (2) of this section as it applies to works carried out in contravention of section 38(1) of that Act (and as if references to consent under that provisions were to consent under subsection (2) of this section).

(2C) Nothing in section 38 of the Commons Act 2006 applies in relation to land to which section 29 of the Act of 1907 applies.]

(3) Notwithstanding anything in subsection (2) of section 30 (power to charge for admission to Trust property) of the Act of 1907 the National Trust may make such reasonable charges as they may from time to time determine for the use by the public of any facilities, services, parking places or other accommodation provided under this section.

(Text 4.37-40, 6.14)

LOCAL GOVERNMENT ACT 1972 (c 70)

122. (1) Subject to the following provisions of this section, a principal council may appropriate for any purpose for which the council are authorised by this or any other enactment to acquire land by agreement any land which belongs to the council and is no longer required for the purpose for which it is held immediately before the appropriation; but the appropriation of land by a council by virtue of this subsection shall be subject to the rights of other persons in, over or in respect of the land concerned.

(2) A principal council may not appropriate under subsection (1) above any land which they may be authorised to appropriate under [section 229 of the Town and Country Planning Act 1990] (land forming part of a common, etc) unless—

(a) the total of the land appropriated, in any particular common, or fuel or field garden allotment (giving those expressions the same meanings as in [the said section 229]) does not in the aggregate exceed 250 square yards, and

(b) before appropriating the land they cause notice of their intention to do so, specifying the land in question, to be advertised in two consecutive weeks in a newspaper circulating in the area in which the land is situated, and consider any objections to the proposed appropriation which may be made to them.

(4) Where land has been acquired under this Act or any other enactment or any statutory order incorporating the Lands Clauses Acts and is subsequently appropriated under this section, any work executed on the land after the appropriation has been effected shall be treated for the purposes of section 68 of the Lands Clauses Consolidation Act 1845 and section 10 of the Compulsory Purchase Act 1965 as having been authorised by the enactment or statutory order under which the land was acquired.

123. (1) Subject to the following provisions of this section, a principal council may dispose of land held by them in any manner they wish.

(2) Except with the consent of the Secretary of State, a council shall not dispose of land under this section, otherwise than by way of a short tenancy, for a consideration other than the best that can reasonably be obtained.

[(2A) A principal council may not dispose under subsection (1) above of any land consisting or forming part of an open space unless before disposing of the land they cause notice of their intention to do so, specifying the land in question, to be advertised in two consecutive weeks in a newspaper circulating in the area in which the land is situated, and consider any objections to the proposed disposal which may be made to them.

(2B) Where by virtue of subsection 2A above a council dispose of land which is held:

(a) for the purposes of section 164 of the Public Health Act 1875 (pleasure grounds) or;

(b) in accordance with section 10 of the Open Spaces Act 1906,

the land shall by virtue of the disposal be freed from any trust arising solely by virtue of its being held in trust for the enjoyment by the public in accordance with the said section 164 or, as the case may be, the said section 10.]

(7) For the purposes of this section a disposal of land is a disposal by way of a short tenancy if it consists:

(a) of the grant of a tenancy not exceeding seven years, or

(b) of the assignment of a tenancy which at the date of the assignment has not more than seven years to run, and in this section 'public trust land' has the meaning assigned to it by section 122(6) above.

[Note: s122(6) was repealed by the Local Government, Planning and Land Act 1980.]

126. (1) Any land belonging to a parish or community council which is not required for the purposes for which it was acquired or has since been appropriated may, subject to the following provisions of this section, be appropriated by the council for any other purpose for which the council are authorised by this or any other public general Act to acquire land by agreement.

(2) In the case of a parish which does not have a separate parish council, any land belonging to the parish meeting which is not required for the purposes for which it was acquired or has since been appropriated may, subject to the following provisions of this section, be appropriated by the parish meeting for any other purpose approved by the Secretary of State.

(3) The appropriation of land by virtue of this section by a parish or community council or by a parish meeting shall be subject to the rights of other persons in, over or in respect of the land concerned. (4) Neither a parish or community council nor a parish meeting may appropriate by virtue of this section any land which they may be authorised to appropriate under [section 229 of the Town and Country Planning Act 1990] (land forming part of a common, etc) unless—

(a) the total of the land appropriated in any particular common, or fuel or field garden allotment (giving those expressions the same meanings as in [the said section 229]) does not in the aggregate exceed 250 square yards, and

(b) before appropriating the land they cause notice of their intention to do so, specifying the land in question, to be advertised in two consecutive weeks in a newspaper circulating in the area in which the land is situated, and consider any objections to the proposed appropriation which may be made to them.

127. (1) subject to the following provisions of this section, a parish or community council, or the parish trustees of a parish acting with the consent of the parish meeting, may dispose of land held by them in any manner they wish.

(2) Except with the consent of the Secretary of State, land shall not disposed of under this section, otherwise than by way of a short tenancy, for a consideration other than the best that can reasonably be obtained.

[(3) Subsections (2A) and (2B) of section 123 above shall apply in relation to the disposal of land under this section as they apply to the disposal of land under that section, with the substitution of a reference to a parish or community council or the parish trustees of a parish meeting for the reference to a principal council in the said subsection (2A).]

(5) For the purposes of this section a disposal of land is a disposal by way of a short tenancy if it consists: ...

(c) of the grant of a tenancy not exceeding seven years, or
(d) of the assignment of a tenancy which at the date of the assignment has not more than seven years to run.

189. (3) The references in section 12 of the Inclosure Act 1857 (prevention of nuisances in town and village greens, etc,) to a churchwarden or overseer of the parish in which the town or village green or land is situated shall be construed—

(a) with respect to a green or land in a parish, as references to the parish council, or, where there is no parish council, the parish meeting;
(b) with respect to a green or land in a community where there is a community council, as references to the community council;
(c) with respect to any other green or land, as references to the council of the district [or Welsh principal area] in which the green or land is situated;

and where those references fall to be construed in accordance with paragraph (c) above the reference in the said section 12 to highways in the parish shall be construed as a reference to highways in the district [or (as the case may be) area].

270. (1) 'open space' has the meaning assigned to it by [section 336 (1) of the Town and Country Planning Act 1990].

'principal area' means a [non-metropolitan county], a district or a London borough [but, in relation to Wales, means a county or county borough].

'principal council' means a council elected for a principal area.

(Text 6.52-54)

ACQUISITION OF LAND ACT 1981 (c 67)

19. (1) In so far as a compulsory purchase order authorises the purchase of any land forming part of a common, open space or fuel or field garden allotment, the order shall be subject to special parliamentary procedure unless the Secretary of State is satisfied—

(a) that there has been or will be given in exchange for such land, other land, not being less in area and being equally advantageous to the persons, if any, entitled to rights of common or other rights, and to the public, and that the land given in exchange has been or will be vested in the persons in whom the land purchased was vested, and subject to the like rights, trusts and incidents as attach to the land purchased, or

[(aa) the land is being purchased in order to secure its preservation or improve its management]

(b) that the land does not exceed 250 square yards in extent or is required for the widening or drainage of an existing highway or partly for the widening and partly for the drainage of such a highway and that the giving in exchange of other land is unnecessary, whether in the interests of the persons, if any, entitled to rights of common or other rights or in the interests of the public, and certifies accordingly.

(2) Where it is proposed to give a certificate under this section the Secretary of State shall [direct the acquiring authority to] give public notice of his intention to do so, and—

(a) after affording opportunity to all persons interested to make representations and objections in relation thereto, and

(b) after causing a public local inquiry to be held in any case where it appears to him to be expedient so to do, having regard to any representations or objections made,

the Secretary of State may, after considering any representations and objections made and, if an inquiry has been held, the report of the person who held the inquiry, give the certificate.

[(2A). Notice under subsection (2) above shall be given in such form and manner as the Secretary of State may direct.]

(3) A compulsory purchase order may provide for—

(a) vesting land given in exchange as mentioned in subsection (1) above in the persons, and subject to the rights, trusts and incidents, therein mentioned, and

(b) discharging the land purchased from all rights, trusts and incidents to which it was previously subject [except where the Secretary of State has given a certificate under subsection (1)(aa) above.]

(4) In this section

'common' includes any land subject to be enclosed under the Inclosure Acts 1845 to 1882, and any town or village green,

'fuel or field garden allotment' means any allotment set out as a fuel allotment, or a field garden allotment, under an Inclosure Act,

'open space' means any land laid out as a public garden, or used for the purposes of public recreation, or land being a disused burial ground.

(Text 2.86, 2.134, 6.1, 6.35-62, 6.77, 7.46)

DYFED ACT 1987 (c xxiv)

42. (1) In this section 'green' means any land registered as a town or village green under the Commons Registration Act 1965.

(2) If on application being made to a district council by the owner or occupier of any residential premises existing or proposed at the date of the application which adjoins a green in the district it appears to the district council that—

(a) the premises lack satisfactory means of vehicular or other access; and

(b) it is not reasonably practicable for the owner or occupier to secure such means of access in any other manner; the council may, with the consent of the Secretary of State, notwithstanding any enactment or rule of law, authorise the owner or occupier to construct and maintain a way giving vehicular or other access to those premises over the green.

(3) An authorisation of an access way under this section may be given on such conditions (which may include conditions requiring the maintenance of the access way, and the provision and maintenance in connection with it of cattle grids or other works) as may be specified in the authorisation and in the consent of the Secretary of State.

(4) The district council may at any time with the consent of the Secretary of State vary the conditions on which an authorisation under this section is given.

(5) A district council may with the consent of the Secretary of State by resolution suspend any rights of recreation over so much of any green as is the subject of an authorisation given under this section, at such times or for such period as may be specified in the resolution but such a resolution shall only have effect while the authorisation is in force.

(6) A district council shall not seek the consent of the Secretary of State to the giving of any authorisation or the passing of any resolution under this section in relation to any green not vested in them without the assent in writing of the person in whom the green is vested.

(7) Where the owner or occupier of any premises to which access is afforded pursuant to an authorisation under this section fails to carry out works required by a condition of the authorisation within the time specified therein or (in the case of works for the maintenance of the access way or of any cattle grids or other works provided in connection therewith) within such reasonable time as may be required by notice in writing given by the district council to the owner or occupier, the district council may carry out the works and recover from that person the expenses reasonably incurred by them in so doing.

(8) A district council may enter into arrangements with any person to whom an authorisation under this section has been given for the carrying out by the council on such terms as may be agreed between the parties of any works authorised or required by the authorisation.

(9) The conditions of an authorisation under this section and the requirements

of a notice under subsection (7) above shall be enforceable against the owner and occupier for the time being of the premises to which access is afforded pursuant to the authorisation and shall be a local land charge on those premises.

(10) Nothing in this section shall authorise the enclosure of any part of a green.

(11) (a) Before seeking the consent of the Secretary of State under any provision of this section in relation to any green not vested in the council for the community to which the application relates is situated, the district council shall consult that community council.
(b) In considering the application for consent made to him under this section the Secretary of State shall have regard to the use normally made of the green by the public or any section thereof and shall refuse his consent if it appears to him that the provision of the access way would prevent or substantially impair such use or would otherwise be detrimental to the neighbourhood where the green is situated.

(Text 7.54)

ROAD TRAFFIC ACT 1988 (c 52)

34. (1) Subject to the provisions of this section, if without lawful authority a person drives a mechanically propelled vehicle:
(a) on to or upon any common land, moorland or land of any other description, not being land forming part of a road, or (b) on any road being a footpath, bridleway or restricted byway, he is guilty of an offence.

(3) It is not an offence under this section to drive a mechanically propelled vehicle on any land within fifteen yards of a road, being a road on which a motor vehicle may lawfully be driven, for the purpose only of parking the vehicle on that land.

(4) A person shall not be convicted of an offence under this section with respect to a vehicle if he proves to the satisfaction of the court that it was driven in contravention of this section for the purpose of saving life or extinguishing fire or meeting any other like emergency.

(5) It is hereby declared that nothing in this section prejudices the operation of—

(a) section 193 of the Law of Property Act 1925 (rights of the public over commons and waste lands), or

(b) any by-laws applying to any land, or affects the law of trespass to land or any right or remedy to which a person may by law be entitled in respect of any such trespass or in particular confers a right to park a vehicle on any land.

(7) In this section ... 'mechanically propelled vehicle' does not include a vehicle falling within paragraph (a), (b) or (c) of section 189(1) of this Act.

(Text 3.37, 4.21, 7.40, 7.48-50)

TOWN AND COUNTRY PLANNING ACT 1990 (c 8)

229. (1) Any local authority may be authorised, by an order made by that authority and confirmed by the Secretary of State, to appropriate for any purpose for which that authority can be authorised to acquire land under any enactment any land for the time being held by them for other purposes.

(2) Subsection (1) applies to land which is or forms part of a common, or fuel or field garden allotment (including any such land which is specially regulated by any enactment, whether public general or local or private), other than land which is Green Belt land within the meaning of the Green Belt (London and Home Counties) Act 1938.

(3) Section 19 of the Acquisition of Land Act 1981 (special provisions with respect to compulsory purchase orders under that Act relating to land forming part of a common, open space or fuel or field garden allotment) shall apply to an order under this section authorising the appropriation of land as it applies to a compulsory purchase order under that Act.

(4) Where land appropriated under this section was acquired under an enactment incorporating the Lands Clauses Acts, any works executed on the land after the appropriation has been effected shall, for the purposes of section 68 of the Lands Clauses Consolidation Act 1845 and section 10 of the Compulsory Purchase Act 1965 be deemed to have been authorised by the enactment under which the land was acquired.

336. (1) 'common' includes any land subject to be enclosed under the Inclosure Acts 1845 to 1882 and any town or village green.

'open space' means any land laid out as a public garden, or used for the purposes of public recreation, or land which is a disused burial ground.

(Text 6.35, 6.53, 7.43)

COUNTRYSIDE AND RIGHTS OF WAY ACT 2000 (c 37)

1. (1) In this Part 'access land' means any land which—

(a) is shown as open country on a map in conclusive form issued by the appropriate countryside body for the purposes of this Part,

(b) is shown on such a map as registered common land,

(c) is registered common land in any area outside Inner London for which no such map relating to registered common land has been issued,

(d) is situated more than 600 metres above sea level in any area for which no such map relating to open country has been issued, or

(e) is dedicated for the purposes of this Part under section 16, but does not (in any of those cases) include excepted land or land which is treated by section 15(1) as being accessible to the public apart from this Act.

(2) In this Part—

'access authority'—

(a) in relation to land in a National Park, means the National Park authority, and
(b) in relation to any other land, means the local highway authority in whose area the land is situated;

'the appropriate countryside body' means—

(b) in relation to Wales, the Countryside Council for Wales;

'excepted land' means land which is for the time being of any of the descriptions specified in Part I of Schedule 1, those descriptions having effect subject to Part II of that Schedule;

'mountain' includes, subject to the following definition, any land situated more than 600 metres above sea level;

'mountain, moor, heath or down' does not include land which appears to the appropriate countryside body to consist of improved or semi-improved grassland;

'open country' means land which—

(a) appears to the appropriate countryside body to consist wholly or predominantly of mountain, moor, heath or down, and
(b) is not registered common land.

(3) In this Part 'registered common land' means—

[(a) land which is registered as common land in the register of common land kept under Part 1 of the Commons Act 2006.]

2. (1) Any person is entitled by virtue of this subsection to enter and remain on any access land for the purposes of open-air recreation, if and so long as—
(a) he does so without breaking or damaging any wall, fence, hedge, stile or gate, and
(b) he observes the general restrictions in Schedule 2 and any other restrictions imposed in relation to the land under Chapter II.

(2) Subsection (1) has effect subject to subsections (3) and (4) and to the provisions of Chapter II.

(3) Subsection (1) does not entitle a person to enter or be on any land, or do anything on any land, in contravention of any prohibition contained in or having effect under any enactment, other than an enactment contained in a local or private Act.

(4) If a person becomes a trespasser on any access land by failing to comply with—
(a) subsection (1)(a),
(b) the general restrictions in Schedule 2, or
(c) any other restrictions imposed in relation to the land under Chapter 11,

he may not, within 72 hours after leaving that land, exercise his right under subsection (1) to enter that land again or to enter other land in the same ownership.

(5) In this section 'owner', in relation to any land which is subject to a farm business tenancy within the meaning of the Agricultural Tenancies Act 1995 or a tenancy to which the Agricultural Holdings Act 1986 applies, means the tenant under that tenancy, and 'ownership' shall be construed accordingly.

15. (1) For the purposes of section 1(1), land is to be treated as being accessible to the public apart from this Act at any time if, but only if, at that time—

(a) section 193 of the Law of Property Act 1925 (rights of the public over commons and waste lands) applies to it,

(b) by virtue of a local or private Act or a scheme made under Part I of the Commons Act 1899 (as read with subsection (2)), members of the public have a right of access to it at all times for the purposes of open-air recreation (however described),

(c) an access agreement or access order under Part V of the National Parks and Access to the Countryside Act 1949 is in force with respect to it, or

(d) the public have access to it under subsection (1) of section 19 of the Ancient Monuments and Archaeological Areas Act 1979 (public access to monuments under public control) or would have access to it under that subsection but for any provision of subsections (2) to (9) of that section.

(2) Where a local or private Act or a scheme made under Part I of the Commons Act 1899 confers on the inhabitants of a particular district or neighbourhood (however described) a right of access to any land for the purposes of open-air recreation (however described), the right of access exercisable by those inhabitants in relation to that land is by virtue of this subsection exercisable by members of the public generally.

16. (1) Subject to the provisions of this section, a person who, in respect of any land, holds—

(a) the fee simple absolute in possession, or

(b) a legal term of years absolute of which not less than 90 years remain unexpired, may, by taking such steps as may be prescribed, dedicate the land for the purposes of this Part, whether or not it would be access land apart from this section.

(2) Where any person other than the person making the dedication holds—

(a) any leasehold interest in any of the land to be dedicated, or

(b) such other interest in any of that land as may be prescribed, the dedication must be made jointly with that other person, in such manner as may be prescribed, or with his consent, given in such manner as may be prescribed.

(3) In relation to a dedication under this section by virtue of subsection (1)(b), the reference in subsection (2)(a) to a leasehold interest does not include a reference to a leasehold interest superior to that of the person making the dedication.

(4) A dedication made under this section by virtue of subsection (1)(b) shall have effect only for the remainder of the term held by the person making the dedication.

(5) Schedule 2 to the Forestry Act 1967 (power for tenant for life and others to enter into forestry dedication covenants) applies to dedications under this section as it applies to forestry dedication covenants.

(6) Regulations may—

(a) prescribe the form of any instrument to be used for the purposes of this section,

(b) enable a dedication under this section to include provision removing or relaxing any of the general restrictions in Schedule 2 in relation to any of the land to which the dedication relates,

(c) enable a dedication previously made under this section to be amended by the persons by whom a dedication could be made, so as to remove or relax any of those restriction in relation to any of the land to which the dedication relates, and

(d) require any dedication under this section, or any amendment of such a dedication by virtue of paragraph (c) to be notified to the appropriate countryside body and to the access authority.

(7) A dedication under this section is irrevocable and, subject to subsection (4), binds successive owners and occupiers of, and other persons interested in, the land to which it relates, but nothing in this section prevents any land from becoming excepted land.

(8) A dedication under this section is a local land charge.

[Note: the form of dedication is prescribed by the Countryside (Dedication of Land) (England) Regulations 2003 (SI 2004) and the Countryside Access (Dedication of Land as Access Land) (Wales) Regulations 2003 (SI 135)).]

SCHEDULE 1

Section 1(2)

EXCEPTED LAND FOR THE PURPOSES OF PART I

PART I

EXCEPTED LAND

1. Land on which the soil is being, or has at any time within the previous 12 months been, disturbed by any ploughing or drilling undertaken for the purposes of planting or sowing crops or trees.

2. Land covered by buildings or the curtilage of such land.

3. Land within 20 metres of a dwelling.

4. Land used as a park or garden.

5. Land used for the getting of minerals by surface working (including quarrying).

6. Land used for the purposes of a railway (including a light railway) or tramway.

7. Land used for the purposes of a golf course, racecourse or aerodrome.

8. Land which does not fall within any of the preceding paragraphs and is covered by works used for the purposes of a statutory undertaking or a telecommunications code system, or the curtilage of any such land.

9. Land as respects which development which will result in the land becoming land falling within any of paragraphs 2 to 8 is in the course of being carried out.

10. Land within 20 metres of a building which is used for housing livestock, not being a temporary or moveable structure.

11. Land covered by pens in use for the temporary reception or detention of livestock.

12. Land habitually used for the training of racehorses.

13. Land the use of which is regulated by by-laws under section 14 of the Military Lands Act 1892 or section 2 of the Military Lands Act 1900.

PART II

SUPPLEMENTARY PROVISIONS

14. In this Schedule—

'building' includes any structure or erection and any part of a building as so defined, but does not include any fence or wall, or anything which is a means of access as defined by section 34; and for this purpose 'structure' includes any tent, caravan or other temporary or moveable structure;

'development' and 'minerals' have the same meaning as in the Town and Country Planning Act 1990;

'ploughing' and 'drilling' include respectively agricultural or forestry operations similar to ploughing and agricultural or forestry operations similar to drilling;

'statutory undertaker' means—

(a) a person authorised by any enactment to carry on any railway, light railway, tramway, road transport, water transport, canal, inland navigation, dock, harbour, pier or lighthouse undertaking or any undertaking for the supply of hydraulic power,
(b) any public gas transporter, within the meaning of Part I of the Gas Act 1986,
(c) any water or sewerage undertaker,
(d) any holder of a licence under section 6(l) of the Electricity Act 1989, or
(e) the Environment Agency, the Post Office or the Civil Aviation Authority;

'statutory undertaking' means—

(a) the undertaking of a statutory undertaker, or
(b) an airport to which Part V of the Airports Act 1986 applies.

15. (1) Land is not to be treated as excepted land by reason of any development carried out on the land, if the carrying out of the development requires planning permission under Part III of the Town and Country Planning Act 1990 and that permission has not been granted.

(2) Subparagraph (1) does not apply where the development is treated by section 191(2) of the Town and Country Planning Act 1990 as being lawful for the purposes of that Act.

16. The land which is excepted land by virtue of paragraph does not include–

(a) any means of access, as defined by section 34, or
(b) any way leading to such a means of access,

if the means of access is necessary for giving the public reasonable access to access land.

17. Land which is habitually used for the training of racehorses is not to be treated by virtue of paragraph 11 as excepted land except -

(a) between dawn and midday on any day, and
(b) at any other time when it is in use for that purpose.

(Text 1.2, 1.11, 2.127, 2.131, 3.15-16, 3.47-48, 4.1, 4.9, 4.18, 4.20, 4.26, 4.30, 4.60, 5 *passim*, 6.26, 6.75, 7.62, 8.3)

COMMONS ACT 2006 (c 26)

PART 1

REGISTRATION

Introductory

1 Registers of common land and greens

Each commons registration authority shall continue to keep—

(a) a register known as a register of common land; and
(b) a register known as a register of town or village greens.

(Text 2.74)

2 Purpose of registers

(1) The purpose of a register of common land is—

(a) to register land as common land; and
(b) to register rights of common exercisable over land registered as common land.

(2) The purpose of a register of town or village greens is—

(a) to register land as a town or village green; and
(b) to register rights of common exercisable over land registered as a town or village green.

3 Content of registers

(1) The land registered as common land in a register of common land is, subject to this Part, to be—
(a) the land so registered in it at the commencement of this section; and
(b) such other land as may be so registered in it under this Part.

(2) The land registered as a town or village green in a register of town or village greens is, subject to this Part, to be—
(a) the land so registered in it at the commencement of this section; and
(b) such other land as may be so registered in it under this Part.

(3) The rights of common registered in a register of common land or town or village greens are, subject to this Part, to be—
(a) the rights registered in it at the commencement of this section; and
(b) such other rights as may be so registered in it under this Part.

(4) The following information is to be registered in a register of common land or town or village greens in respect of a right of common registered in it—
(a) the nature of the right;
(b) if the right is attached to any land, the land to which it is attached;
(c) if the right is not so attached, the owner of the right.

(5) Regulations may—
(a) require or permit other information to be included in a register of common land or town or village greens;
(b) make provision as to the form in which any information is to be presented in such a register.

(6) Except as provided under this Part or any other enactment—
(a) no land registered as common land or as a town or village green is to be removed from the register in which it is so registered;
(b) no right of common registered in a register of common land or town or village greens is to be removed from that register.

(7) No right of common over land to which this Part applies is to be registered in the register of title.

(Text 2.29)

4 Commons registration authorities

(1) The following are commons registration authorities—
(a) a county council in England;
(b) a district council in England for an area without a county council;
(c) a London borough council; and
(d) a county or county borough council in Wales.

(2) For the purposes of this Part, the commons registration authority in relation to any land is the authority in whose area the land is situated.

(3) Where any land falls within the area of two or more commons registration authorities, the authorities may by agreement provide for one of them to be the

commons registration authority in relation to the whole of the land.

(Text 2.26)

5 Land to which Part 1 applies

(1) This Part applies to all land in England and Wales, subject as follows.

(2) This Part does not apply to—
(a) the New Forest; or
(b) Epping Forest.

(3) This Part shall not be taken to apply to the Forest of Dean.

(4) If any question arises under this Part whether any land is part of the forests mentioned in this section it is to be referred to and decided by the appropriate national authority.

(Text 2.7, 2.83)

Registration of rights of common

6 Creation

(1) A right of common cannot at any time after the commencement of this section be created over land to which this Part applies by virtue of prescription.

(2) A right of common cannot at any time after the commencement of this section be created in any other way over land to which this Part applies except—
(a) as specified in subsection (3); or
(b) pursuant to any other enactment.

(3) A right of common may be created over land to which this Part applies by way of express grant if—
(a) the land is not registered as a town or village green; and
(b) the right is attached to land.

(4) The creation of a right of common in accordance with subsection (3) only has effect if it complies with such requirements as to form and content as regulations may provide.

(5) The creation of a right of common in accordance with subsection (3) does not operate at law until on an application under this section—
(a) the right is registered in a register of common land; and
(b) if the right is created over land not registered as common land, the land is registered in a register of common land.

(6) An application under this section to register the creation of a right of common consisting of a right to graze any animal is to be refused if in the opinion of the commons registration authority the land over which it is created would be unable to sustain the exercise of—
(a) that right; and
(b) if the land is already registered as common land, any other rights of common registered as exercisable over the land.

(Text 2.45-46)

7 Variation

(1) For the purposes of this section a right of common is varied if by virtue of any disposition—

(a) the right becomes exercisable over new land to which this Part applies instead of all or part of the land over which it was exercisable;

(b) the right becomes exercisable over new land to which this Part applies in addition to the land over which it is already exercisable;

(c) there is any other alteration in what can be done by virtue of the right.

(2) A right of common which is registered in a register of common land or town or village greens cannot at any time after the commencement of this section be varied so as to become exercisable over new land if that land is at the time registered as a town or village green.

(3) A right of common which is registered in a register of town or village greens cannot at any time after the commencement of this section be varied so as to extend what can be done by virtue of the right.

(4) The variation of a right of common which is registered in a register of common land or town or village greens—

(a) only has effect if it complies with such requirements as to form and content as regulations may provide; and

(b) does not operate at law until, on an application under this section, the register is amended so as to record the variation.

(5) An application under this section to record a variation of a right of common consisting of a right to graze any animal is to be refused if in the opinion of the commons registration authority the land over which the right is or is to be exercisable would, in consequence of the variation, be unable to sustain the exercise of—

(a) that right; and

(b) if the land is already registered as common land, any other rights of common registered as exercisable over the land.

(Text 2.58-61)

8 Apportionment

(1) Regulations may make provision as to the amendments to be made to a register of common land or town or village greens where a right of common which is registered in a register of common land or town or village greens as attached to any land is apportioned by virtue of any disposition affecting the land.

(2) Regulations under subsection (1) may provide that a register is only to be amended when—

(a) a disposition relating to an apportioned right itself falls to be registered under this Part; or

(b) the register falls to be amended under section 11.

(3) Where at any time—

(a) a right of common which is registered in a register of common land or town or village greens as attached to any land has been apportioned by virtue of any disposition affecting the land, and

(b) no amendments have been made under subsection (1) in respect of the apportionment of that right, the rights of common subsisting as a result of the apportionment shall be regarded as rights which are registered in that register as attached to the land to which they attach as a result of the apportionment.

(Text 2.62-65)

9 Severance

(1) This section applies to a right of common which—

(a) is registered in a register of common land or town or village greens as attached to any land; and

(b) would, apart from this section, be capable of being severed from that land.

(2) A right of common to which this section applies is not at any time on or after the day on which this section comes into force capable of being severed from the land to which it is attached, except—

(a) where the severance is authorised by or under Schedule 1; or

(b) where the severance is authorised by or under any other Act.

(3) Where any instrument made on or after the day on which this section comes into force would effect a disposition in relation to a right of common to which this section applies in contravention of subsection (2), the instrument is void to the extent that it would effect such a disposition.

(4) Where by virtue of any instrument made on or after the day on which this section comes into force—

(a) a disposition takes effect in relation to land to which a right of common to which this section applies is attached, and

(b) the disposition would have the effect of contravening subsection (2), the disposition also has effect in relation to the right notwithstanding anything in the instrument to the contrary.

(5) Where by virtue of any instrument made on or after the day on which this section comes into force a right of common to which this section applies falls to be apportioned between different parts of the land to which it is attached, the instrument is void to the extent that it purports to apportion the right otherwise than rateably.

(6) Nothing in this section affects any instrument made before, or made pursuant to a contract made in writing before, the day on which this section comes into force.

(7) This section and Schedule 1 shall be deemed to have come into force on 28 June 2005 (and an order under paragraph 2 of that Schedule may have effect as from that date).

(Text 2.67-70)

10 Attachment

(1) This section applies to any right of common which is registered in a register of common land or town or village greens but is not registered as attached to any land.

(2) The owner of the right may apply to the commons registration authority for the right to be registered in that register as attached to any land, provided that—
- (a) he is entitled to occupy the land; or
- (b) the person entitled to occupy the land has consented to the application.

(Text 2.76)

11 Re-allocation of attached rights

(1) Where—
- (a) a right of common is registered in a register of common land or town or village greens as attached to any land, and
- (b) subsection (2), (3) or (4) applies in relation to part of the land ('the relevant part'), the owner of the land may apply to the commons registration authority for the register to be amended so as to secure that the right does not attach to the relevant part.

(2) This subsection applies where the relevant part is not used for agricultural purposes.

(3) This subsection applies where planning permission has been granted for use of the relevant part for purposes which are not agricultural purposes.

(4) This subsection applies where—
- (a) an order authorising the compulsory purchase of the relevant part by any authority has been made in accordance with the Acquisition of Land Act 1981 (c 67) (and, if the order requires to be confirmed under Part 2 of that Act, has been so confirmed);
- (b) the relevant part has not vested in the authority; and
- (c) the relevant part is required for use other than use for agricultural purposes.

(5) Regulations may for the purposes of subsections (2) to (4) make provision as to what is or is not to be regarded as use of land for agricultural purposes.

(6) Regulations may provide that an application under this section is not to be granted without the consent of any person specified in the regulations.

(Text 2.77)

12 Transfer of rights in gross

The transfer of a right of common which is registered in a register of common land or town or village greens but is not registered as attached to any land—
- (a) only has effect if it complies with such requirements as to form and content as regulations may provide; and
- (b) does not operate at law until, on an application under this section, the

transferee is registered in the register as the owner of the right.

(Text 2.79)

13 Surrender and extinguishment

(1) The surrender to any extent of a right of common which is registered in a register of common land or town or village greens—

(a) only has effect if it complies with such requirements as to form and content as regulations may provide; and

(b) does not operate at law until, on an application under this section, the right is removed from the register.

(2) The reference in subsection (1) to a surrender of a right of common does not include a disposition having the effect referred to in section 7(1)(a).

(3) A right of common which is registered in a register of common land or town or village greens cannot be extinguished by operation of common law.

(Text 2.80-82, 6.8)

Registration, deregistration and exchange of land

14 Statutory dispositions

(1) Regulations may make provision as to the amendment of a register of common land or town or village greens where by virtue of any relevant instrument—

(a) a disposition is made in relation to land registered in it as common land or as a town or village green; or

(b) a disposition is made in relation to a right of common registered in it.

(2) Regulations may provide that, where—

(a) by virtue of any relevant instrument a disposition is made in relation to land registered as common land or as a town or village green,

(b) by virtue of regulations under subsection (1) the land ceases to be so registered, and

(c) in connection with the disposition other land is given in exchange, the land given in exchange is to be registered as common land or as a town or village green.

(3) In this section, 'relevant instrument' means—

(a) any order, deed or other instrument made under or pursuant to the Acquisition of Land Act 1981 (c 67);

(b) a conveyance made for the purposes of section 13 of the New Parishes Measure 1943 (No. 1);

(c) any other instrument made under or pursuant to any enactment.

(4) Regulations under this section may require the making of an application to a commons registration authority for amendment of a register of common land or town or village greens.

(5) Regulations under this section may provide that a relevant instrument, so

far as relating to land registered as common land or as a town or village green or to any right of common, is not to operate at law until any requirement for which they provide is complied with.

(Text 2.86, 6.1, 6.83)

15 Registration of greens

(1) Any person may apply to the commons registration authority to register land to which this Part applies as a town or village green in a case where subsection (2), (3) or (4) applies.

(2) This subsection applies where—

(a) a significant number of the inhabitants of any locality, or of any neighbourhood within a locality, have indulged as of right in lawful sports and pastimes on the land for a period of at least 20 years; and

(b) they continue to do so at the time of the application.

(3) This subsection applies where—

(a) a significant number of the inhabitants of any locality, or of any neighbourhood within a locality, indulged as of right in lawful sports and pastimes on the land for a period of at least 20 years;

(b) they ceased to do so before the time of the application but after the commencement of this section; and

(c) the application is made within the period of two years beginning with the cessation referred to in paragraph (b).

(4) This subsection applies (subject to subsection (5) where—

(a) a significant number of the inhabitants of any locality, or of any neighbourhood within a locality, indulged as of right in lawful sports and pastimes on the land for a period of at least 20 years;

(b) they ceased to do so before the commencement of this section; and

(c) the application is made within the period of five years beginning with the cessation referred to in paragraph (b).

(5) Subsection (4) does not apply in relation to any land where—

(a) planning permission was granted before 23 June 2006 in respect of the land;

(b) construction works were commenced before that date in accordance with that planning permission on the land or any other land in respect of which the permission was granted; and

(c) the land—

(i) has by reason of any works carried out in accordance with that planning permission become permanently unusable by members of the public for the purposes of lawful sports and pastimes; or

(ii) will by reason of any works proposed to be carried out in accordance with that planning permission become permanently unusable by members of the public for those purposes.

(6) In determining the period of 20 years referred to in subsections (2)(a), (3)(a) and (4)(a), there is to be disregarded any period during which access to the land was prohibited to members of the public by reason of any enactment.

(7) For the purposes of subsection (2)(b) in a case where the condition in subsection (2)(a) is satisfied—

(a) where persons indulge as of right in lawful sports and pastimes immediately before access to the land is prohibited as specified in subsection (6), those persons are to be regarded as continuing so to indulge; and

(b) where permission is granted in respect of use of the land for the purposes of lawful sports and pastimes, the permission is to be disregarded in determining whether persons continue to indulge in lawful sports and pastimes on the land 'as of right'.

(8) The owner of any land may apply to the commons registration authority to register the land as a town or village green.

(9) An application under subsection (8) may only be made with the consent of any relevant leaseholder of, and the proprietor of any relevant charge over, the land.

(10) In subsection (9)—

'relevant charge' means—

(a) in relation to land which is registered in the register of title, a registered charge within the meaning of the Land Registration Act 2002 (c 9);

(b) in relation to land which is not so registered—

(i) a charge registered under the Land Charges Act 1972 (c 61); or

(ii) a legal mortgage, within the meaning of the Law of Property Act 1925 (c 20), which is not registered under the Land Charges Act 1972;

'relevant leaseholder' means a leaseholder under a lease for a term of more than seven years from the date on which the lease was granted.

(Text 7.63, 7.67-73)

16 Deregistration and exchange: applications

(1) The owner of any land registered as common land or as a town or village green may apply to the appropriate national authority for the land ('the release land') to cease to be so registered.

(2) If the release land is more than 200 square metres in area, the application must include a proposal under subsection (3).

(3) A proposal under this subsection is a proposal that land specified in the application ('replacement land') be registered as common land or as a town or village green in place of the release land.

(4) If the release land is not more than 200 square metres in area, the application may include a proposal under subsection (3).

(5) Where the application includes a proposal under subsection (3)—

(a) the replacement land must be land to which this Part applies;

(b) the replacement land must not already be registered as common land or as a town or village green; and

(c) if the owner of the release land does not own the replacement land, the owner of the replacement land must join in the application.

(6) In determining the application, the appropriate national authority shall have regard to—

(a) the interests of persons having rights in relation to, or occupying, the release land (and in particular persons exercising rights of common over it);
(b) the interests of the neighbourhood;
(c) the public interest;
(d) any other matter considered to be relevant.

(7) The appropriate national authority shall in a case where—

(a) the release land is not more than 200 square metres in area, and
(b) the application does not include a proposal under subsection (3), have particular regard under subsection (6) to the extent to which the absence of such a proposal is prejudicial to the interests specified in paragraphs (a) to (c) of that subsection.

(8) The reference in subsection (6)(c) to the public interest includes the public interest in—

(a) nature conservation;
(b) the conservation of the landscape;
(c) the protection of public rights of access to any area of land; and
(d) the protection of archaeological remains and features of historic interest.

(9) An application under this section may only be made with the consent of any relevant leaseholder of, and the proprietor of any relevant charge over—

(a) the release land;
(b) any replacement land.

(10) In subsection (9) 'relevant charge' and 'relevant leaseholder' have the meanings given by section 15(10).

(Text 2.88-91, 6.1, 6.83, 7.47)

17 Deregistration and exchange: orders

(1) Where the appropriate national authority grants an application under section 16 it must make an order requiring the commons registration authority to remove the release land from its register of common land or town or village greens.

(2) Where the application included a proposal to register replacement land, the order shall also require the commons registration authority—

(a) to register the replacement land as common land or as a town or village green in place of the release land; and
(b) to register as exercisable over the replacement land any rights of common which, immediately before the relevant date, are registered as exercisable over the release land.

(3) A commons registration authority must take such other steps on receiving an order under this section as regulations may require.

(4) Where immediately before the relevant date any rights of common are registered as exercisable over the release land, those rights are on that date extinguished in relation to that land.

(5) Where immediately before the relevant date any rights are exercisable over the release land by virtue of its being, or being part of, a town or village green—
(a) those rights are extinguished on that date in respect of the release land; and
(b) where any replacement land is registered in its place, those rights shall become exercisable as from that date over the replacement land instead.

(6) Where immediately before the relevant date the release land was registered as common land and any relevant provision applied in relation to it—
(a) the provision shall on that date cease to apply to the release land; and
(b) where any replacement land is registered in its place, the provision shall on that date apply to the replacement land instead.

(7) An order under this section may contain—
(a) provision disapplying the effect of subsection (5)(b) or (6)(b) in relation to any replacement land;
(b) supplementary provision as to the effect in relation to any replacement land of—
(i) any rights exercisable over the release land by virtue of its being, or being part of, a town or village green;
(ii) any relevant provision;
(c) supplementary provision as to the effect in relation to the release land or any replacement land of any local or personal Act.

(8) In subsections (6) and (7) 'relevant provision' means a provision contained in, or made under—
(a) section 193 of the Law of Property Act 1925 (c 20);
(b) a scheme under the Metropolitan Commons Act 1866 (c 122);
(c) an Act under the Commons Act 1876 (c 56) confirming a provisional order of the Inclosure Commissioners;
(d) a scheme under the Commons Act 1899 (c 30);
(e) section 1 of the Commons Act 1908 (c 44).

(9) In this section, 'relevant date' means the date on which the commons registration authority amends its register as required under subsections (1) and (2).

(10) Regulations may make provision for the publication of an order under this section.

(Text 2.92-93, 6.1, 6.83, 7.47)

Conclusiveness and correction of the registers

18 Conclusiveness

(1) This section applies to land registered as common land, or as a town or village green, which is registered as being subject to a right of common.

(2) If the land would not otherwise have been subject to that right, it shall be deemed to have become subject to that right, as specified in the register, upon its registration.

(3) If the right is registered as attached to any land, the right shall, if it would not otherwise have attached to that land, be deemed to have become so attached upon registration of its attachment.

(4) If the right is not registered as attached to any land, the person registered as the owner of the right shall, if he would not otherwise have been its owner, be deemed to have become its owner upon his registration.

(5) Nothing in subsection (2) affects any constraint on the exercise of a right of common where the constraint does not appear in the register.

(6) It is immaterial whether the registration referred to in subsection (2), (3) or (4) occurred before or after the commencement of this section.

(Text 2.24, 2.97, 2.100-103)

19 Correction

(1) A commons registration authority may amend its register of common land or town or village greens for any purpose referred to in subsection (2).

(2) Those purposes are—
(a) correcting a mistake made by the commons registration authority in making or amending an entry in the register;
(b) correcting any other mistake, where the amendment would not affect—
(i) the extent of any land registered as common land or as a town or village green; or
(ii) what can be done by virtue of a right of common;
(c) removing a duplicate entry from the register;
(d) updating the details of any name or address referred to in an entry;
(e) updating any entry in the register relating to land registered as common land or as a town or village green to take account of accretion or diluvion.

(3) References in this section to a mistake include—
(a) a mistaken omission, and
(b) an unclear or ambiguous description, and it is immaterial for the purposes of this section whether a mistake was made before or after the commencement of this section.

(4) An amendment may be made by a commons registration authority—
(a) on its own initiative; or
(b) on the application of any person.

(5) A mistake in a register may not be corrected under this section if the authority considers that, by reason of reliance reasonably placed on the register by any person or for any other reason, it would in all the circumstances be unfair to do so.

(6) Regulations may make further provision as to the criteria to be applied in determining an application or proposal under this section.

(7) The High Court may order a commons registration authority to amend its

register of common land or town or village greens if the High Court is satisfied that—

(a) any entry in the register, or any information in an entry, was at any time included in the register as a result of fraud; and

(b) it would be just to amend the register.

(Text 2.40, 2.104-107)

Information etc

20 Inspection

(1) Any person may inspect and make copies of, or of any part of—

(a) a register of common land or town or village greens;

(b) any document kept by a commons registration authority which is referred to in such a register;

(c) any other document kept by a commons registration authority which relates to an application made at any time in relation to such a register.

(2) The right in subsection (1) is subject to regulations which may, in particular—

(a) provide for exceptions to the right;

(b) impose conditions on its exercise.

(3) Conditions under subsection (2)(b) may include conditions requiring the payment of a fee (which may be a fee determined by a commons registration authority).

(Text 2.29, 2.109)

21 Official copies

(1) An official copy of, or of any part of—

(a) a register of common land or town or village greens,

(b) any document kept by a commons registration authority which is referred to in such a register, or

(c) any other document kept by a commons registration authority which relates to an application made at any time in relation to such a register, is admissible in evidence to the same extent as the original.

(2) Regulations may make provision for the issue of official copies and may in particular make provision about—

(a) the form of official copies;

(b) who may issue official copies;

(c) applications for official copies;

(d) the conditions to be met by applicants for official copies.

(3) Conditions under subsection (2)(d) may include conditions requiring the payment of a fee (which may be a fee determined by a commons registration authority).

(Text 2.32, 2.110)

Transitory and transitional provision

22 Non-registration or mistaken registration under the 1965 Act

Schedule 2 (non-registration or mistaken registration under the Commons Registration Act 1965 (c 64)) has effect.

23 Transitional

(1) Schedule 3 (transitional provision) has effect.

(2) Nothing in Schedule 3 affects the power to make transitional provision and savings in an order under section 56; and an order under that section may modify any provision made by that Schedule.

Supplementary

24 Applications etc

(1) Regulations may make provision as to the making and determination of any application for the amendment of a register of common land or town or village greens under or for the purposes of this Part.

(2) Regulations under subsection (1) may in particular make provision as to—
(a) the steps to be taken by a person before making an application;
(b) the form of an application;
(c) the information or evidence to be supplied with an application;
(d) the fee payable on an application (which may be a fee determined by the person to whom the application is made);
(e) the persons to be notified of an application;
(f) the publication of an application;
(g) the making of objections to an application;
(h) the persons who must be consulted, or whose advice must be sought, in relation to an application;
(i) the holding of an inquiry before determination of an application;
(j) the evidence to be taken into account in making a determination and the weight to be given to any evidence;
(k) the persons to be notified of any determination;
(l) the publication of a determination;
(m) the amendments to be made by a commons registration authority to a register of common land or town or village greens pursuant to a determination;
(n) the time at which any such amendments are to be regarded as having been made.

(3) In the case of an application made for the purposes of any of—
(a) sections 6 to 8, 12 and 13,
(b) paragraph 1 or 3 of Schedule 1,
(c) paragraph 2 or 3 of Schedule 2, and
(d) paragraph 2(5)(a) of Schedule 3, regulations under subsection (1) may make provision as to the persons entitled to make the application.

(4) An application made for the purposes of any of—
- (a) sections 6, 7, 10, 11, 12, 13 and 15, and
- (b) paragraph 1 or 3 of Schedule 1, shall, subject to any provision made by or under this Part, be granted.

(5) Regulations under subsection (1) may include provision for the appropriate national authority to appoint a person to discharge any or all of its functions in relation to an application made to it under section 16.

(6) Regulations may make provision as to the making and determination of any proposal by a commons registration authority to amend a register on its own initiative pursuant to section 19, Schedule 2 or paragraph 2(5)(b) of Schedule 3.

(7) Regulations under subsection (6) may in particular make provision as to—
- (a) the persons to be notified of a proposal;
- (b) the publication of a proposal (and the information or evidence to be published with a proposal);
- (c) the making of objections to a proposal;
- (d) the persons who must be consulted, or whose advice must be sought, in relation to a proposal;
- (e) the holding of an inquiry before determination of a proposal;
- (f) the evidence to be taken into account in making a determination and the weight to be given to any evidence;
- (g) the persons to be notified of any determination;
- (h) the publication of a determination;
- (i) the amendments to be made by a commons registration authority to a register of common land or town or village greens pursuant to a determination.

(8) Regulations under this section may include provision for—
- (a) the appropriate national authority to appoint persons as eligible to discharge functions of a commons registration authority in relation to applications made to, or proposals made by, the commons registration authority; and
- (b) the appointment of one or more of those persons to discharge functions of the commons registration authority in the case of any description of application or proposal.

(9) Regulations under this section may provide for the Church Commissioners to act with respect to any land or rights belonging to an ecclesiastical benefice of the Church of England which is vacant.

(Text 2.33, 2.47, 2.125, 2.130, 2.141)

25 Electronic registers

(1) Regulations may require or permit the whole or any part of a register kept under this Part to be kept in electronic form.

(2) Regulations under subsection (1) may include provision as to—
- (a) requirements to be complied with in relation to the recording of information in electronic form;

(b) the certification of information recorded in electronic form (including the status of print-outs of such information).

(3) Regulations under subsection (1) may also include provision as to the process of converting a register, or part of a register, into electronic form.

(4) The provision referred to in subsection (3) includes in particular provision—
(a) as to the publicity to be given to such a conversion;
(b) requiring a provisional electronic version to be made available for inspection and comment;
(c) as to the holding of an inquiry in relation to any question arising as a result of the conversion.

(Text 2.34, 2.143)

PART 2

MANAGEMENT

Commons councils

26 Establishment

(1) The appropriate national authority may, for any area or areas of land to which this section applies, establish a body corporate to carry out functions conferred under this Part.

(2) This section applies to any land that—
(a) is registered as common land; or
(b) is registered as a town or village green and is subject to rights of common.

(3) A body corporate established under this section is to be known as a 'commons council'.

(4) A commons council is to be established by order.

(5) An order establishing a commons council must specify—
(a) the name of the council;
(b) the area or areas of land for which the council is established.

27 Procedure for establishment

(1) This section applies where the appropriate national authority proposes to make an order under section 26 establishing a commons council.

(2) The appropriate national authority must—
(a) publish a draft of the proposed order in such manner as it thinks fit; and
(b) invite representations about it.

(3) The appropriate national authority may cause a local inquiry to be held.

(4) The appropriate national authority may not make the proposed order unless, having regard to—
(a) any representations received pursuant to subsection (2)(b), and
(b) the result of any local inquiry held under subsection (3), it is satisfied that

there is substantial support for the making of the order.

(5) For the purposes of subsection (4) the appropriate national authority must have particular regard to representations received pursuant to subsection (2)(b) from—

(a) persons having rights (other than rights of common) in relation to, or occupying, land specified in the draft order;
(b) persons who are entitled to exercise rights of common (and in particular persons exercising rights of common) over any such land; and
(c) persons with functions under an enactment which relate to the maintenance or management of any such land.

Status and constitution of commons councils

28 Status

(1) A commons council is not to be regarded as the servant or agent of the Crown or as enjoying any status, immunity or privilege of the Crown.

(2) The property of a commons council is not to be regarded as the property of, or as property held on behalf of, the Crown.

(3) A commons council is not to be regarded as an authority to which section 28G of the Wildlife and Countryside Act 1981 (c 69) applies.

29 Constitution

(1) The appropriate national authority must by regulations prescribe standard terms as to the constitution and administration of commons councils (in this Part, the 'standard constitution').

(2) The terms of the standard constitution apply to every commons council, subject as follows.

(3) An order under section 26 may also make provision as to the constitution and administration of a commons council.

(4) Provision which may be made under subsection (3) includes in particular—

(a) provision supplementary to any term of the standard constitution;
(b) provision disapplying any such term;
(c) provision replacing any such term.

(5) Where in relation to a commons council—

(a) provision is made under subsection (3) that is inconsistent with any term of the standard constitution, and
(b) any such term has not been expressly disapplied under that subsection, the provision made under subsection (3) prevails, to the extent of the inconsistency, over the term of the standard constitution.

(6) Terms of the standard constitution prescribed by regulations under subsection (1) may be amended by further regulations under that subsection; and this section applies in relation to such terms as amended as it applies in relation to the terms as first prescribed.

30 Constitution: supplementary

(1) This section applies in relation to terms as to the constitution and administration of a commons council contained in—
- (a) the standard constitution; or
- (b) an order under section 26.

(2) The terms may in particular include terms as to—
- (a) the membership of the council;
- (b) participation in the council by persons other than members;
- (c) the proceedings of the council;
- (d) the keeping and publication of accounts, annual reports and other information relating to the council.

(3) The terms referred to in subsection (2)(a) include in particular terms as to—
- (a) the appointment of members (by election or otherwise);
- (b) the term for which members are appointed;
- (c) co-option of members;
- (d) the conduct of members;
- (e) resignation and disqualification of members;
- (f) termination and renewal of membership;
- (g) payment of allowances to members.

(4) The terms referred to in subsection (2)(b) include in particular terms as to—
- (a) entitlement to elect members;
- (b) entitlement to attend meetings.

(5) The terms referred to in subsection (2)(c) include in particular terms as to—
- (a) the frequency of meetings;
- (b) voting procedures at meetings;
- (c) committees and subcommittees.

(6) The terms referred to in subsection (2)(d) include in particular terms as to—
- (a) the appointment of auditors;
- (b) the preparation and publication of accounts;
- (c) the preparation and publication of annual reports.

(7) Subject to any terms made of the kind referred to in subsection (2)(c), a commons council may regulate its own proceedings.

Functions of commons councils

31 Functions

(1) An order under section 26 is to confer on a commons council functions relating to any one or more of the following—
- (a) the management of agricultural activities on the land for which the council is established;
- (b) the management of vegetation on the land;
- (c) the management of rights of common on the land.

(2) The functions conferred on a commons council under subsection (1) must

be those the appropriate national authority considers appropriate in the case of that council.

(3) The functions which may be conferred on a commons council under subsection (1) include in particular functions of—

(a) making rules relating to agricultural activities, the management of vegetation and the exercise of rights of common on the land for which the council is established;
(b) making rules relating to the leasing or licensing of rights of common;
(c) preparing and maintaining a register of grazing;
(d) establishing and maintaining boundaries;
(e) removing unlawful boundaries and other encroachments;
(f) removing animals unlawfully permitted to graze.

(4) Rules made by virtue of subsection (3)(a) may have the effect of—

(a) limiting or imposing conditions on the exercise of rights of common over, or the exercise of rights to use the surplus of, the land for which the council is established;
(b) requiring the provision of information to the commons council in relation to the exercise of those rights.

(5) In exercising a function conferred under subsection (3)(f), a commons council may—

(a) dispose of any animal it removes; and
(b) recover from the owner of the animal the costs that it may reasonably incur in removing and disposing of it.

(6) A commons council must discharge its functions having regard to—

(a) any guidance given by the appropriate national authority; and
(b) the public interest in relation to the land for which it is established.

(7) The reference in subsection (6)(b) to the public interest includes the public interest in—

(a) nature conservation;
(b) the conservation of the landscape;
(c) the protection of public rights of access to any area of land; and
(d) the protection of archaeological remains and features of historic interest.

32 Ancillary powers

(1) A commons council has the power to do anything which it considers will facilitate, or is conducive or incidental to, the carrying out of its functions.

(2) The power conferred by subsection (1) includes power to—

(a) enter into agreements;
(b) prepare and adopt management plans;
(c) raise money (including by applying for funds from any source);
(d) acquire or dispose of land;
(e) employ staff.

(3) The power of a commons council to raise money as specified in subsection

(2)(c) includes power to require the payment of fees in connection with—
(a) the exercise of rights of common over, or the exercise of rights to use the surplus of, the land for which the council is established, and
(b) participation in the council, and any such fees owed to the council may be recovered as a debt due to it.

33 Consent

(1) Subject to subsections (2) and (3), nothing in this Part authorises a commons council to do anything on the land for which it is established without the consent of a person with an interest in the land, where that person's consent would otherwise be required.

(2) A commons council does not need the consent of a person who has a right of common over the land for which it is established in order to do anything on the land.

(3) A commons council does not need the consent of any other person with an interest in the land for which it is established in order to do anything on the land where what is proposed to be done could be done without that person's consent by any person who has a right of common over the land.

(4) Where a commons council wishes to obtain the consent of any person with an interest in the land for which the council is established in respect of anything it proposes to do on the land, it may serve a notice on him.

(5) A notice under subsection (4) must specify—
  (a) what the commons council proposes to do;
  (b) the time within which the person on whom it is served may object (which may not be less than 28 days after service of the notice); and
  (c) the manner in which he may object.

(6) If the person on whom a notice under subsection (4) is served does not object within the time and in the manner specified in the notice, he is to be regarded as having given his consent in relation to the proposal specified in the notice.

(7) Where a commons council proposes to serve a notice on a person under subsection (4) but is unable after reasonable enquiry to ascertain his name or proper address—
  (a) the council may post the notice on the land; and
  (b) the notice is to be treated as having been served on the person at the time the notice is posted.

(8) An order under section 26 may make further provision as to the form and service of notices under subsection (4).

(9) For the purposes of this section, a person with an interest in any land is a person who—
  (a) owns the land; or
  (b) is entitled to exercise any right over the land.

34 Enforcement of rules

(1) A person who breaches a rule to which subsection (2) applies is guilty of an offence.

(2) This subsection applies to a rule which—
- (a) is made with the consent of the appropriate national authority pursuant to a function of making rules conferred on a commons council under section 31; and
- (b) specifies that a person who contravenes it is guilty of an offence under this section.

(3) A person guilty of an offence under subsection (1) is liable on summary conviction to—
- (a) a fine not exceeding level 4 on the standard scale; and
- (b) in the case of a continuing offence, to a further fine not exceeding one half of level 1 on the standard scale for each day during which the offence continues after conviction.

(4) A commons council may bring proceedings in relation to an offence under subsection (1) in respect of breach of any rule made by it to which subsection (2) applies.

(5) A commons council may apply to a county court for an order to secure compliance with any rule that it has made pursuant to a function of making rules conferred on it under section 31.

(6) But a commons council may only make an application under subsection (5) for the purpose of securing compliance with a rule to which subsection (2) applies if it is of the opinion that proceedings for an offence under subsection (1) would provide an ineffectual remedy against the person who has failed to comply with the rule.

(7) On an application under subsection (5) the court may make such an order as it thinks fit.

35 Rules: supplementary

(1) Any power to make rules conferred on a commons council under section 31 includes power to vary or revoke the rules made by the council.

(2) An order under section 26 conferring a power to make rules may provide for the procedure to be followed in the exercise of the power (and may in particular require the consent of the appropriate national authority to be obtained before rules are made).

(3) The appropriate national authority may by direction revoke any rule made by a commons council.

(4) A direction under subsection (3) must set out the reason why the rule is being revoked.

(5) Before revoking any rule under subsection (3) the appropriate national

authority must consult—
- (a) the commons council; and
- (b) any other person it thinks appropriate.

Commons councils: supplementary

36 Consequential provision

(1) The appropriate national authority may by order under section 26 make any provision specified in subsection (2) if it appears to the authority desirable to do so in consequence of functions conferred on a commons council in relation to any land.

(2) The provision referred to in subsection (1) is provision to—
- (a) vary or abolish the jurisdiction so far as relating to the land of any court of a description referred to in Part 1 of Schedule 4 to the Administration of Justice Act 1977 (c 38) (certain ancient courts);
- (b) vary or revoke any regulations or arrangement made under the Commons Act 1908 (c 44);
- (c) vary or revoke any scheme made under the Commons Act 1899 (c 30), or any arrangement arising under such a scheme;
- (d) vary or revoke any Act made under the Commons Act 1876 (c 56) confirming a provisional order of the Inclosure Commissioners or any arrangement arising under such an Act;
- (e) vary or revoke any local or personal Act, or any scheme or arrangement under such an Act, which relates to the management or maintenance of, or the exercise of rights of common over, the land.

(3) The appropriate national authority may not under subsection (1) make provision specified in subsection (2)(c) to (e) to the extent that to do so would have the effect of abolishing or restricting a right of access of whatever nature exercisable by members of the public generally or by any section of the public.

(Text 4.12, 4.19, 4.34, 4.51, 4.55, 4.57)

37 Variation and revocation of establishment orders

(1) The appropriate national authority may by order under section 26 revoke a previous order under that section establishing a commons council only if it is satisfied that—
- (a) the council has ceased to operate;
- (b) the council is failing to discharge its functions in an effective manner; or
- (c) the council is, in discharging its functions, failing to have sufficient regard to the public interest as required by section 31.

(2) An order under section 26 revoking a previous order under that section may include—
- (a) provision for the transfer of rights, property and liabilities of the commons council;
- (b) provision amending any enactment previously amended under section 36 in relation to the council.

(3) Section 27 applies to an order under section 26 varying or revoking a

previous order under that section as it applies to an order under that section establishing a commons council (but as if the references in section 27 to land specified in the order were to land affected by the variation or revocation).

(Text 4.50-51)

PART 3

WORKS

38 Prohibition on works without consent

(1) A person may not, except with the consent of the appropriate national authority, carry out any restricted works on land to which this section applies.

(2) In subsection (1) 'restricted works' are—
- (a) works which have the effect of preventing or impeding access to or over any land to which this section applies;
- (b) works for the resurfacing of land.

(3) The reference to works in subsection (2)(a) includes in particular—
- (a) the erection of fencing;
- (b) the construction of buildings and other structures;
- (c) the digging of ditches and trenches and the building of embankments.

(4) For the purposes of subsection (2)(b) works are for the resurfacing of land if they consist of the laying of concrete, tarmacadam, coated roadstone or similar material on the land (but not if they consist only of the repair of an existing surface of the land made of such material).

(5) This section applies to—
- (a) any land registered as common land;
- (b) land not so registered which is—
  - (i) regulated by an Act made under the Commons Act 1876 (c 56) confirming a provisional order of the Inclosure Commissioners; or
  - (ii) subject to a scheme under the Metropolitan Commons Act 1866 (c 122) or the Commons Act 1899 (c 30);
- (c) land not falling within paragraph (a) or (b) which is in the New Forest and is subject to rights of common.

(6) The prohibition in subsection (1) does not apply to—
- (a) works on any land where those works, or works of a description which includes those works, are carried out under a power conferred in relation to that particular land by or under any enactment;
- (b) works on any land where the works are carried out under a power conferred by or under any enactment applying to common land;
- (c) works authorised under a scheme under the Metropolitan Commons Act 1866 or the Commons Act 1899 without any requirement for any person to consent to the works;
- (d) works for the installation of electronic communications apparatus for the purposes of an electronic communications code network.

(7) In subsection (6)(a) the reference to an enactment does not include Part 2 of this Act.

(8) For the purposes of subsection (6)(b), an enactment applies to common land if it is expressed to apply (generally) to—

(a) registered common land;

(b) common land; or

(c) any common or commons, commonable land, land subject to inclosure under any enactment or other land of a similar description.

(9) Subject to the following provisions of this Part, consent given to works under subsection (1) of this section constitutes consent for the purposes of that subsection only.

(Text 3.10-11, 3.20, 4.3, 6.1, 6.62-71)

39 Consent: general

(1) In determining an application for consent under subsection (1) of section 38 in relation to works on land to which that section applies, the appropriate national authority shall have regard to—

(a) the interests of persons having rights in relation to, or occupying, the land (and in particular persons exercising rights of common over it);

(b) the interests of the neighbourhood;

(c) the public interest;

(d) any other matter considered to be relevant.

(2) The reference in subsection (1)(c) to the public interest includes the public interest in—

(a) nature conservation;

(b) the conservation of the landscape;

(c) the protection of public rights of access to any area of land; and

(d) the protection of archaeological remains and features of historic interest.

(3) Consent may be given under section 38(1)—

(a) in relation to all or part of the proposed works;

(b) subject to such modifications and conditions relating to the proposed works as the appropriate national authority thinks fit.

(4) In considering the effect in relation to any land of proposed works under this section, the appropriate national authority may consider that effect in conjunction with the effect in relation to that land of any other works for which consent has previously been given under section 38(1) above or section 194 of the Law of Property Act 1925 (c 20).

(5) Where the appropriate national authority imposes any modification or condition in relation to any consent given under section 38(1), it may on the application of any person carrying out or proposing to carry out works in accordance with the consent vary or revoke that modification or condition.

(6) Regulations may specify a time limit for the making of applications under subsection (5).

(7) Consent may be given under section 38(1) in relation to works which have been commenced or completed; and any consent so given has effect from the time of commencement of the works.

(Text 6.65, 6.69)

40 Consent: procedure

(1) Regulations may make provision as to the procedure to be followed in the making and determination of applications under sections 38(1) and 39(5).

(2) Regulations under this section may in particular include provision—
(a) as to the steps to be taken by an applicant before submitting an application;
(b) as to the form and content of an application;
(c) as to the procedure to be followed in making an application;
(d) as to the evidence to be supplied in support of an application;
(e) as to the fees payable in relation to an application;
(f) as to the steps to be taken by the appropriate national authority upon receipt of an application;
(g) for the appointment by the appropriate national authority of a person to discharge any (or all) of its functions in relation to the determination of an application;
(h) for the making of representations or objections in relation to an application;
(i) for the holding of a hearing or local inquiry in relation to an application;
(j) for the publication of a determination of an application and the notification of interested persons.

(Text 6.72)

41 Enforcement

(1) Where any works are carried out on land to which section 38 applies in contravention of subsection (1) of that section, any person may apply to the county court in whose area the land is situated.

(2) On an application under this section the court may make an order—
(a) in any case, for removal of the works and restoration of the land to the condition it was in before the works were carried out;
(b) in a case where consent has been given under section 38(1) but the works have not been carried out in accordance with any term of that consent, for the works to be carried out in such manner and subject to such conditions as the order may specify.

(Text 6.73)

42 Schemes

(1) This section applies in relation to works on relevant land where, by virtue of section 38(1), the works may not be carried out without the consent of the appropriate national authority.

(2) In subsection (1) 'relevant land' means land which is subject to—
(a) a scheme under the Metropolitan Commons Act 1866 (c 122) which is in force at the commencement of this section; or

(b) a scheme under the Commons Act 1899 (c 30) which is in force at the commencement of this section.

(3) Where—

(a) any provision of the scheme referred to in subsection (2) would also prohibit the carrying out of the works, and

(b) the scheme does not allow for any person to consent to the works to be carried out, the works do not contravene that provision if they are carried out with (and in accordance with the terms of) the consent of the appropriate national authority under section 38(1) and of any owner of the land (if not the person carrying out the works).

(4) Regulations may make provision as to the procedure to be followed in obtaining the consent of an owner under subsection (3) (and may include provision for the consent of an owner to be regarded as having been given where he has not objected within a period of time specified in the regulations).

(5) Where any provision of the scheme referred to in subsection (2) would also prohibit the carrying out of the works without the consent of the appropriate national authority—

(a) consent given under section 38(1) is to be regarded as consent given under the scheme; and

(b) consent may not be sought separately under the scheme.

(Text 6.74)

43 Power to exempt

(1) The appropriate national authority may by order provide that section 38 is not to apply to—

(a) the carrying out by a specified person of specified works on specified land; or

(b) the carrying out by a specified person, or a person of a specified description, of works of a specified description on—

(i) any land; or

(ii) land of a specified description.

(2) The appropriate national authority may only make an order under subsection (1)(a) if it is satisfied that the works specified in the order are necessary or expedient for any of the purposes in subsection (4).

(3) The appropriate national authority may only make an order under subsection (1)(b) if it is satisfied that works of the description specified in the order are likely to be necessary or expedient on any land, or on land of the description specified in the order, for any of the purposes in subsection (4).

(4) The purposes referred to in subsections (2) and (3) are—

(a) use of land by members of the public for the purposes of open-air recreation pursuant to any right of access;

(b) the exercise of rights of common;

(c) nature conservation;

(d) the protection of archaeological remains or features of historic interest;

(e) the use of the land for sporting or recreational purposes.

(5) Where—

(a) any land was at any time before the commencement of this section land to which section 194 of the Law of Property Act 1925 (c 20) applied, but

(b) at any such time that section ceased to apply to the land by virtue of subsection (3)(a) of that section, the appropriate national authority may by order provide that section 38 is not to apply to the carrying out of works, or works of a description specified in the order, on that land.

(6) Where any land is the subject of a resolution under section 194(3)(b) of the Law of Property Act 1925 (c 20) immediately before the commencement of this section, the appropriate national authority may by order provide that section 38 is not to apply to the carrying out of works, or works of a description specified in the order, on that land.

(7) An order under this section may provide that section 38 is not to apply only if the works to which the order relates are carried out in accordance with the terms of the order.

(8) In subsection (1) 'specified' means specified in an order under that subsection.

(Text 6.75)

44 Supplementary

(1) Schedule 4 (which makes supplementary provision relating to works on common land) has effect.

(2) A national authority may for any purpose specified in subsection (3) by order amend—

(a) any local or personal Act passed before this Act which contains provision for that authority to consent to works on land which is common land; and

(b) any Act made under the Commons Act 1876 (c 56) confirming a provisional order of the Inclosure Commissioners which contains provision for that authority to consent to works on land to which the Act applies.

(3) The purposes referred to in subsection (2) are—

(a) that of securing that sections 39 and 40 apply to an application for the consent referred to in paragraph (a) or (b) of subsection (2) as they apply to an application for consent under section 38(1);

(b) that of securing that section 41 applies in relation to the carrying out of works in contravention of the provision referred to in paragraph (a) or (b) of subsection (2) as it applies to works carried out in contravention of section 38(1).

(4) In subsection (2)—

'national authority' means—

(a) the Secretary of State; and

(b) the National Assembly for Wales;

'common land' means—

(a) any land registered as common land; and

(b) any land not so registered which is subject to a scheme under the Metropolitan Commons Act 1866 (c 122) or the Commons Act 1899 (c 30).

(Text 6.76)

PART 4

MISCELLANEOUS

Intervention powers

45 Powers of local authorities over unclaimed land

(1) This section applies where—
  (a) land is registered as common land or a town or village green;
  (b) no person is registered in the register of title as the owner of the land; and
  (c) it appears to a local authority in whose area the land or any part of it is situated that the owner cannot be identified.

(2) The local authority may—
  (a) take any steps to protect the land against unlawful interference that could be taken by an owner in possession of the land; and
  (b) institute proceedings against any person for any offence committed in respect of the land (but without prejudice to any power exercisable apart from this section).

(3) In this section 'local authority' means—
  (a) a county, district or parish council in England;
  (b) a London borough council; and
  (c) a county, county borough or community council in Wales.

(Text 2.38, 2.51, 2.53, 4.63)

46 Powers relating to unauthorised agricultural activities

(1) This section applies where it appears to the appropriate national authority that—
  (a) a person is carrying out, or causing to be carried out by virtue of any arrangements, an agricultural activity on land which—
    (i) is registered as common land; or
    (ii) is registered as a town or village green and is subject to rights of common;
  (b) the activity is unauthorised; and
  (c) the activity is detrimental to—
    (i) the interests of persons having rights in relation to, or occupying, the land; or
    (ii) the public interest.

(2) The appropriate national authority may, subject to the following provisions of this section, serve a notice on the person requiring him to do any one or more of the following—
  (a) within such reasonable period as may be specified in the notice to stop carrying out the activity, or stop causing it to be carried out, to the extent that it is unauthorised;
  (b) not to carry out, or cause to be carried out, any other unauthorised agricultural activity on the land which would be detrimental to the matters specified in subsection (1)(c)(i) and (ii);

(c) to supply the authority with such information relating to agricultural activities on the land carried out, or caused to be carried out, by him as it may reasonably require.

(3) Before serving a notice under this section the appropriate national authority must, to the extent that it is appropriate and practicable in all the circumstances to do so—

(a) notify the persons specified in subsection (4) of its intention to serve the notice; and
(b) publicise its intention to do so (in such manner as it thinks fit).

(4) The persons referred to in subsection (3)(a) are—

(a) any commons council for the land;
(b) any other person with functions under any enactment which relate to the maintenance or management of the land; and
(c) any person appearing to the authority to own or occupy the land.

(5) Any notification or publication under subsection (3) may specify a period within which representations about the proposed notice may be made.

(6) In deciding whether to serve a notice under this section the appropriate national authority must have regard to—

(a) any criminal or civil proceedings that have been or may be commenced in relation to the activity; and
(b) any steps taken by a commons council in relation to the activity.

(7) If a person on whom a notice is served under this section fails to comply with it—

(a) the appropriate national authority may apply to a county court for an order requiring him to do so; and
(b) the court may make such an order for the purpose of securing compliance with the notice as it thinks fit.

(8) For the purposes of this section, activity is unauthorised if the person carrying it out or causing it to be carried out—

(a) has no right or entitlement by virtue of his ownership or occupation of the land, or pursuant to any right of common, to do so; or
(b) is not doing so with the authority of the person or persons entitled to give such authority.

(9) The reference in subsection (1)(c)(ii) to the public interest includes the public interest in—

(a) nature conservation;
(b) the conservation of the landscape;
(c) the protection of public rights of access to any area of land; and
(d) the protection of archaeological remains and features of historic interest.

(10) Section 123(1) to (5) of the Environment Act 1995 (c 25) applies in relation to the service of a notice under this section as it applies in relation to the service of a notice under that Act.

(Text 4.65)

Abolition of powers of approvement and inclosure etc

47 Approvement

(1) The Commons Act 1285 (13 Edw 1 c 46) (power of approvement) shall cease to have effect.

(2) Any power of approvement of a common which subsists at common law is abolished.

48 Inclosure

(1) Section 147 of the Inclosure Act 1845 (c 118) (power to exchange common land for other land) shall cease to have effect.

(2) The following shall cease to have effect—
  (a) section 2 of the Gifts for Churches Act 1811 (c 115);
  (b) in section 2 of the School Sites Act 1841 (c 38), the words from 'Provided also, that where any portion' to 'such conveyance;';
  (c) in section 1 of the Literary and Scientific Institutions Act 1854 (c 112), the words from 'Provided also' to the end.

49 Notice of inclosure

(1) Section 31 of the Commons Act 1876 (c 56) (three months' notice of claim to inclose to be given in local papers) shall cease to have effect.

(2) In section 3 of the Metropolitan Commons Act 1878 (c 71), for 'Sections thirty and thirty-one' substitute 'Section 30'.

Commons Act 1899

50 Schemes under the Commons Act 1899

(1) The Commons Act 1899 (c 30) is amended as follows.

(2) In section 1 (power of councils to make schemes for the regulation of commons)—
  (a) in subsection (1), for the words from 'their district' to the end substitute 'in the public interest';
  (b) after that subsection insert—
  '(1A) In subsection (1), the reference to the public interest includes the public interest in—
    (a) nature conservation;
    (b) the conservation of the landscape;
    (c) the protection of public rights of access to any area of land; and
    (d) the protection of archaeological remains and features of historic interest.'

(3) In that section, in subsection (3), omit the words from ', and for' to the end.

(4) In that section, after subsection (3) insert—
  '(4) Regulations under subsection (3) may—
    (a) prescribe alternative forms;

(b) permit exceptions or modifications to be made to any prescribed form.'

(5) In section 2 (procedure for making scheme)—

(a) for subsections (1) to (3) and the first paragraph of subsection (4) substitute—

'(1) A council is to make and approve a scheme under this Part of this Act in the prescribed manner.';

(b) renumber the second paragraph of subsection (4) as subsection (2).

(6) For section 9 (power to amend scheme) substitute—

'9 Power to amend or revoke scheme

(1) A scheme under this Part of this Act for any common may, in prescribed circumstances, be amended in the prescribed manner.

(2) A scheme under this Part of this Act for any common may, where a new scheme is made under this Part of this Act for the whole of that common, be revoked in the prescribed manner.'

(7) For section 10 (byelaws) substitute—

'10 Byelaws

(1) A council which has made a scheme under this Part of this Act in relation to any common may make byelaws for the prevention of nuisances and the preservation of order on the common.

(2) Sections 236 to 238 of the Local Government Act 1972 (which relate to the procedure for making byelaws, authorise byelaws to impose fines not exceeding level 2 on the standard scale, and provide for the proof of byelaws in legal proceedings) apply to all byelaws under this section.'

(Text 4.13, 4.20)

Vehicular access

51 Vehicular access

Section 68 of the Countryside and Rights of Way Act 2000 (c 37) shall cease to have effect.

(Text 3.12, 3.38, 3.44)

PART 5

SUPPLEMENTARY AND GENERAL

Amendments and repeals

52 Minor and consequential amendments

Schedule 5 (minor and consequential amendments) has effect.

53 Repeals

Schedule 6 (repeals, including consequential repeals and repeals of spent and obsolete enactments) has effect.

(Text 2.5, 2.14, 2.19, 2.111, 2.120, 3.14, 3.38, 3.44, 4.15, 6.7, 7.18)

54 Power to amend enactments relating to common land or greens

(1) The appropriate national authority may by order amend any relevant Act so as to secure that—

(a) a provision of that Act applying to common land does not apply to land to which Part 1 applies and which is not registered as common land;

(b) such a provision applies to either or both of the following—

(i) land registered as common land, or particular descriptions or areas of such land;

(ii) land to which Part 1 does not apply, or particular descriptions or areas of such land.

(2) The appropriate national authority may by order amend any relevant Act so as to secure that—

(a) a provision of that Act which is expressed to apply to a town or village green does not apply to land to which Part 1 applies and which is not registered as a town or village green;

(b) such a provision applies to either or both of the following—

(i) land registered as a town or village green, or particular descriptions or areas of such land;

(ii) land to which Part 1 does not apply, or particular descriptions or areas of such land.

(3) In this section, 'relevant Act' means any public general Act passed before this Act.

(4) For the purposes of subsection (1) a provision applies to common land if it is expressed to apply (generally) to common land, any common or commons, commonable land, land subject to inclosure under any enactment or other land of a similar description.

(Text 2.74)

55 Power to amend enactments conferring functions on national authorities

(1) A national authority may by order amend or repeal any provision of a local or personal Act passed before this Act which applies to common land for any of the following purposes—

(a) to remove any function of the national authority which relates to the common land;

(b) to transfer such a function from the national authority to another person;

(c) to remove a requirement that the national authority be consulted, or that its consent be obtained, in respect of—

(i) any act or omission relating to the common land; or

(ii) any act or omission of a person concerned with the management of the common land;

(d) to substitute for a requirement referred to in paragraph (c) a requirement that a person other than the national authority be consulted, or his consent obtained, in relation to the act or omission.

(2) In subsection (1), 'common land' means—
(a) any land registered as common land or as a town or village green;
(b) any land referred to in section 5(2); and
(c) any land not falling within paragraph (a) or (b) which is subject to a scheme under the Metropolitan Commons Act 1866 (c 122) or the Commons Act 1899 (c 30).

(3) A national authority may by order amend or repeal any provision of an Act made under the Commons Act 1876 (c 56) confirming a provisional order of the Inclosure Commissioners for any of the following purposes—
(a) to remove any function of the national authority which relates to land to which the Act applies;
(b) to transfer such a function from the national authority to another person;
(c) to remove a requirement that the national authority be consulted, or that its consent be obtained, in respect of—
  (i) any act or omission relating to land to which the Act applies; or
  (ii) any act or omission of a person concerned with the management of such land;
(d) to substitute for a requirement referred to in paragraph (c) a requirement that a person other than the national authority be consulted, or his consent obtained, in relation to the act or omission.

(4) In this section 'national authority' means—
(a) the Secretary of State; and
(b) the National Assembly for Wales.

(Text 2.1)

Commencement and transitional provision

56 Commencement

(1) The preceding provisions of this Act, except section 9 and Schedule 1 and sections 54 and 55, come into force in accordance with provision made by order by the appropriate national authority.

(2) Sections 54 and 55 come into force at the end of the period of two months beginning with the day on which this Act is passed.

57 Severance: transitional

(1) In relation to any area of England and Wales, the reference in subsection (1) of section 9 to a register of common land or town or village greens shall, during the relevant period in relation to that area, be read as a reference to such a register kept under the Commons Registration Act 1965 (c 64).

(2) Subparagraph (6) of paragraph 1 of Schedule 1 shall not have effect in relation to a right of common severed (in accordance with that paragraph) from land in any area of England and Wales during the relevant period in relation to that area.

(3) In this section, the 'relevant period', in relation to an area of England and

Wales, is the period which—
(a) begins with the coming into force of this section; and
(b) ends with the coming into force of section 1 in relation to that area.

(4) This section is deemed to have come into force on 28 June 2005.

58 Natural England

Any reference in a provision of this Act to Natural England shall, in relation to any time after the coming into force of that provision but before the coming into force of section 1(4) of the Natural Environment and Rural Communities Act 2006, be read as a reference to English Nature.

General

59 Orders and regulations

(1) An order or regulations under this Act may make—
(a) transitional, consequential, incidental and supplemental provision or savings;
(b) different provision for different purposes or areas.

(2) An order or regulations under this Act, other than an order under section 17, must be made by statutory instrument.

(3) A statutory instrument containing regulations under section 29(1) or an order under section 54 or 55 may not be made by the Secretary of State (alone or jointly with the National Assembly for Wales) unless a draft has been laid before and approved by a resolution of each House of Parliament.

(4) Subject to subsection (3), a statutory instrument containing any order or regulations made under this Act by the Secretary of State (alone or jointly with the National Assembly for Wales) other than an order under section 56 shall be subject to annulment in pursuance of a resolution of either House of Parliament.

60 Crown application

(1) This Act (and any provision made under it) binds the Crown.

(2) This section does not impose criminal liability on the Crown in relation to an offence under section 34(1).

(3) Subsection (2) does not affect the criminal liability of persons in the service of the Crown.

61 Interpretation

(1) In this Act—
'appropriate national authority' means—
(a) the Secretary of State, in relation to England; and
(b) the National Assembly for Wales, in relation to Wales;
'commons council' means a commons council established under Part 2;
'land' includes land covered by water;
'nature conservation' means the conservation of flora and fauna and

geological and physiographical features;
'regulations' means regulations made by the appropriate national authority;
'register of title' means the register kept under section 1 of the Land Registration Act 2002 (c 9);
'right of common' includes a cattlegate or beastgate (by whatever name known) and a right of sole or several vesture or herbage or of sole or several pasture, but does not include a right held for a term of years or from year to year.

(2) In this Act—
(a) any reference to land registered as common land or a town or village green is to land so registered in a register of common land or town or village greens;
(b) any reference to a register of common land or town or village greens is to such a register kept under Part 1 of this Act.

(3) In this Act—
(a) references to the ownership or the owner of any land are references to the ownership of a legal estate in fee simple in the land or to the person holding that estate;
(b) references to land registered in the register of title are references to land the fee simple of which is so registered.

62 Short title

This Act may be cited as the Commons Act 2006.

63 Extent

This Act extends to England and Wales only.

SCHEDULES

SCHEDULE 1 (Section 9)

AUTHORISED SEVERANCE

Severance by transfer to public bodies

1 (1) A right of common to which section 9 applies may on or after the day on which this Schedule comes into force be severed permanently from the land to which it is attached by being transferred on its own to—
(a) any commons council established for the land over which the right is exercisable;
(b) Natural England (where the land or any part of it is in England); or
(c) the Countryside Council for Wales (where the land or any part of it is in Wales).

(2) Where a person proposes to sever a right of common to which section 9 applies by a transfer under subparagraph (1)(b) or (c), Natural England or the Countryside Council for Wales as the case may be must—
(a) give notice of the proposal to the owner of the land over which the right is exercisable unless his name and address cannot reasonably be ascertained;

(b) in a case where there is no commons council established for the land, give notice of the proposal to such persons (if any) as they consider represent the interests of persons exercising rights of common over the land.

(3) A notice under subparagraph (2) must be given at least two months before the transfer and must—

(a) specify the name and address of the owner of the land to which the right is attached;

(b) describe the right proposed to be transferred, giving such details as regulations may specify;

(c) state the proposed consideration for the transfer; and

(d) give such other information as regulations may specify.

(Text 2.71)

(4) Where a right of common to which section 9 applies is exercisable over land for which a commons council is established, the right may only be severed by a transfer under subparagraph (1)(b) or (c) if that council consents to the transfer.

(5) In a case where there is no commons council established for the land over which a right of common to which section 9 applies is exercisable, the appropriate national authority may by order provide that a person with functions of management conferred by any enactment in relation to that land is to be regarded, for any or all purposes of this paragraph, as a commons council established for the land.

(6) The severance of a right of common by its transfer under subparagraph (1)—

(a) only has effect if the transfer complies with such requirements as to form and content as regulations may provide; and

(b) does not operate at law until, on an application under this Schedule, the transferee is registered as the owner of the right in the register of common land or of town or village greens in which the right is registered.

(Text 2.71)

Temporary severance by letting or leasing

2 (1) A right of common to which section 9 applies may, on or after the day on which this Schedule comes into force, to any extent be severed temporarily from the land to which it is attached by virtue of the right, or all or part of the land, being leased or licensed on its own in accordance with—

(a) provision made by order by the appropriate national authority; or

(b) rules made in relation to the land by a commons council under section 31.

(2) Provision under subparagraph (1)(a) and rules referred to in subparagraph (1)(b) may be framed by reference to—

(a) particular land or descriptions of land;

(b) descriptions of persons to whom rights of common may be leased or licensed.

(3) Where—

(a) provision under subparagraph (1)(a) applies in relation to any land, and

(b) rules referred to in subparagraph (1)(b) also apply in relation to that land and are inconsistent with that provision,

the rules prevail over that provision, to the extent of the inconsistency, in relation to that land.

(4) The appropriate national authority may by order provide that the leasing or licensing of a right of common (whether authorised by provision under subparagraph (1)(a) or by rules referred to in subparagraph (1)(b)) must comply with such requirements as to form and content as the order may provide.

(Text 2.72)

Severance authorised by order

3 (1) The appropriate national authority may by order make provision authorising rights of common to which section 9 applies to be severed permanently from the land to which they are attached by transfer in accordance with that provision.

(2) Provision under subparagraph (1) is to be framed by reference to—

(a) particular land over which the rights of common are exercisable, or

(b) particular descriptions of such land, and may authorise transfers to particular persons, particular descriptions of persons or any person.

(3) The appropriate national authority must, before making any provision under subparagraph (1) in relation to any land, consult such persons (if any) as it considers represent the interests of—

(a) persons who own the land;

(b) persons who exercise rights of common over the land.

(4) Provision under subparagraph (1) may include provision securing that the owner of any land over which a right of common is exercisable is to be notified, and his consent obtained, before the right may be transferred.

(5) Provision referred to in subparagraph (4) may include—

(a) provision as to the circumstances in which notification may be regarded as having been given; or

(b) provision as to the circumstances in which consent may be regarded as having been obtained.

(6) Provision referred to in subparagraph (5)(b) may include—

(a) provision for consent to be regarded as having been obtained if it is withheld unreasonably;

(b) provision for the circumstances in which consent is to be regarded as withheld unreasonably;

(c) provision for the resolution of disputes.

(7) The severance of a right of common by its transfer under provision under subparagraph (1)—

(a) only has effect if the transfer complies with such requirements as to form and content as regulations may provide; and

(b) does not operate at law until, on an application under this Schedule, the transferee is registered as the owner of the right in the register of common land or of town or village greens in which the right is registered.

(8) Provision under subparagraph (1) may include provision to secure the result that where—

(a) the person to whom the right of common is transferred is the owner of land to which rights of common are attached, and
(b) those rights are exercisable over the same land, or substantially the same land, as the right of common being transferred, the transferee must, when making an application as specified in subparagraph (7)(b), apply to the commons registration authority for the right to be registered as attached to the land referred to in paragraph (a).

(Text 2.71)

SCHEDULE 2 (Section 22)

NON-REGISTRATION OR MISTAKEN REGISTRATION UNDER THE 1965 ACT

Introductory

1 In this Schedule 'the 1965 Act' means the Commons Registration Act 1965 (c 64).

Non-registration of common land

2 (1) If a commons registration authority is satisfied that any land not registered as common land or as a town or village green is land to which this paragraph applies, the authority shall, subject to this paragraph, register the land as common land in its register of common land.

(2) This paragraph applies to any land which—

(a) was not at any time finally registered as common land or as a town or village green under the 1965 Act;
(b) is land which is—
  (i) regulated by an Act made under the Commons Act 1876 (c 56) confirming a provisional order of the Inclosure Commissioners;
  (ii) subject to a scheme under Metropolitan Commons Act 1866 (c 122) or the Commons Act 1899 (c 30);
  (iii) regulated as common land under a local or personal Act; or
  (iv) otherwise recognised or designated as common land by or under an enactment;
(c) is land to which this Part applies; and
(d) satisfies such other conditions as regulations may specify.

(3) A commons registration authority may only register land under subparagraph (1) acting on—

(a) the application of any person made before such date as regulations may specify; or

(b) a proposal made and published by the authority before such date as regulations may specify.

(Text 2.118)

Non-registration of town or village green

3 (1) If a commons registration authority is satisfied that any land not registered as a town or village green or as common land is land to which this paragraph applies, the authority shall, subject to this paragraph, register the land as a town or village green in its register of town or village greens.

(2) This paragraph applies to any land which—
(a) on 31 July 1970 was land allotted by or under any Act for the exercise or recreation of the inhabitants of any locality;
(b) was not at any time finally registered as a town or village green or as common land under the 1965 Act;
(c) continues to be land allotted as specified in paragraph (a);
(d) is land to which this Part applies; and
(e) satisfies such other conditions as regulations may specify.

(3) A commons registration authority may only register land under subparagraph (1) acting on—
(a) the application of any person made before such date as regulations may specify; or
(b) a proposal made and published by the authority before such date as regulations may specify.

(Text 2.119, 7.8, 7.55)

Waste land of a manor not registered as common land

4 (1) If a commons registration authority is satisfied that any land not registered as common land or as a town or village green is land to which this paragraph applies, the authority shall, subject to this paragraph, register the land as common land in its register of common land.

(2) This paragraph applies to land which at the time of the application under subparagraph (1) is waste land of a manor and where, before the commencement of this paragraph—
(a) the land was provisionally registered as common land under section 4 of the 1965 Act;
(b) an objection was made in relation to the provisional registration; and
(c) the provisional registration was cancelled in the circumstances specified in subparagraph (3), (4) or (5).

(3) The circumstances in this subparagraph are that—
(a) the provisional registration was referred to a Commons Commissioner under section 5 of the 1965 Act;
(b) the Commissioner determined that, although the land had been waste land of a manor at some earlier time, it was not such land at the time of the determination because it had ceased to be connected with the manor; and

(c) for that reason only the Commissioner refused to confirm the provisional registration.

(4) The circumstances in this subparagraph are that—

(a) the provisional registration was referred to a Commons Commissioner under section 5 of the 1965 Act;

(b) the Commissioner determined that the land was not subject to rights of common and for that reason refused to confirm the provisional registration; and

(c) the Commissioner did not consider whether the land was waste land of a manor.

(5) The circumstances in this subparagraph are that the person on whose application the provisional registration was made requested or agreed to its cancellation (whether before or after its referral to a Commons Commissioner).

(6) A commons registration authority may only register land under subparagraph (1) acting on—

(a) the application of any person made before such date as regulations may specify; or

(b) a proposal made and published by the authority before such date as regulations may specify.

(Text 2.124, 4.29)

Town or village green wrongly registered as common land

5 (1) If a commons registration authority is satisfied that any land registered as common land is land to which this paragraph applies, the authority shall, subject to this paragraph, remove the land from its register of common land and register it in its register of town or village greens.

(2) This paragraph applies to land where—

(a) the land was provisionally registered as common land under section 4 of the 1965 Act;

(b) the provisional registration became final; but

(c) immediately before its provisional registration, the land was a town or village green within the meaning of that Act as originally enacted.

(3) A commons registration authority may only remove and register land under subparagraph (1) acting on—

(a) the application of any person made before such date as regulations may specify; or

(b) a proposal made and published by the authority before such date as regulations may specify.

(Text 7.56, 7.60)

Buildings registered as common land

6 (1) If a commons registration authority is satisfied that any land registered as common land is land to which this paragraph applies, the authority shall, subject to this paragraph, remove that land from its register of common land.

(2) This paragraph applies to land where—
- (a) the land was provisionally registered as common land under section 4 of the 1965 Act;
- (b) on the date of the provisional registration the land was covered by a building or was within the curtilage of a building;
- (c) the provisional registration became final; and
- (d) since the date of the provisional registration the land has at all times been, and still is, covered by a building or within the curtilage of a building.

(3) A commons registration authority may only remove land under subparagraph (1) acting on—
- (a) the application of any person made before such date as regulations may specify; or
- (b) a proposal made and published by the authority before such date as regulations may specify.

(Text 2.128)

Other land wrongly registered as common land

7 (1) If a commons registration authority is satisfied that any land registered as common land is land to which this paragraph applies, the authority shall, subject to this paragraph, remove the land from its register of common land.

(2) This paragraph applies to land where—
- (a) the land was provisionally registered as common land under section 4 of the 1965 Act;
- (b) the provisional registration of the land as common land was not referred to a Commons Commissioner under section 5 of the 1965 Act;
- (c) the provisional registration became final; and
- (d) immediately before its provisional registration the land was not any of the following—
  - (i) land subject to rights of common;
  - (ii) waste land of a manor;
  - (iii) a town or village green within the meaning of the 1965 Act as originally enacted; or
  - (iv) land of a description specified in section 11 of the Inclosure Act 1845 (c 118).

(3) A commons registration authority may only remove land under subparagraph (1) acting on—
- (a) the application of any person made before such date as regulations may specify; or
- (b) a proposal made and published by the authority before such date as regulations may specify.

(Text 2.129)

Buildings registered as town or village green

8 (1) If a commons registration authority is satisfied that any land registered as a town or village green is land to which this paragraph applies, the authority shall, subject to this paragraph, remove that land from its register of town or village greens.

(2) This paragraph applies to land where—

(a) the land was provisionally registered as a town or village green under section 4 of the 1965 Act;

(b) on the date of the provisional registration the land was covered by a building or was within the curtilage of a building;

(c) the provisional registration became final; and

(d) since the date of the provisional registration the land has at all times been, and still is, covered by a building or within the curtilage of a building.

(3) A commons registration authority may only remove land under subparagraph (1) acting on—

(a) the application of any person made before such date as regulations may specify; or

(b) a proposal made and published by the authority before such date as regulations may specify.

(Text 7.57)

Other land wrongly registered as town or village green

9 (1) If a commons registration authority is satisfied that any land registered as a town or village green is land to which this paragraph applies, the authority shall, subject to this paragraph, remove the land from its register of town or village greens.

(2) This paragraph applies to land where—

(a) the land was provisionally registered as a town or village green under section 4 of the 1965 Act;

(b) the provisional registration of the land as a town or village green was not referred to a Commons Commissioner under section 5 of the 1965 Act;

(c) the provisional registration became final; and

(d) immediately before its provisional registration the land was not—

(i) common land within the meaning of that Act; or

(ii) a town or village green.

(3) For the purposes of subparagraph (2)(d)(ii), land is to be taken not to have been a town or village green immediately before its provisional registration if (and only if)—

(a) throughout the period of 20 years preceding the date of its provisional registration the land was, by reason of its physical nature, unusable by members of the public for the purposes of lawful sports and pastimes; and

(b) immediately before its provisional registration the land was not, and at the time of the application under this paragraph still is not, allotted by or under any Act for the exercise or recreation of the inhabitants of any locality.

(4) A commons registration authority may only remove land under subparagraph (1) acting on—

(a) the application of any person made before such date as regulations may specify; or

(b) a proposal made and published by the authority before such date as regulations may specify.

(Text 7.59)

Costs

10 (1) Regulations may make provision as to the payment of costs which pursuant to an application under this Schedule are incurred by the applicant, an objector or the person determining the application.

(2) That provision may in particular include provision—

(a) for the payment of costs by the applicant, an objector or a commons registration authority;

(b) for the person determining an application or the appropriate national authority to determine who is liable to pay costs and how much they are liable to pay.

(Text 7.61)

(Text for whole schedule 2.25, 2.85, 2.117)

SCHEDULE 3 (Section 23)

REGISTRATION: TRANSITIONAL PROVISION

Interpretation

1 In this Schedule 'the 1965 Act' means the Commons Registration Act 1965 (c 64).

Transitional period for updating registers

2 (1) Regulations may make provision for commons registration authorities, during a period specified in the regulations ('the transitional period'), to amend their registers of common land and town or village greens in consequence of qualifying events which were not registered under the 1965 Act.

(2) The following are qualifying events for the purposes of this Schedule—

(a) the creation of a right of common (by any means, including prescription), where occurring in relation to land to which this Part applies at any time—

(i) after 2 January 1970; and

(ii) before the commencement of this paragraph;

(b) any relevant disposition in relation to a right of common registered under the 1965 Act, or any extinguishment of such a right, where occurring at any time—

(i) after the date of the registration of the right under that Act; and

(ii) before the commencement of this paragraph;

(c) a disposition occurring before the commencement of this paragraph by virtue of any relevant instrument in relation to land which at the time of the disposition was registered as common land or a town or village green under the 1965 Act;

(d) the giving of land in exchange for any land subject to a disposition referred to in paragraph (c).

(3) In subparagraph (2)(b) 'relevant disposition' means—

(a) the surrender of a right of common;

(b) the variation of a right of common;

(c) in the case of a right of common attached to land, the apportionment or severance of the right;

(d) in the case of a right not attached to land, the transfer of the right.

(4) In subparagraph (2)(c) 'relevant instrument' means—

(a) any order, deed or other instrument made under or pursuant to the Acquisition of Land Act 1981 (c 67);

(b) a conveyance made for the purposes of section 13 of the New Parishes Measure 1943 (No. 1);

(c) any other instrument made under or pursuant to any enactment.

(5) Regulations under this paragraph may include provision for commons registration authorities to amend their registers as specified in subparagraph (1)—

(a) on the application of a person specified in the regulations; or

(b) on their own initiative.

(6) Regulations under subparagraph (5)(b) may include provision requiring a commons registration authority to take steps to discover information relating to qualifying events, including in particular requiring an authority to—

(a) carry out a review of information already contained in a register of common land or town or village greens;

(b) publicise the review;

(c) invite persons to supply information for, or to apply for amendment of, the register.

(Text 2.133)

3 At the end of the transitional period, any right of common which—

(a) is not registered in a register of common land or town or village greens, but

(b) was capable of being so registered under paragraph 2,

is by virtue of this paragraph at that time extinguished.

4 (1) Regulations may make provision for commons registration authorities to amend their registers of common land or town or village greens after the end of the transitional period, in circumstances specified in the regulations, in consequence of qualifying events.

(2) Regulations under this paragraph may provide that paragraph 3 is to be treated as not having applied to any right of common which is registered

pursuant to the regulations.

5 Regulations under paragraph 2 or 4 may in particular include provision as to what is or is not to be regarded as severance of a right of common for the purposes of those regulations.

Effect of repeals

6 The repeal by this Act of section 1(2)(b) of the 1965 Act does not affect the extinguishment of rights of common occurring by virtue of that provision.

7 The repeal by this Act of section 21(1) of the 1965 Act does not affect the application of section 193 of the Law of Property Act 1925 (c 20) in relation to any land.

(Text 4.27, 4.30, 6.7)

Ownership of common land or town or village green

8 (1) Where the ownership of any land is registered in any register under the 1965 Act immediately before the commencement of this Schedule the ownership shall, subject to this Part, continue to be registered in that register.

(2) Where the ownership of land continues to be registered in a register of common land or town or village greens pursuant to subparagraph (1), if the commons registration authority is notified by the Chief Land Registrar that the land has been registered in the register of title, the authority shall—

(a) remove the registration of ownership; and

(b) indicate in the register in such manner as may be specified in regulations that the land has been registered in the register of title.

(3) Regulations may require commons registration authorities—

(a) to remove registration of ownership of land from their registers of common land and town or village greens;

(b) to keep or otherwise deal with documents received by them in connection with the registration of ownership of land in such manner as the regulations may specify.

(Text 2.44)

Vesting of unclaimed land

9 (1) The repeal by this Act of section 8 of the 1965 Act does not affect the vesting of land in any local authority (within the meaning of that Act) occurring by virtue of that provision.

(2) Unless land so vesting is regulated by a scheme under the Commons Act 1899 (c 30), sections 10 and 15 of the Open Spaces Act 1906 (c 25) (power to manage and make byelaws) shall continue to apply to it as if the local authority had acquired the ownership under that Act of 1906.

(Text for whole schedule 5.3)

SCHEDULE 4 (Section 44)

WORKS: SUPPLEMENTARY

Metropolitan commons

1 In section 5 of the Metropolitan Commons Act 1866 (c 122) (prohibition on inclosure), after 'inclosure of a metropolitan common' substitute 'which is under the control and management of a London borough council'.

2 (1) The Schedule to the Ministry of Housing and Local Government Provisional Order Confirmation (Greater London Parks and Open Spaces) Act 1967 (c xxix) is amended as follows.

(2) In article 12 (restriction on powers in relation to commons), in paragraph (1) omit '(which consent the Minister may give in such cases as he thinks fit)'.

(3) In that article, after paragraph (2) insert—

'(2A) Sections 39 and 40 of the Commons Act 2006 apply in relation to an application for consent under paragraph (1) as they apply in relation to an application for consent under section 38(1) of that Act.

(2B) Section 41 of that Act applies in relation to the carrying out of works in contravention of paragraph (1) as it applies to works carried out in contravention of section 38(1) of that Act (and as if references to consent under that provision were to consent under paragraph (1)).'

(4) Omit paragraph (3) of that article.

(5) In article 17 (street improvement), in paragraph (1), after 'enactment' insert 'or in any scheme made under, or confirmed by, any enactment'.

(6) In that article—

(a) in paragraph (2), omit the words from 'and the Minister' to the end;

(b) after that paragraph insert—

'(2A) Where an application is made for consent under paragraph (2) in the case of any common, section 40 of the Commons Act 2006 applies in relation to the application as it applies in relation to an application for consent under section 38(1) of that Act.

(2B) Where an application is made for consent under paragraph (2) in any other case, the Minister before giving any consent shall have regard to any representations made to him in the manner specified in paragraph (3).';

(c) in paragraph (3), after 'paragraph (2)' insert 'in a case to which paragraph (2B) applies'.

National Trust property

3 (1) Section 29 of the National Trust Act 1907 (c cxxxvi) (powers exercisable over common or commonable land) is amended as follows.

(2) Renumber the existing provision as subsection (1).

(3) In that subsection, for 'consists of common or commonable land' substitute 'is land to which this section applies'.

(4) After that subsection insert—

'(2) This section applies to—

(a) any land registered as common land;

(b) land not so registered which is—

(i) regulated by an Act made under the Commons Act 1876 confirming a provisional order of the Inclosure Commissioners; or

(ii) subject to a scheme under the Metropolitan Commons Act 1866 or the Commons Act 1899; and

(c) land not falling within paragraph (a) or (b) which is in the New Forest and is subject to rights of common.'

4 (1) Section 23 of the National Trust Act 1971 (c vi) (powers over common land) is amended as follows.

(2) In subsection (2), omit the words from ', and in giving' to the end.

(3) After that subsection insert—

'(2A) Sections 39 and 40 of the Commons Act 2006 apply in relation to an application for consent under subsection (2) of this section as they apply in relation to an application for consent under section 38(1) of that Act.

(2B) Section 41 of that Act applies in relation to the carrying out of works in contravention of subsection (2) of this section as it applies to works carried out in contravention of section 38(1) of that Act (and as if references to consent under that provision were to consent under subsection (2) of this section).

(2C) Nothing in section 38 of the Commons Act 2006 applies in relation to land to which section 29 of the Act of 1907 applies.'

New parishes

5 In section 15 of the New Parishes Measure 1943 (No 1) (land subject to rights of common), in subsection (1), for the words from 'without the consent' to the end substitute 'without the consent of the Secretary of State and sections 39 and 40 of the Commons Act 2006 apply in relation to an application for such consent as they apply in relation to an application for consent under section 38(1) of that Act.'

Transitional provision

6 In its application to any works carried out on or after 28 June 2005 but before the day on which section 38(1) above comes into force, section 194(2) of the Law of Property Act 1925 (c 20) shall have effect as if the words 'interested in the common' were omitted.

(Text 6.33, 6.76)

7 The prohibition in section 38(1) does not apply to works carried out in connection with the taking or working of minerals if—

(a) the works were granted planning permission under any enactment before the commencement of section 38;

(b) the works are carried out in accordance with that planning permission in the period allowed for the works to be carried out (subject to any extension of time granted before or after the commencement of that section).

SCHEDULE 5 (Section 52)

MINOR AND CONSEQUENTIAL AMENDMENTS

Countryside Act 1968 (c 41)

1 (1) The Countryside Act 1968 is amended as follows.

(2) In section 9(6), for the definition of 'common land' substitute—

'"common land" means—

(a) land registered as common land in a register of common land kept under Part 1 of the Commons Act 2006;

(b) land to which Part 1 of that Act does not apply and which is subject to rights of common within the meaning of that Act;'.

(3) In Schedule 2, in paragraph 7, for the words from 'section 22(1)' to the end substitute 'the principal section'.

Animals Act 1971 (c 22)

2 In section 11 of the Animals Act 1971, for the definitions of 'common land' and 'town or village green' substitute—

'"common land" means—

(a) land registered as common land in a register of common land kept under Part 1 of the Commons Act 2006;

(b) land to which Part 1 of that Act does not apply and which is subject to rights of common within the meaning of that Act;

"town or village green" means land registered as a town or village green in a register of town or village greens kept under Part 1 of the Commons Act 2006;'.

Wildlife and Countryside Act 1981 (c 69)

3 In section 52(2C) of the Wildlife and Countryside Act 1981—

(a) for 'common land' (in the first place where it occurs) substitute 'subject to rights of common (within the meaning of the Commons Act 2006)';

(b) for the words from 'the commoners' to the end of the subsection substitute 'the persons with such rights or any of them and any commons council established under Part 2 of the Commons Act 2006 for that land'.

Norfolk and Suffolk Broads Act 1988 (c 4)

4 In Schedule 3 to the Norfolk and Suffolk Broads Act 1988, in paragraph

38(1)(d), for 'section 9 of the Commons Registration Act 1965' substitute 'section 45 of the Commons Act 2006'.

Criminal Justice and Public Order Act 1994 (c 33)

5 In section 61(9) of the Criminal Justice and Public Order Act 1994—

(a) for the definition of 'common land' substitute—
'"common land" means—

(a) land registered as common land in a register of common land kept under Part 1 of the Commons Act 2006; and

(b) land to which Part 1 of that Act does not apply and which is subject to rights of common as defined in that Act;';

(b) in the definition of 'commoner', for the words from 'as defined' to the end substitute 'as so defined;';

(c) in the definition of 'the local authority', for 'section 9 of the Commons Registration Act 1965' substitute 'section 45 of the Commons Act 2006'.

Environment Act 1995 (c 25)

6 In Schedule 9 to the Environment Act 1995, in paragraph 1—

(a) in subparagraph (2)(d), for 'section 9 of the Commons Registration Act 1965' substitute 'section 45 of the Commons Act 2006';

(b) in subparagraph (6), for 'the Commons Registration Act 1965' substitute 'Part 1 of the Commons Act 2006'.

Countryside and Rights of Way Act 2000 (c 37)

7 (1) The Countryside and Rights of Way Act 2000 is amended as follows.

(2) In section 1, in subsection (3)—

(a) for paragraph (a) substitute 'land which is registered as common land in a register of common land kept under Part 1 of the Commons Act 2006.';

(b) omit paragraph (b).

(3) In that section, omit subsection (4).

(4) In section 45(1), in the definition of 'rights of common', for 'the Commons Registration Act 1965' substitute 'the Commons Act 2006'.

(5) In section 46(2), for 'section' substitute 'subsection'.

Land Registration Act 2002 (c 9)

8 (1) The Land Registration Act 2002 is amended as follows.

(2) In section 27(2)(d), for 'the Commons Registration Act 1965 (c 64)' substitute 'Part 1 of the Commons Act 2006'.

(3) In section 33(d), for 'the Commons Registration Act 1965 (c 64)' substitute 'Part 1 of the Commons Act 2006'.

(4) In Schedule 3, in paragraph 3(1), for 'the Commons Registration Act 1965 (c 64)' substitute 'Part 1 of the Commons Act 2006'.

THE COMMONS (SEVERANCE OF RIGHTS) (ENGLAND) ORDER 2006 (SI 2006 NO 2145)

Made..3rd August 2006

Laid before Parliament..7th August 2006

Coming into force...9th September 2006

The Secretary of State, in exercise of the powers conferred upon him by section 9(2) and (7), section 59(1) and section 61(1) of, and paragraph 2(1)(a) of Schedule 1 to, the Commons Act 2006, makes the following Order:

Citation, commencement and application

1. —(1) This Order may be cited as the Commons (Severance of Rights) (England) Order 2006, and shall come into force on 9th September 2006 but shall have effect as from 28th June 2005.

(2) This Order applies in relation to England.

Temporary severance of right of common

2. —(1) A right of common to graze animals to which section 9(1) of the Commons Act 2006 applies may be temporarily severed from the land to which it is attached—

(a) by leasing or licensing the right of common on its own, provided that the period of the lease or licence does not exceed two years; or

(b) by leasing or licensing the land, or part of the land, to which the right of common is attached, without the right of common.

(2) Where a right of common is temporarily severed from any land pursuant to paragraph (1)(b), any disposal of the retained right of common on or after the grant of the lease or licence of the land and before its termination shall be of no effect unless—

(a) the disposal is made to the grantee of the lease or licence of the land; and

(b) the disposal is made for a period expiring not more than two years from the expiry of the lease or licence of the land.

(3) References in this article to a right of common, in relation to a right of common to graze more than one animal, include a right to graze a proportion of the number of animals that may be grazed by virtue of that right of common.

(Text 2.72)

THE COMMONS ACT 2006 (COMMENCEMENT NO 1, TRANSITIONAL PROVISIONS AND SAVINGS) (ENGLAND) ORDER 2006 (SI 2006 NO 2504)

Made ....11th September 2006

The Secretary of State, in exercise of the powers conferred upon him by sections 56(1) and 59(1) of the Commons Act 2006, makes the following Order:

Citation, interpretation and application

1. —(1) This Order may be cited as the Commons Act 2006 (Commencement No. 1, Transitional Provisions and Savings) (England) Order 2006.

(2) In this Order—
'the 1965 Act' means the Commons Registration Act 1965;
'the 2006 Act' means the Commons Act 2006.

(3) This Order applies in relation to England only.

Commencement of provisions

2. The following provisions of the 2006 Act shall come into force on 1st October 2006—

(a) section 45 (powers of local authorities over unclaimed land);
(b) section 47 (approvement);
(c) section 49 (notice of inclosure);
(d) section 51 (vehicular access);
(e) in Schedule 3 (registration: transitional provision), paragraph 9 (vesting of unclaimed land), and section 23 insofar as it relates to that paragraph;
(f) in Schedule 4 (works: supplementary), paragraph 6 (transitional provision), and section 44(1) insofar as it relates to that paragraph;
(g) in Schedule 5 (minor and consequential amendments), subparagraph (5) of paragraph 7 (Countryside and Rights of Way Act 2000 (c37)) and subparagraph (1) of paragraph 7 insofar as it relates to subparagraph (5), and section 52 insofar as it relates to those provisions;
(h) the following entries in Part 1 of Schedule 6 (repeals relating to registration), and section 53 insofar as it relates to those entries—
(i) Commons Registration Act 1965, to the extent of repealing sections 8, 9 and 13(a);
(ii) Local Government Act 1972, section 189(1) and (2);
(iii) Local Government Act 1985, Schedule 8, paragraph 10(6);
(iv) Dartmoor Commons Act 1985, section 8;
(v) Common Land (Rectification of Registers) Act 1989;
(vi) Countryside and Rights of Way Act 2000, section 46(1);
(vii) Greenham and Crookham Commons Act 2002, section 33(1);
(i) the following entries in Part 2 of Schedule 6 (repeals relating to works), and section 53 insofar as it relates to those entries—
(i) Metropolitan Commons Act 1866, section 21;
(ii) Commons Act 1876, in section 30, the words from 'Any person aggrieved' to

the end of the section;

(iii) Commons Act 1899, section 21;

(iv) Compulsory Purchase Act 1965, in Schedule 7, the entry relating to the Commons Act 1899;

(j) the following entries in Part 3 of Schedule 6 (repeals relating to approvement and inclosure) and section 53 insofar as it relates to those entries—

(i) Commons Act 1285;

(ii) Law of Commons Amendment Act 1893.

Transitional provisions and savings

3. —(1) In relation to any area of England, the reference in section 45(1) of the 2006 Act to land being registered as common land or a town or village green shall, until the coming into force of section 1 of that Act in relation to that area, be taken as a reference to land being so registered under the 1965 Act.

(2) Where, before 1st October 2006, a Commons Commissioner makes a direction under section 8(2) or (3) of the 1965 Act for a registration authority to register a person as the owner of land, but the registration authority does not comply with the direction before that date—

(a) the direction shall continue to have effect on and after 1st October 2006 notwithstanding the repeal of section 8(2) and (3); and

(b) if the direction is for a local authority to be registered as the owner of land, on the registration being made section 8(4) of the 1965 Act shall apply as if it had not been repealed.

(3) In relation to any area of England, section 13(a) of the 1965 Act and regulations made under it (a) shall, until the coming into force of section 14 of the 2006 Act in relation to that area, continue to have effect insofar as they relate to land which ceases to be common land or a town or village green by virtue of any instrument made under or pursuant to an enactment.

(4) Where, in relation to any land other than land referred to in paragraph (3)—

(a) an application is made before 1st October 2006 to a registration authority, pursuant to regulations under section 13(a) of the 1965 Act, for land to be removed from the register as a result of that land having ceased to be common land or a town or village green, and

(b) the registration authority does not determine the application before that date, the registration authority shall continue to deal with the application on and after 1st October 2006 as if section 13(a) had not been repealed.

(Text 2.51, 2.111, 3.44, 4.20, 6.33, 6.76)

Bibliography

All statements of the law in the following works should be treated as of historic interest only, unless there are revised editions following the Commons Act 2006.

Six Essays on Commons Preservation by R Hunter et al (Sampson Low, Son and Marston 1867)

Our Common Land by Octavia Hill (Macmillan 1877)

Rights of Common by J Williams (Sweet 1880)

English Commons and Forests by G Shaw-Lefevre (Cassell 1894) revised as:
Commons, Forests and Footpaths by Lord Eversley (Cassell 1910)

Index to Local and Personal Acts (HMSO 1949) Class IX (1) *Inclosures and Allotments;* (2) *Open Spaces, Commons and Parks*

Royal Commission on Common Land 1955-58 (Cmnd 462) (HMSO 1958)

The Common Lands of England and Wales by L Dudley Stamp and W G Hoskins (Collins, New Naturalist 1963)

The Commons, Open Spaces and Footpaths Preservation Society 1865-1965: A Short History by W H Williams (Commons, Open Spaces and Footpaths Preservation Society 1965)

An Outline of the Law Relating to Common Land and Public Access to the Countryside by B Harris and G Ryan (Sweet and Maxwell 1967)

Commons and Village Greens by D R Denman, R A Roberts and H J F Smith (L Hill 1967)

The Law of Commons by I Campbell (Commons, Open Spaces and Footpaths Preservation Society 1971) revised as:

The Law of Commons and Village Greens by I Campbell and P Clayden
(Commons, Open Spaces and Footpaths Preservation Society 1980)

Our Common Land by P Clayden
(Commons, Open Spaces and Footpaths Preservation Society 1985 and 2003)

Common Land: Preparations for Comprehensive Legislation: Report of an interdepartmental working party 1975-77 (Department of the Environment 1978)

A Domesday of English Enclosure Acts and Awards by W E Tate and M E Turner (University of Reading 1978)

The Common Ground by Richard Mabey (Hutchinson 1980) (part 2, chapter 3)

Back to the Land by Jan Marsh (Quartet 1982) (chapter 3)

The Common Lands of Wales: Problems and Opportunities by J W Aitchison (University

College of Wales, Aberystwyth 1983)

The Future of Common Land and Its Management: Report of Conference held 2 June 1983 (Open Spaces Society 1983)

Common Land in Wales, Wales Countryside Forum (Countryside Commission 1984)

Report of the Common Land Forum (Countryside Commission 1986)

The Law of Commons by G D Gadsden (Sweet & Maxwell 1988)

A Practitioner's Guide to Common Land and the Commons Registration Act 1965 by Ros Oswald (ESC Publishing, Oxford 1989)

Halsbury's Laws of England, fourth edition reissue 1991, vol 6, paras 501-783 (pages 193-341). Halsbury is a standard legal work and contains a long summary of the law of commons and village greens

Getting Greens Registered (Open Spaces Society 1995, revised edition 2007)

Index to Local and Personal Acts (TSO 1996) vols 1797-1849 A-K and L-Z; vols 1850-1995 A-E, F-L, M-R and S-Z

Halsbury's *Statutes of England and Wales,* fourth edition, vol 7 (2002 reissue) *Commons*. Other relevant statutes will be found in vol 32 (2001 reissue) *Open Spaces and National Heritage*, vol 26 (2002 reissue) London and vol 25 (2001 reissue) *Local Government*

Common Land Policy Statement 2002 (Defra 2002)

A Common Purpose: A guide to agreeing management on common land (The National Trust, Natural England and the Open Spaces Society 2005).

Index

Numbers in *italics* refer to statutes printed in the book. Otherwise, the numbers refer to paragraphs in the text.

abandonment of rights 2.4
Abergwesyn Commons, Powys 1.32
access agreement/order 3.47, 4.41-44, 5,12
access, *de facto* 1.14, 4.63, 6.46, 6.51
access, *de jure* 1.2, 1.11, 1.23, 1.31, 2.127, 2.131, 3.15, 3.47-48, chapters 4 and 5 *passim*, 6.75, 6.79-80
access, definition 6.12
access land 2.128, 2.132, 5.1
  dedication of 5.15-17
  maps of 5.7-9
  right of access over 5.10-14
Acquisition of Land Act 1981 2.86, 2.134, 6.1, 6.35-62, 6.77, 7.46, *144*
Administration of Justice Act 1977 4.53-55
adverse possession 2.57
Allendale, Northumberland 1.33
allotments—see fuel allotments, recreation allotments
amendment of registers 2.86-94
animals, commonable 2.4
  entire 4.56
appendant right of common 2.4
apportionment of rights 2.62-65, 2.133
appropriation 6.38, 6.43-62, 7.46-47
appurtenant right of common 2.4
Ashdown Forest, East Sussex 1.18, 2.9
Attachment of rights 2.63, 2.76
Austenwood Common, Buckinghamshire 2.84, 4.17

Banstead, Surrey 1.8, 1.19, 3.26-27
Beastgates 2.1-2
Berkhamsted, Hertfordshire 1.8, 1.19
Beverley, East Yorkshire 1.33
Bexhill Down, East Sussex 1.18, 4.9
Black Mountain, Carmarthenshire 1.30
Blackdown, Mendips 1.25
Blackdown, West Sussex 1.20

Blackheath 1.16, 4.5
Bodmin Moor, Cornwall 1.24, 4.56
boroughs 4.20
Bowden Down, Devon 6.34
Box Hill Common, Wiltshire 2.122
Bradford, West Yorkshire 1.33
Bramshott, Hampshire 1.20
Bransbury, Hampshire 1.21
Brecon Beacons 1.30, 1.32
Brentor, Devon 6.34
Bretherdale, Cumbria 6,21
Bringsty, Herefordshire 1.29
Bromyard Downs, Herefordshire 1.29
Bucklebury Common, West Berkshire 4.17
buildings—see common land (works), village greens (encroachments)
Burnham Beeches, Buckinghamshire 4.6
Burrington, Mendips 1.25
by-laws 2.7, 4.4, 4.10, 4.16, 4.21-23, 4.35, 7.27, 7.40-41

Cadnam, Hampshire 1.21
camping 4.21
car parking 4.15, 7.36-45
car parks 2.129, 4.37, 4.46, 6.10, 6.15, 6.26, 7.58
caravans 4.61
Caravan Sites and Control of Development Act 1960 4.61, *130*
cattlegates 2.1-2
Cemaes, Courts Leet and Baron, Pembrokeshire 4.53
Central Electricity Generating Board 2.82
Charities Act 1993 7.8
Charity Commissioners 7.7-8
Chewton Common, Dorset 2.123
Chipping Sodbury, South Gloucestershire 1.25
Chiswick Commons 4.5
Chobham Common, Surrey 4.45, 6.27
Church Commissioners 2.86, 2.134, 4.5
Clee Hills, Shropshire 1.28
Cleeve Hill, Gloucestershire 1.25
Clent Hills, Worcestershire 1.28, 4.9
Cliffe, Kent 1.17
Clifton and Durdham Downs (Bristol) Act 1861 4.32
Clinton Devon estate 1.23

coal 2.12
Coal Industry Act 1994 2.12
Coity Wallia, Bridgend 4.11
Coldharbour Common, Surrey 6.25
Common Council of the City of London 4.64
common land
  acquisition by local authorities 4.2-8, 4.45-47
  buildings registered as 2.129
  compulsory acquisition 2.86, 3.22, 6.35, 6.47, 6.54, 6.56, 6.60-62, 6.77
  creation 2.45-49
  definition 2.14, 2.120-121, 6.4
  de-registration 2.88-94
  exchange 2.86, 2.88-94, 2.132, 3.22, 6.1, 6.35-62, 6.77-82
  fencing 3.17, 4.37-38, 6.1-34, 6.66
  management 1.11, 4.1-69
  new 2.45-49
  owner (and see lord of the manor) 1.1, 2.2, 2.31, 2.36-44, 2.50-51, 2.57-58, 2.83, 2.88, 2.139, 3.1-16, 3.26-28, 3.36, 3.39, 4.9, 4.13-16, 4.23, 4.26, 4.37, 4.51, 4.65, 5.11, 5.15, 6.22, 6.31, 6.54, 6.68
  protection 4.13, 6.1-76
  rectification of registers 2.17, 2.85, 2.112-144
  trespassers on 4.62-64
  works 3.10-11, 3.17-21, 4.3, 4.15, 4.37-38, 6.2-34, 6.63-76
  wrong registration of 2.129-131
Common Land Forum 1.11, 2.55, 3.16, 7.30, 7.38, 7.44
Common Land Policy Statement 1.12, 2.37, 2.45, 2.57, 2.125, 4.50, 4.57, 7.28, 7.39, 7.45
Common Land (Rectification of Registers) Act 1989 2.20, 2.111-116
Common Land (Rectification of Registers) Regulations 1990 2.113
common rights—see rights of common
commoners, rights of 3.17-22, 3.26-27
Commons Act 1876, 1.8, 2.83, 2.94, 3.40-41, 4.9-12, 6.19, 6.21-22, 6.30-31, 6.64, 7.7, 7.37-40, 7.49-50, 7.52-53, *120*
  s 7 6.30-31, *120*
  s 10 6.22, *121*
  s 11 6.19
  s 19 7.7, *121*
  s 29 7.24, 7.37-40, 7.49-50, 7.52-53, *122*
  s30 3.41, 6.32
  s37, *122*
Commons Act 1899 2.83, 2.94, 2.118, 3.40, 3.47, 4.13-19, 4.51, 4.61, 5.5, 6.64, 6.67, 6.74, 7.7-8, 7.29, *122*

Commons Act 1908 2.94, 4.51, 4.56-57, *128*
Commons Act 2006
- Part 1 2.34, 2.63-64, 2.118, 4.31, 4.62, 5.3, 6.1-6, 7.55, *153*
- Part 2 1.11, 4.50-51, *168*
- Part 3 2.54, 6.63-76, *175*
- Part 4, *180*
- Part 5, *183*
- s1 2.74, *153*
- s3 2.29, *154*
- s4 2.26, *154*
- s5 2.7, 2.83, *155*
- s6 2.45-6, *155*
- s7 2.58-61, *156*
- s8 2.62-65, *156*
- s9 2.67-70, *157*
- s10 2.76, *158*
- s11 2.77, *158*
- s12 2.79, *158*
- s13 2.80-82, 6.8, *159*
- s14 2.86, 6.1, 6.83, *159*
- s15 7.63, 7.67-73, *160*
- s16 2.88-91, 6.1, 6.83, 7.47, *161*
- s17 2.92-3, 6.1, 6.83, 7.47, *162*
- s18 2.24, 2.97, 2.100-103, *163*
- s19 2.40, 2.104-107, *164*
- s20 2.29, 2.109, *165*
- s21 2.32, 2.110, *165*
- s24 2.33, 2.47, 2.125, 2.130, 2.141, *166*
- s25 2.34, 2.143, *167*
- s26-35 4.51, *168*
- s36 4.12, 4.19, 4.34, 4.51, 4.55, 4.57, *174*
- s37 4.50-51, *174*
- s38 3.10-11, 3.20, 4.3, 6.62-71, *175*
- s39 6.65, 6.69, *176*
- s40 6.72, *177*
- s41 6.73, *177*
- s42 6.74, *177*
- s43 6.75, *178*
- s44 6.76, *179*
- s45 2.38, 2.51, 2.53, 4.63, *180*
- s46 4.65, *180*

s50 4.13, 4.20, *182*
s51 3.12, 3.38, 3.44, *183*
s53 2.5, 2.14, 2.19, 2.111, 2.120, 3.14, 3.38, 3.44, 4.15, 6.7, 7.18, *183*
s54 2.74, *184*
s55 2.1, *184*
sch1 2.71-72, *187*
sch2 2.17, 2.25, 2.85, 2.98, 2.117-119, 2.124, 2.128-129, 4.29, 7.8, 7.55-57, 7.59, 7.60, 7.61, *190*
sch3 2.43, 2.133, 4.27, 4.30, 5.3, 6.7, *195*
sch4 6.33, 6.76, *198*
Commons (Severance of Rights) (England) Order 2006 2.72, *202*
Commons Act 2006 (Commencement No 1, Transitional Provisions and Savings) (England) Order 2006 2.51, 2.111, 3.44, 4.20, 6.33, 6.76, *203*
commons commissioners—see registration
commons councils 3.24, 4.12, 4.19, 4.34, 4.50-51
Commons Preservation Society—see Open Spaces Society
commons registration—see registration
Commons Registration Act 1965 1.11, 2.36-42, 2.95-96
Commons Registration (East Sussex) Act 1994 2.28
Commons Registration (General) Regulations 1966 3.11
Commons (Schemes) Regulations 1982 4.15
Commons (Severance of Rights) (England) Order 2006 2.66-75
community councils—see local councils
compensation 3.22, 4.14, 4.62
compulsory purchase 2.77, 3.22, 6.35-62, 6.77, 7.60
Compulsory Purchase Act 1965 3,22, *131*
conservators 1.17, 1.18, 1.23, 1.25, 1.29, 4.5, 4.9, 4.10
corporation, as commoner 3.34
Corporation of London (Open Spaces) Act 1878 4.6
Corpus Christi College, Oxford 2.95-96
couchancy—see levancy
Countryside Act 1968 4.48-49, *138*
Countryside Agency 5.7
Countryside and Rights of Way Act 2000 1.2, 1.11, 2.127, 2.131, 3.15-16, 3.38, 3.44, 3.47-48, 4.1, 4.9, 4.18, 4.20, 4.26, 4.30, 4.41-44, 4.60, 5.1-18, 6.26, 6.75, 6.80, 7.53, 7.62, 7.67, 8.3, *148*
Countryside and Rights of Way Act 2000 (Commencement No 5) (Wales) Order 2006 4.20
Countryside Council for Wales 2.71, 5.7
county councils 2.26, 2.51, 4.28, 4.64, 6.8, 6.32, 6.34, 6.75, 6.79, 7.5, 7.25, 7.29, 7.42
county borough councils 2.26, 2.51, 2.55, 4.28, 4.64, 6.8, 6.32, 7.29, 7.42

courts baron 4.53-55
  leet 1.3, 1.33, 4.53
  manorial 1.10, 4.51-55
Criminal Damage Act 1971 2.51, 7.40
Criminal Justice and Public Order Act 1994 4.62-64
Crown commons 4.58-60
Crown Estate Commissioners 1.31, 4.58, 6.28
custom 2.4, 2.102, 3.29, 7.1-3, 7.9-24, 7.31-32

Dartmoor, Devon, 1.23, 2.7, 3.24, 4.31, 4.53, 4.59
Dartmoor Commoners' Council 4.31
Dartmoor Commons Act 1985 1.23, 2.67, 3.24, 4.31, 4.59
dedication of land as access land 5.15-17
deeds of declaration 1.31, 4.20, 4.23-26, 4.30
Department for Environment, Food and Rural Affairs (Defra) 1.11, 3.25, 6.16, 6.19, 6.48, 6.79, 6.82, 7.53, 8.4, 8.6
Dilke, Sir Charles 1.8
district councils 2.26, 2.51, 2.55, 3.20, 4.8, 4.13, 4.17, 4.28, 4.33, 4.61, 4.64, 6.32-34, 6.75, 7.5, 7.29, 7.42
Duchy of Cornwall 1.23, 4.59
Durdham Downs, Bristol 4.32, 6.43
dwelling house 2.112, 2.114-115
Dwr Cymru 1.31
Dyfed Act 1987 7.54, *146*

easements 3.3, 3.11-14, 3.36-45, 7.50-53
East Sussex County Council 2.28
enclosure—see inclosure
environmental impact assessment (EIA) 6.39
Environmental Protection Act 1990 2.52
Epping Forest 1.19, 2.83, 2.118, 3.31, 4.5-6, 7.55
Epping Forest Acts 1878-80 4.5-6
Esher, Surrey 2.84, 6.47-48
estovers, right of 2.3, 2.9, 3.29
Eversley, Lord 1.8
excepted land 5.2, 5.4, 5.16
exchange land 6.1, 6.35, 6.40-62, 6.77-81, 7.46-47
exemption order 2.83-85, 6.6
Exmoor 1.23, 1.25
express grant 2.45-47

Farthing Down, Surrey 2.84, 3.4, 4.6

fencing—see common land; village greens
fires 4.21
Fordham Heath, Essex 6.49-50
Forest of Dean, Gloucestershire 2.83, 2.118, 3.24, 7.55
Forestry Act 1967 3.10, 6.38
Forestry Commission 1.21, 4.31
Forrabury, Cornwall 1.24
fuel allotments 1.7, 6.60

game, taking of 3.5-6
garden 2.112-116, 2.128, 7.37, 7.58
gates—see stints
government departments 4.5, 4.58, 6.37
Gower, Swansea 1.32
grant—see prescription
grant (creation) of rights 2.45-48
gravel 1.7, 2.12, 3.4, 3.26, 4.47, 7.31
grazing rights 2.2-7, 2.66, 2.72, 2.75, 3.7, 3.23-25, 3.35, 4.31, 6.15
Greater London Council 2.26, 2.85
Greenham and Crookham Commons Act 2002 2.49, 2.67, 3.24, 4.33
Greenwich, Royal Manor of 4.5
gross, right of common in 2.4, 2.66, 2.76, 2.79, 2.101, 2.133, 3.29

Half Moon, Hampshire 1.21
Hampshire County Council 2.122
Hampstead Heath 1.16, 4.5-4.7
Hampstead Heath Act 1871 4.5
Hatherleigh Moor, Devon 1.23
hefting 1.33
Henfield, West Sussex 1.20
Hergest Ridge, Herefordshire 1.29
Hexhamshire, Northumberland 1.33, 7.71
High Court 2.40, 4.22, 4.38, 6.19, 6.55, 7.6, 7.67-68
Hightown, Hampshire 1.21
highway 2.23, 4.4, 4.64, 6.35, 6.41, 7.32-33
Highways Act 1980 4.4, 6.26, 6.35
High Wycombe, Buckinghamshire 6.59, 7.6
Hindhead, Surrey 1.19
High Court 2.40, 2.107-8, 4.22, 4.38, 6.19, 6.55, 7.6, 7.67-68, 7.71
horse riding 4.22, 4.46
House of Lords 2.11, 2.66, 2.122, 2.124, 3.14, 3.37, 3.39, 3.41, 7.3, 7.19, 7.34, 7.50, 7.68, 7.69, 7.71

Housing Act 1985 6.35
Huxley, Thomas 1.8

Ilkley Moor, Bradford, West Yorkshire 1.33
inclosure 1.4-8, 6.67
Inclosure Act 1845 1.7, 2.129, 6.1, 6.78-82, 7.5-6, *118*
Inclosure Act 1857 7.24, 7.35-36, 7.38, 7.40, 7.49-50, 7.52-53, *119*
inclosure acts 1.5-7, 7.5
inclosure awards 3.29, 7.4-5, 7.8
inclosure commissioners 6.30
inhabitants 1.7, 3.20, 3.30-34, 3.48, 4.09, 4.18,6.21, 6.31, 7.1-2, 7.4-5, 7.9, 7.16-18, 7.26, 7.31, 7.43, 7.49, 7.63, 7.67
Itchingwood Common, Surrey 4.43

jus spatiandi 7.12

Ladydale Meadow, Leek, Staffordshire 7.67
Lake District 1.33, 2.6, 4.58, 6.21
Land Registration Acts 2.31, 2.36, 2.42-43, 2.82
Land Registry 2.31, 2.36, 2.41-43, 2.57, 2.63, 3.43
Langholme Meadow, Bedford 6.44
Law of Property Act 1922 2.16, 2.123, 4.54
Law of Property Act 1925
  s 62 2.66
  s 193 1.10, 2.93-94, 2.138, 3,37, 3.39, 3.42, 3.47, 4.20-30, 4.36, 4.49, 4.58, 4.61, 5.5, 6.12-13, 6.32, 6.75, 6.80, 7.29, 7.49-50, *128*
  s 194 1.10, 3.11 4.15, 4.27, 4.37, 6.2-34, 6.63, 6.65, 6.71, 6.76, *129*
levancy and couchancy, rules of 2.66
Liddaton Down, Devon 6.34
Limitation Act 1980 2.39, 2.56
litter 1.21, 2.53
Llanbister and Moelfre Common, Powys 6.28
Lleyn, Gwynedd 1.32
local authorities 1.9, 2.44, 2.50-57, 2.85, 2.140, 4.5, 4.9, 4.20, 4.32, 4.39, 4.45-48, 4.63-64, 6.37-38, 6.52, 7.27-30, 7.68
local councils 2.51-52, 2.55, 3.34, 4.5, 4.16, 4.45, 7.5, 7.25, 7.29-30, 7.42-43
Local Government Act 1894 3.20, 7.5, 7.42,
Local Government Act 1972 2.52, 4.16, 4.20, 6.52-54, *142*
Local Government (Miscellaneous Provisions) Act 1976 7.42
Local Government Act 2000 2.52
locality 7.2, 7.9, 7.16-18, 7.63
London borough councils 2.26

London (City of) Corporation 1.4, 4.6
London Government Reorganisation (Hampstead Heath) Order 1989, 4.7
Long Mynd, Shropshire 1.28
lord of the manor 1.3, 1.7, 2.15, 2.121, 3.4, 3.26, 4.9, 4.46-47, 6.32, 7.1
lost modern grant 3.12-14
Ludshott, Hampshire 1.20
Lytchett Minster bypass, Dorset 6.60

Malvern Hills 1.29
manor 1.3, 2.14-17, 2.95, 2.120-125, 3.32, 4.29, 4.46-47, 4.54, 7.1
manorial courts—see courts
manorial waste—see waste of the manor
maps of access land 5.7-9
Marstakes, East Sussex 1.18
Mendips 1.25
Merton, Statute of 1.3
metropolitan commons 4.2-8, 6.76
Metropolitan Commons Act 1866 1.8, 2.83, 2.94, 2.118, 4.2, 5.1, 6.67, 6.74, *120*
metropolitan district councils 4.28, 6.75, 7.42
Mill, John Stuart 1.8
Minchinhampton Common, Gloucestershire 1.25, 5.4
minerals 2.12, 3.4
Ministry of Housing and Local Government Provisional Order Confirmation (Greater London Parks and Open Spaces) Act 1967 4.3-4, 6.14, *132*
Mynydd Maen, Caerphilly/Torfaen 1.32

National Assembly for Wales 6.8, 6.16, 6.28, 6.40, 6.61, 6.79, 6.82, 7.54
national parks 1.12, 4.13, 4.61, 6.21
National Parks and Access to the Countryside Act 1949 2.52, 3.47, 4.41-44, 5.12
National park authorities 1.9, 1.32, 4.13, 4.61
National Trust 1.9, 1.19, 1,21, 1.24-25, 1.32, 3.18, 4.1, 4.22, 4.35-40, 5.4, 5.18, 6.62, 6.76
National Trust Act 1907 4.35-40, *126*
National Trust Act 1971 3.40, 4.37-40, 6.14, *142*
Natural England 2.71, 4.1, 5.7, 5.18
nature conservation 1.19, 4.13, 4.69, 6.49, 6.70, 6.75
Newcastle Town Moor 1.33
New Forest, Hampshire 1.21-2, 2.7, 2.83, 2.118, 3.24, 4.31, 6.64
New Roads and Street Works Act 1991 4.4
North York Moors 1.33
Northam Burrows, Devon 1.23, 3.33

open country 5.7
open space 1.3, 1.8-9, 2.85, 3.47, 4.3-4, 4.6-7, 4.35, 4.45, 6.25, 6.35, 6.43-44, 6.46, 6.51-52, 6.59-60, 7.25, 7.42, 7.68
Open Spaces Act 1906 4.45, 7.25, 7.29, 7.42, *124*
Open Spaces Society (Commons Preservation Society) 1.8, 1.10, 1.19, 1.25, 1.31, 2.141, 3.16, 4.1-2, 4.4, 4.33, 4.38, 6.47-48, 6.60, 6.79-80, 7.54, 7.72
order of limitations 4.23-24, 7.29
Otmoor, Oxfordshire 1.6
ownership—see common land, village greens, lord of the manor

pannage, right of 2.3, 2.8
parish councils—see local councils
pasture, right of 2.4-7, 2.116, 3.27-28
Pennines 1.14, 2.6
piscary, right of 2.3, 2.11
Plaitford, Hampshire 1.21
Potboilers 1.23
Pot wallopers 1.23
prescription 2.45, 2.132, 3.12, 3.14, 3.36-38, 3.42, 7.12, 7.48-50, 7.69
Prescription Act 1832 3.12, 3.36, *117*
Principal authority 2.53
provisional order 2.94, 2.118, 3.40, 3.47, 4.3, 4.9-12, 4.20, 5.5, 6.64, 6.76, 7.5
public access—see access
Public Health Act 1875 7.6
public open space—see open space

quantification of rights 2.104, 3.23-25, 3.29
Quantocks, Somerset 1.25

rabbits 3.6
re-allocation of rights of common 2.77-78
rectification of registers—see registration
recreation allotments 1.7, 2.85, 7.4-8
recreation, rights of—see village greens
registration (see also Commons Registration Act 1965, Commons Act 2006)
amendment of registers 2.86-94, 6.78
applications 2.18, 2.33, 2.37, 2.39, 2.47, 2.59, 2.65, 2.78, 2.87-92, 2.104, 2.106, 2.109-110, 2.117-19, 2.124-126, 2.128-130, 2.135, 2.138, 2.141-142, 5.3, 7.8, 7.23, 7.55-61, 7.63-64, 7.66-67, 7.71, 7.73
authorities 2.18, 2.26-28, 2.30, 2.36, 2.38, 2.47, 2.60, 2.92, 2.104, 2.108, 2.117-119, 2.124-126, 2.128-130, 2.132, 2.135-136, 2.141, 4.31, 4.57, 7.55-57, 7.59
commons commissioners 2.14, 2.19-20, 2.37, 2.50, 2.95, 2.114-115, 2.120,

2.124, 2.129, 3.32-34, 7.6, 7.13, 7.20, 7.22-23, 7.25, 7.59
copies of entries 2.30, 2.32, 2.109-110
date of 2.95
exemptions 2.83-85
failure to register 2.39, 2.48, 4.27, 6.7, 7.3
High Court 2.40, 2.107-108
land 2.31, 2.42-43, 2.95, 2.139
objections 2.18-19
ownership 2.15, 2.20-22, 2.31, 2.36-44, 7.25
period 2.18-25, 2.36, 2.48, 2.82, 7.3, 7.55
procedure 2.18-25
provisional 2.18, 2.124, 2.128-129, 7.57, 7.59-60
rectification of registers 2.20, 2.111-116, 2.128, 7.58
registers 2.29-35
regulations 2.29, 2.32-34, 2.36, 2.46-47, 2.58, 2.62-64, 2.78-80, 2.86-87, 2.106, 2.109-110, 2.113, 2.118-119, 2.124-126, 2.128-130, 2.132, 2.135-137, 2.139, 2.141-143, 3.11, 7.56-57, 7.59-60, 8.6
Commons Registration (General) Regulations 1966 3.11
rights 2.18-25, 4.27, 6.7
search 2.35
restricted works 3.10-11, 6.64
rights of common
abandonment 2.4
appendant 2.4
apportionment 2.62-65, 2.133
appurtenant 2.4
attachment 2.63, 2.76
creation 2.45-49, 2.132, 3.23
definition 2.1-13
destruction 2.48, 2.75, 2.80-81, 2.132, 2.137, 3.30, 4.27, 4.32, 6.7-8, 7.3
exercise 2.47, 2.59-61, 2.63, 2.102, 3.4, 3.12, 3.20-22, 3.26-27, 3.35, 4.31, 4.33, 6.51, 6.75
express grant 2.45-47
extinguishment—see destruction
greens (over) 7.31
gross 2.4, 2.66, 2.76, 2.79, 2.101, 2.133, 3.29
licence of 2.72, 3.35
nature of (see estovers, pannage, pasture, piscary, soil, turbary)
prescription 2.4, 2.45, 2.132, 3.12
re-allocation of 2.77-78
quantification 2.104, 3.23-25, 3.29
registration 2.18-25, 4.27, 6.7

severance 2.64, 2.66-75, 2.100, 2.133, 3.35
sufficiency of land 3.26-28
surrender 2.61, 2.64, 2.80-82, 2.133, 4.28, 6.8
vicinage, by reason of 2.7
rights of way, private (see easement)
Road Traffic Act 1988 3.37, 4.21, 7.40, 7.48-50, *147*
Road Traffic Regulation Act 1984 7.42
Roundthwaite, Cumbria 6.21
Royal Commission on Common Land 1.11, 1.29, 3.16, 8.1, 8.3
Roydon Common, Norfolk 4.24

Sandlings, Suffolk 1.26
sans nombre 2.5
Secretary of State 4.3-4, 4.10, 4.14-15, 4.23, 4.25, 4.28, 4.37-38, 4.48, 4.56-57, 6.2, 6.8, 6.10, 6.12, 6.15, 6.17-21, 6.23, 6.25-27, 6.30-32, 6.34, 6.40-41, 6.43, 6.46-48, 6.50, 6.52-54, 6.56-57, 7.44, 7.53
sea-sand 2.13
Sea-Sand (Devon and Cornwall) Act 1609 2.13
Selborne, Hampshire 1.21
severance 2.64, 2.66-75, 2.100, 2.133, 3.35
several vesture, pasture or herbage 2.1-2
shooting—see sporting rights
site of special scientific interest (SSSI) 1.12, 1.18, 1.21, 4.33
Snowdonia National Park 1.32, 4.58
soil, right of common in 2.12-13
sole vesture, pasture or herbage 2.2
Southampton Common 4.32, 6.10, 6.12
Southampton Marsh Act 1844 4.32
special parliamentary procedure 6.35, 6.40, 6.42, 6.56-62
Spitchwick Court Leet and Baron, Devon 4.53
sporting rights 3.5-6
Stafford Common, Swansea 6.8
Stanhope, Durham 1.33
Statutory Orders (Special Procedure) Acts 1945 and 1965 6.56
Stedham Common, West Sussex 6.26-27
Stelling Minnis, Kent 1.17
stints 1.23,1.25, 1.33, 2.2
stitchmeal 1.24
Stockbridge, Hampshire 1.21
Stonehenge 3.46, 7.12
Stourpaine, Dorset 7.4
straying 2.7

street 4.4
Studland, Kent 1.17
Sunningwell, Oxfordshire 7.19, 7.69-70
Surrey County Council 4.45
Tebay, Cumbria 6.21
Temple Ham Meadow, Gloucestershire 2.95
tenant 2.104, 5.11, 7.71
Therfield Heath, Hertfordshire 4.9
Thursley, Surrey 1.19
timber 3.3, 3.8-10
Torrington Common, Devon 1.23
Torver Commons, Cumbria 4.58
Town and Country Planning Act 1990 3.10, 6.35, 6.53, 7.43, *148*
Town and Country Planning Acts 3.2
town greens - see village greens
Town Moor, Newcastle 1.33
Transport and Works Act 1992 6.35
Trap Grounds, Oxford 7.3, 7.34, 7.50
trees 2.8-9, 2.52, 3.3, 3.8-10, 4.35, 6.30
trespass 2.51, 3.3, 3.15-16, 3.39, 4.62-64, 5.11, 7.1, 7.41
Tunbridge Wells, Kent 1.17
Tunbridge Wells Improvement Act 1890 1.17
turbary, right of 2.3, 2.10, 6.49

unclaimed land 2.50-57, 7.25
unitary councils - see principal authorities
University of Wales 1.32
urban district 4.20

vehicles 3.21, 3.37-45, 4.62, 5.12, 7.36, 7.41-45, 7.49-54
venville rights 1.23
Verderers 1.21
vicinage, right of common by reason of 2.7
village greens
  appropriation of 6.53, 7.46-47
  buildings, registration of 7.57-58
  compulsory acquisition 6.35, 6.77, 7.7
  customary rights over 7.2-3, 7.9-24
  damage 7.34-39
  definition 7.1, 7.4-24, 7.46
  driveways across 7.48-54

encroachment 7.34-39
exchange of 6.54, 6.77-82, 7.7-8, 7.46-47
fencing 7.37
highways and 7.32
management 4.13, 7.29-30
new 2.99, 2.141, 7.28, 7.63-73
non-registration of 7.55
owner 7.25-30, 7.40-41, 7.45, 7.48-50, 7.66, 7.68-69, 7.71, 7.73
recreation rights 7.4-24
registration of land 7.2, 7.13
registration of ownership 7.25-28
rights of common over 7.31
unclaimed land 7.25
vehicles 7.40-45, 7.48-54
wrong registration 7.56

Washington First Forum 7.68
waste of the manor 2.14-17, 2.25, 2.95, 2.120-125, 2.129, 4.30, 4.45, 6.4, 7.1
Welsh Water Authority 1.31
West Berkshire District Council 4.17, 4.33
Wimbledon and Putney Commons Act 1871 4.5
Wimbledon Common 1.8, 1.16
Whinash, Cumbria 6.21
Winton and Kaber Fell, Cumbria 4.9-10
Wisley Common, Surrey 6.19, 6.46
Withypool, Somerset 1.25
Woolbeding, West Sussex 1.20
Wycombe Rye, Buckinghamshire 6.59, 7.6